THE END
OF COLLEGE

THE END
OF COLLEGE

CREATING THE FUTURE OF LEARNING AND THE UNIVERSITY OF EVERYWHERE

Kevin Carey

RIVERHEAD BOOKS
a member of Penguin Group (USA)
New York
2015

RIVERHEAD BOOKS
Published by the Penguin Group
Penguin Group (USA) LLC
375 Hudson Street
New York, New York 10014

USA · Canada · UK · Ireland · Australia
New Zealand · India · South Africa · China

penguin.com
A Penguin Random House Company

Library of Congress Cataloging-in-Publication Data

Carey, Kevin, date.
The end of college : creating the future of learning and the university of everywhere / Kevin Carey.
p.   cm.
ISBN 978-1-59463-205-1
1. Distance education.   2. Education, Higher.   3. Internet in higher education.   I. Title.
LC5800.C36   2015   2014026978
371.35'8—dc23

Printed in the United States of America
1   3   5   7   9   10   8   6   4   2

Book design by Meighan Cavanaugh

For Corinne

CONTENTS

THE END
OF COLLEGE

1

The Secret of Life

The Japanese television crew and excitable LA producer were the first signs that something unusual was happening at MIT.

It was a warm evening in April, barely a week after a pair of mad bombers had terrorized the city of Boston and shot a campus security guard dead in front of Building 46, the glass-and-stone complex I was standing inside. Most colleges name their structures after wealthy donors. MIT likes to keep things rational, so when the Brain and Cognitive Sciences Complex was completed in 2005, the administration just gave it the next number in line. As I walked through the building's ninety-foot-high atrium toward a nearby lecture hall, I recognized many of the students who had, like me, spent much of the last semester learning about genetics from one of the smartest people in the world.

Introduction to Biology—*The Secret of Life* is a mandatory course for all MIT freshmen. It's taught by a professor named Eric Lander, who is a walking advertisement for the triumphs of American higher education. Born in the working-class Flatlands neighborhood of Brooklyn, Lander tested into Stuyvesant High, an elite New York City public school, where he discovered an aptitude for math. From there it was a rapid climb up the ladder of academic meritocracy: International Math Olympiad, Princeton valedictorian at age twenty, Rhodes Scholarship, Harvard professorship, MacArthur "Genius" award.

But unlike some of his monastic colleagues, Eric Lander was a sociable person with eclectic intellectual tastes. Pure mathematics were beautiful and thrilling, but they were also a solitary pursuit. Lander liked to interact with other smart people and dive into whole new fields. First he switched from exploring math to teaching economics at Harvard Business School. Then a connection with an MIT biologist led him to the field that would become his calling: uncovering the mysteries of genetics. Lander led the Human Genome Project, which created the historic first complete sequence of human DNA. He went on to cochair President Obama's Council of Advisors on Science and Technology and found a multidisciplinary medical research center. When the *Boston Globe* listed the 150 most important things ever done at MIT, Lander and his work ranked second, after the guy who invented the World Wide Web.

Lander is also a very good teacher. Many great scholars are inept in the classroom. Their intense, internal focus works against them when it comes to forming connections with students. Lander is outgoing, personable, and almost as good at lecturing as he is at discovering new ways to unravel the meaning of human DNA. As I entered the lecture hall where his class would take place, a group of freshmen had already staked out seats in the front row. One, a young woman named Abbey, was standing expectantly by her desk, holding a cupcake in a plastic box. Abbey grew up in a suburb of Salt Lake City. Her father said he would only pay for her to attend two colleges other than Brigham Young: Harvard and MIT. So she aced her college boards and made the trip to Cambridge, Massachusetts. As Lander reached his lectern, she walked up to him, face flushing, and gave him the cupcake. "Happy anniversary!" she said, before quickly turning back to her seat. Because of this class, she later told me, she plans to major in chemical and biological engineering.

I settled into a seat in the back row, flipped up the desk, and pulled out my study materials. After two months of watching Lander lecture, my class notebook was almost full. We had begun with the building blocks of biochemistry before proceeding on a long voyage of intellectual discovery, through Mendelian genetics, Crick and Watson's double helix, and the modern age of biotechnology. Lander used a storyteller's flair for drama as he worked through complex explanations of biochemistry, genetic mutation, and RNA transcription. When his tales reached a point of crucial discovery (often involving a Nobel Prize awarded to one of his MIT colleagues), you could see sparks of enthusiasm in his eyes—even from the last row.

After each lecture, my fellow students and I would retreat to our laptops to tackle MIT's famously challenging "problem sets," exercises meant to test and solidify the knowledge we had gained in class. I found myself staying up late at night, trying to make sense of RNA base pair chains and a list of stop codons, restriction enzymes, and plasmids. But I could always ask other students or teaching assistants for help—MIT encourages this—and I eventually made it through the assignments. At the end of the semester, I passed the two midterms and the final with a respectable 87 percent average. In exchange, MIT gave me an official university document certifying that I had completed Introduction to Biology—*The Secret of Life.*

Yet I was not, and never have been, an MIT undergraduate. I did not fill out a college application or financial aid form or write a personal essay explaining why my life-altering experience founding a shelter for homeless marmots made me uniquely qualified to attend MIT. In fact, until that evening, I had never set foot on the MIT campus in my life. Nor did I pay MIT any tuition, which runs over $42,000 per year, plus another $15,000 for books, fees, and room and board. The entire Secret of Life course—lectures, problem sets, class forums, exams, and certificate—was totally free.

And I wasn't the only one. At the same time, all around the world, tens of thousands of other students were taking *The Secret of Life* for free. There were doctors and medical students from South America, a group of high schoolers in Greece, a seventy-two-year-old retired chemist living in the Netherlands, a Sri Lankan college dropout, a full-time homemaker in India, a Ukrainian software engineer, and a nurse in the Philippines. One young woman wrote on the class message board, "My dad is letting me take this instead of my regular 8th grade science. I am 13 years old." Most of them had never been to the United States and could not imagine experiencing, or affording, an elite American education. But they were, in most of the ways that mattered, doing exactly that.

That's why, throughout Lander's lecture that evening, a small team of camera operators from Japan's NHK (Japan Broadcasting Corporation) television network prowled the sides and back of the lecture hall, shooting a news documentary under the direction of a California-based TV producer eager to get shots of Lander and his students at work. It's also why the Japanese camera techs had to work around an entirely different production crew that was also in the room, filming Lander from a variety of angles in digital HD.

The class was being produced by a brand-new online educational organization jointly run by MIT and Harvard University. For the better part of the last 150 years, those two institutions have sat, less than two miles apart, at the zenith of global higher education. They are bitter rivals for the world's best scholars and students. Yet they had, in this time and place, decided to put their rivalries aside.

This unlikely collaboration came about because higher education now stands at the brink of transformation by information technology. Harvard and MIT are accelerating seismic forces that threaten colleges that have stood, largely unchanged, for decades or more. These historic developments will liberate hundreds of millions of people around the world, creating ways of learning that have never existed before. They will also upend a cornerstone of the American meritocracy, fundamentally altering the way our society creates knowledge and economic opportunity.

Whether they know it or not, Harvard and MIT are helping to build a new and unprecedented institution: the University of Everywhere.

The University of Everywhere is where students of the future will go to college. Parts of it will be familiar to anyone who's gotten a great college education, because some aspects of human learning are eternal. But in many respects, it will be like nothing that has come before.

At the University of Everywhere, educational resources that have been scarce and expensive for centuries will be abundant and free. Anything that can be digitized—books, lecture videos, images, sounds, and increasingly powerful digital learning environments—will be available to anyone in the world with an Internet connection.

The idea of "admission" to college will become an anachronism, because the University of Everywhere will be open to everyone. It won't, in fact, be a single place or institution at all. The next generation of students will not waste their teenage years jostling for spots in a tiny number of elitist schools. Their educational experience will come from dozens of organizations, each specializing in different aspects of human learning.

The University of Everywhere will span the earth. The students will come from towns, cities, and countries in all cultures and societies, members of a growing global middle class who will transform the experience of higher education.

These students will be educated in digital learning environments of unprecedented sophistication. The University of Everywhere will solve the basic problem that has bedeviled universities since they were first invented over a millennium ago: how to provide a personalized, individual education to large numbers of people at a reasonable price. The intense tutorial education that has historically been the province of kings and princes will be available to anyone in the world.

That personalization will be driven by advances in artificial intelligence and fueled by massive amounts of educational data. Information about student learning will be used to continually adapt and improve people's educational experience based on their unique strengths, needs, flaws, and aspirations.

The University of Everywhere will not be devoid of people, however. In fact, learners and educators will be all around us. The new digital learning environments will be designed by education engineers collaborating across organizations and cultures, sharing insights and tools in a way that far surpasses what any single college professor can accomplish alone. Students will be part of rich global communities as small as a half dozen people working intently together and as large as millions of students contending with timeless questions and monuments of human thinking at the same time.

Learning at the University of Everywhere will be challenging. There will be no more "gentleman's Cs," no grade inflation, no more slacking through late adolescence in a haze, confident that social connections and inertia will see you through. Standards of excellence will rise to the highest common denominator of the most talented and motivated students in the world. The new digital learning environments will be designed to stimulate the kind of sustained hard work that authentic education always requires.

Traditional college credentials, based on arbitrary amounts of time spent in obsolete institutions, will fade into memory. Instead of four-year bachelor's degrees and two-year associate's degrees, students will accumulate digital evidence of their learning throughout their lives, information that will be used to get jobs, access new educational opportunities, and connect with other learners. People will control their personal educational identities instead of leaving that crucial information in the hands of organizations acting from selfish interests.

Enrollment in the University of Everywhere will be lifelong, a fundamental aspect of modern living. Instead of checking into a single college for a few years on the cusp of adulthood, people will form relationships with learning organizations that last decades based on their personal preferences, circumstances, and needs. Unlike today, belonging to a learning organization will not involve massive expenses and crippling amounts of debt.

Some of those organizations will have the names of colleges and universities that we know today. Traditional institutions that move quickly and adapt to the opportunities of information technology will become centers of learning in the networked University of Everywhere. Those that cannot change will disappear. The story of higher education's future is a tale of ancient institutions in their last days of decadence, creating the seeds of a new world to come.

I SIGNED UP FOR *The Secret of Life* because I was both intensely curious and increasingly fearful about the future of American higher education. As a child, I was immersed in traditional university life. My father was a PhD computer scientist who taught at a large public university in Connecticut. While raising three children, my mother got her doctorate in education from the same institution. There was never a question of whether I would follow them to college, only where I would enroll.

Fortunately, a middle-class family in the late 1980s could still send their children to a good public university without breaking the bank. A scholarship helped cover tuition at a selective state school in New York, and I emerged four years later with a bachelor's degree and a clear path in front of me. Some of my peers came from well-off families while others were first-generation students from single-parent, working-class households. In all my time there I never once heard the words "student loan."

But as I grew older and began to study America's education system in depth, it became clear that the affordable college of my youth was a historical relic. Colleges in the United States have become, by a wide margin, the most expensive in the world. Since I first enrolled, inflation-adjusted tuition at public universities has more than tripled, rising much faster than the average family income. The only way parents and students have been able to make up the difference is debt. By 2004, Americans owed nearly $250 billion in student loans, which at the time was considered to be an alarming sum. By comparison, outstanding credit card debt then stood at $700 billion, the hangover of a ravenous consumer culture with a taste for easy credit.

Over the next eight years, student loan debt quadrupled, passing $1 trillion, leaving credit cards in the dust. The share of twenty-five-year-olds with student loans increased by 60 percent. In the early 1990s, most undergraduates were able to avoid borrowing entirely. By 2012, 71 percent of students graduated with an average debt of nearly $30,000. Leaving school with swollen loans during the worst economic crisis in generations, many students found they couldn't afford the monthly payments. They put off buying homes because more borrowing was impossible. They defaulted on their loans in larger numbers, bringing repo men to their doors.

I also came to realize how unusual my college experience had been. Only a third of working-age American adults have a bachelor's degree, a percentage that grew slowly, and in some years not at all, throughout the 1990s and 2000s even as other industrialized nations were achieving dramatic increases in the percentage of adults with degrees. In part, this was because many American students were falling off the path to graduation. Less than 40 percent of students enrolling for the first time at a four-year college actually graduate in four years. Even allowing an extra two years for changed majors, illnesses, and other circumstances, fewer than two-thirds graduate within *six* years.

And these are only the averages, which include places like Harvard and MIT, where nearly everyone graduates unless they drop out to found a multibillion-dollar software company. On the other end of the spectrum, hundreds of colleges and universities fail to graduate even a third of their students within six years. In urban centers like Chicago, Detroit, and Washington, D.C., some colleges graduate less than 10 percent of minority students on time. Attrition rates resemble those of soldiers sent over the top in World War I.

At two-year community colleges, where nearly half of all Americans start higher education, the numbers are also dire. Only 34 percent graduate or transfer to another school within three years of enrolling. Although most students starting community college say they want a bachelor's degree, only 11.6 percent earn one within six years.

According to the U.S. Census, there are almost 35 million college dropouts in America over the age of twenty-five. Many of them have large student loans yet no access to the well-paying jobs that require a college degree.

At least, most people have assumed, those who did graduate from college had the knowledge and skills they need to survive in an increasingly perilous economy. This, too, turns out to be wrong. In 2005 a U.S. Department of Education study of adult literacy found that the majority of college graduates couldn't do things like compare and contrast the viewpoints in two newspaper editorials. Fourteen percent of college graduates scored at only the "basic" level of literacy: good enough to read grade-school books but not much more. The results showed a sharp decline from the same exams given a decade before. The study was written up in the *New York Times*—and then disappeared from the public debate without a trace.

In late 2010, I met a New York University sociologist named Richard Arum at a coffee shop near my office in downtown Washington, D.C. He had just completed a book, *Academically Adrift: Limited Learning on College Campuses*, that would be published a few months later. It described a four-year study of how much students at a diverse group of colleges and universities had actually learned while they were in school. The results were shocking. Arum and his coauthor, Josipa Roksa, found that 45 percent of students made no gains on a widely used test of critical thinking, analytic reasoning, and communication skills during their first two years in college. Thirty-six percent made no statistically significant gains over the entire four years. "American higher education," they wrote, "is characterized by limited or no learning for a large proportion of students."

The evidence continued to pile up. In 2013 the nonprofit Organisation for Economic Co-operation and Development published a groundbreaking study that compared the literacy, numeracy, and problem-solving skills of adults in different countries. Fully 38 percent of American college graduates failed to meet at least the third level on a five-level assessment of numeracy that involves solving problems with math and performing "basic analysis of data and statistics." Only 19 percent met the fourth level, compared to the average of 25 percent in other industrialized nations. Americans have long been told that our colleges and universities are the best in the world. It turns out that when it comes to college student learning, we are decidedly mediocre.

One of the big reasons is that colleges have been demanding less and less of students over time. A study published by the National Bureau of Economic Research found that in 1961, full-time college students worked more or less full-time, devoting forty hours a week to studying and attending class. By 2003, the average had fallen to twenty-seven hours—even though, over the same time period, the percentage of all class grades given an A rose from 15 to 43 percent. Nearly 20 percent of students reported studying less than five hours a week outside of class.

These alarming trends came at a time when the abstract statistics I pored over in my job at a D.C. think tank had become very personal. A few months before I met with Richard Arum and learned about his damning findings, my wife and I had our first child. Suddenly those long-term trends of rapidly escalating tuition led to a specific, unavoidable destination: In eighteen years, my daughter would graduate from high school. Like her parents and our parents before us, I expected her to go to college. How much would it cost? The numbers were mind-boggling. Over four years, the bill would be $122,000 for an average public university, in today's dollars, after adjusting for inflation. The typical private university would be nearly double that, $228,000. That was if she beat the odds and finished in four years. And even if she did, would it be worth it? A quarter of a million dollars for "limited or no learning"?

Yet, even as the tuition trends and research studies were piling up, something else was happening that gave me reason to be hopeful. When my father let me tag along on trips to his university laboratory in the

1970s, computers were housed in six-foot-high metal cabinets powered by thick electrical cables. Times have changed since then. Over the following decades, the technology revolution radically altered broad swaths of the economy. Organizations that were in the business of controlling access to information that could be digitized—sounds, words, and images—found themselves challenged by upstart competitors. People around the world who were once isolated from the centers of culture and commerce suddenly became connected through information networks and computers that are getting cheaper and more powerful by the year. Information technology became interwoven into the social, economic, and cultural fabric of modern life.

I sensed that the University of Everywhere was out there, somewhere, waiting in the near future, a blurred outline that was beginning to come into view.

So when MIT and Harvard joined a handful of other world-class universities by offering complete versions of their highly sought-after courses for free, online, I decided to find out for myself if the digital future of higher learning had finally arrived. I asked Anant Agarwal, the former director of MIT's computer science and artificial intelligence laboratory and the recently installed CEO of edX, the joint Harvard-MIT online effort, to recommend a course to take. As an undergraduate political science and graduate public policy major who studied education policy for a living, I wanted something completely outside of my expertise, so that the experience was as close to that of a newly enrolled student as possible. I was also interested in taking a course that would show off what the edX online education system could do. Agarwal recommended a class starting in a few weeks, taught by one of MIT's most esteemed professors: Eric Lander.

2

A Sham, a Bauble, a Dodge

College admission has become a rite of passage in American life, a chance for parents to spend the last precious months before their children finally leave the nest in a state of constant bewilderment and frustration, sorting through mountains of college brochures, filling out invasively detailed financial aid applications, constructing intricate college visit itineraries, and endlessly hassling their teenagers to please, please, finish writing their "personal essay."

Signing up for *The Secret of Life*, by contrast, took all of two minutes. I used my laptop computer to search for "edX," selected the class from a list of available courses, typed in a username and password, and was done. Clicking on the course title opened up the edX "learning management system," which consisted of several neatly arranged menus surrounding a video of Eric Lander standing in front of a whiteboard in the lecture hall that I would eventually visit in person several months later.

I was, at that point, still skeptical about the idea of taking an entire MIT-caliber course online. Like most people, I had ridden the wave of technological change as neither an early nor a late adopter. I had a love/hate relationship with my smartphone—so convenient and useful, so endlessly distracting. I liked reading detective novels on my Kindle but still loved browsing the stacks at my local bookstore and leaving with a full bag of books that would surely make me a smarter, better person. My music CDs had long since been thrown in a closet, but the sound in my earbuds still didn't measure up to what came from my old stereo gear.

College, meanwhile, seemed to occupy a more exalted plane of existence. I knew that education was much more complicated than simply reproducing words or sounds. *The Secret of Life* would help me understand what could be replicated in a free class offered entirely on my laptop, and what was unavoidably left out.

The course itself was a faithful digital translation of the education that all MIT undergraduates receive. The math, science, and engineering prodigies who win admission to MIT are required to complete a core curriculum called the General Institute Requirements. It consists of six introductory courses in biology, chemistry, physics, and mathematics. There are a few options in the sense that MIT offers an extra-hard version of chemistry for students who spent their high school years knee-deep in beakers and Erlenmeyer flasks, but otherwise there is no testing out with AP credits or otherwise avoiding the core curriculum. The courses are hard enough that, even given the kind of people who are admitted to MIT, the university prohibits freshmen from taking more than four of them in one term. First-semester freshmen don't even receive letter grades and cannot fail; the only options are "pass" or no grade at all.

The educational model for the MIT courses is straightforward: Students attend lectures and discussion sections every week, read supplementary materials, complete problem sets, and takes exams.

To produce *The Secret of Life*, MIT installed several professional-grade high-definition video cameras in the lecture hall where Eric Lander was teaching freshmen the standard Introduction to Biology course. Because MIT also numbers its classes and majors in an orderly fashion (the Mechanical Engineering major is called "Course 2," Biology is "Course 7," and the first biology class is designated "7.01"), the experimental online course was designated "7.00x." The videos were posted on edX a few weeks after the live lectures occurred. Other than the short time delay, the thousands of students taking 7.00x online proceeded through the course in exactly the same way as the select students at MIT.

The edX system allows you to download the videos or stream them onto your laptop, tablet, or smartphone. Once you press "Play" and Lander begins to talk, the text of his lecture starts to scroll down a window to the right of the video, keeping time with the lecture itself. You can pause at any time and read back through what he just said or click on the text, which rewinds the video to that point in the lecture.

I quickly realized that 7.00x was nothing like the AP biology course I had taken in high school. At MIT, professors assume you know all of that already and dive right into the good stuff: genetics and the underlying code of life. As a rule, I'm a reader: I usually find listening to people explain things to be frustrating, unless I can interrupt them and ask questions. But Lander's lectures were engrossing. The course was an intricate story of discovery, during which students learn the fundamental principles and intellectual unification of genetics and biology.

We began with four one-hour lectures on biochemistry, starting with the composition of cells and moving quickly through various types of molecular bonding. From there we went into protein structures and the various interesting and complicated ways that amino acids behave and interact. Then we covered enzymes and biochemical reactions, how molecules move through transition states of various energy profiles, and how enzymes help them along. All of this came together in a lengthy explanation of biochemical pathways, with the elaborate glycolysis process as the main example.

Molecular biology is a visual subject, and the lectures primarily consisted of Lander covering whiteboard after whiteboard with diagrams and explaining what they mean. I carefully copied his diagrams into my notebook, making annotations at crucial points and pausing the video to back up, read, and listen again when a concept wasn't clear. He was the pedagogue, the master, and I was the acolyte receiving wisdom and information.

In doing this, Lander and I were engaged in a kind of educational interaction that dates back to the very beginning of modern higher education. The university as we know it today—the institution that is failing to help so many students learn and graduate even as it charges them ever-increasing amounts of money—did not appear, fully formed, from the ether. It emerged from particular historical circumstances and evolved, often strangely, over time. And it turns out that information technology has been part of that story from the very beginning. The nature of the deeply flawed modern university has been shaped, century by century, by the way technology has mediated the balance of power between students and their masters. Only now have the scales finally begun to tip in students' favor.

THE ARCHETYPICAL LIBERAL ARTS major is classics, the study of how the Greeks and Romans invented much of Western civilization. Notably, the ancients accomplished this without universities themselves. We may think of Raphael's magnificent fresco in the Vatican's Apostolic Palace showing Plato and Aristotle surrounded by fellow philosophers, but its title, *The School of Athens*, was added centuries after the painting itself was completed. The classical world had teachers and students but no deans or departments or diplomas—no places of higher learning as we know them today.

The first modern university wasn't created until 1088, more or less, in Bologna, Italy. It's still there, and when I visited the University of Bologna's campus in autumn 2012, it seemed entirely familiar. Throngs of young people wearing backpacks and blue jeans laughed and flirted outside bars and cafés near academic buildings clad with red roofs and orange plaster walls. There was a bookstore, paper signs with little tear-off stubs advertising apartments for rent, and bicycles locked to street-side poles.

The area had a certain worn-in look that comes from having tens of thousands of students circulate through every year. A plaque on the administration building declared that it is the *Alma Mater Studiorum*—the "Nourishing Mother of Education."

As a city, Bologna is like Florence without the Uffizi, Michelangelo's *David*, and 95 percent of the tourists, which is to say it's a wonderful place to live and learn. You can spend hours under the covered walkways wandering through shops, galleries, and restaurants. Local businesses sell cheap food and drinks, and articles in the city newspaper denounce student drunkenness. After visiting Bologna, Charles Dickens remarked that "there is a grave and learned air about the city, and pleasant gloom upon it." It's the original college town.

Everything about the University of Bologna reinforces the idea that colleges are eternal institutions, unchanged through enemy sackings, plagues, papal feuds, and world wars. This is an idea that modern universities are eager to reinforce, with their founding dates stamped in bold type on ancient-looking seals. In a society that worships youth and modernity, universities stand out for their pride in antiquity. We have always been here, they imply, very much like this, and so we will always be.

But in truth the first university was a very different beast from the ones we know today. Even the University of Bologna's founding date is something of an approximation. All we know for sure is that in 1888 the civic leaders of Bologna decided that they wanted to celebrate the university's eight hundredth anniversary. Still, it's reasonably certain that in the late eleventh century a group of students in Bologna got together and decided to pool their resources—financial, intellectual, and spiritual—in order to learn.

Europe then was emerging from the Dark Ages. The wisdom that was the true subject of Raphael's fresco—in the center, Aristotle holds a copy of his *Nicomachean Ethics*, Plato his dialogue *Timaeus*—had begun to return to Europe, after centuries in exile, transported onto the continent by the Islamic scholars of Spain. Along with philosophy came Euclidean geometry, Arabic numerals, and rediscovered Roman law. Goods and people began to circulate through the European economy, along with a desire for knowledge.

Young people eager to learn congregated in cities. In Bologna they organized themselves into associations based on national origin, first to better bargain with greedy landlords. Next the students hired teachers, on terms that would be unimaginable to today's tenured professors. Standards for teaching were established in code and contract. Professors were never allowed to skip classes and were required to begin and finish on time. They had to post a security deposit if they left the city and were obligated to proceed through the entire curriculum over the course of a year. If fewer than five students showed up for a lecture, the professor was fined, on the theory that it must have been a bad lecture.

Professors responded by forming organizations of their own. Today, we use the words "college" and "university" somewhat interchangeably. But in the beginning, a university was a collection of scholars, or students— *universitas scholarium*—while a "college" was a guild of masters. The academic guilds administered tests for admission, and those who passed got a license to teach—the first "college" degrees.

The balance of power favoring the students was short-lived. The second major European university, in Paris, was organized around the professors, and the pattern has changed little since. The University of Paris grew out of the cathedral school at Notre Dame in the middle of the twelfth century. The faculty there grouped themselves by discipline: canon law, arts, theology, and medicine.

This idea of the university thrived because it had the weight of supply and demand on its side. As Europe gradually moved toward renaissance and enlightenment, knowledge and wisdom were scarce and precious resources. There were only two ways to get them in an educational setting: listen to a master speak, or read words written in a book. Universities were able to accumulate a critical mass of books and masters, usually in a city that served as a hub of communications and commerce. There were few such places, and the people who owned the intellectual capital could decide who would be allowed to access it and on what terms.

So students came to listen to the likes of Peter Abelard, the great French scholastic philosopher whose doomed love affair with Heloise became the stuff of legend and song. A prodigy and champion logician, Abelard attracted throngs to his lectures and public debates in Paris and the surrounding wilderness, where students would camp for days to hear the master speak. He was, as the medieval historian Charles Homer Haskins wrote, "bold, original, lucid, sharply polemical, always fresh and stimulating, and withal 'able to move to laughter the minds of serious men.'" Abelard reached the height of his fame just as the University of Paris emerged, exemplifying the idea of professor-centered education.

The idea soon germinated elsewhere. In 1167, England's Henry II forbade English students from studying at the University of Paris. Scholars, masters, and books began congregating at Oxford instead. Violent clashes between students and the local townspeople prompted the university to build dormitories, which evolved into a new meaning of "college": independent places where students lived under the supervision of masters. By 1264, Balliol, Merton, and University colleges had been built, all of which continue to operate today along with thirty-five other Oxford University colleges. The colleges were largely autonomous, raised their own money, and were responsible for teaching and student life. The university administered exams and granted degrees. Cambridge University was founded not long after, by a charter from Henry III. It, too, adopted the college model.

The medieval university worked in this way for the next few centuries, expanding to more locations in Europe and beyond. It was not always the center of intellectual life—the great artists and scholars of the Renaissance did not work at universities—but it continued to grow, adapting to the last great information technology revolution in higher education before the current one: Johannes Gutenberg's invention of the printing press in the mid-fifteenth century.

This was not the first time that teachers had been confronted with new learning technology. Millennia before, another invention had upset those wedded to traditional teaching methods: the written word. In the *Phaedrus*, Socrates tells the story of a conversation between two gods, Theuth and Thamus. Theuth was "the inventor of many arts, such as arithmetic and calculation and geometry and astronomy and draughts and dice, but his great discovery was the use of letters." Thamus was god of all Egypt, and said this about Theuth's prized invention:

> "O most ingenious Theuth, the parent or inventor of an art is not always the best judge of the utility or inutility of his own inventions. . . . [Y]ou who are the father of letters, from a paternal love of your own children have been led to attribute to them a quality which they cannot have; for this discovery of yours will create forgetfulness in learners' souls, because they will not use their memories; they will trust to the external written characters and not remember of themselves. The specific which you have discovered is an aid not to memory, but to reminiscence, and you give your disciples not truth, but only the semblance of truth; they will be hearers of many things and will have learned nothing; they will appear to be omniscient and will generally know nothing; they will be tiresome company, having the show of wisdom without the reality."

Socrates distrusted learning from books. Students reading words, he argued, would gain only shadows of the author's original insight and, worse, not understand the difference. Anyone who has suffered in the tiresome company of a book-read pedant and his shows of wisdom would probably concede that Socrates had a point.

He was, however, shortsighted about the long-term net benefits of books to human civilization. Without written words, complexities of human thinking are limited to what can be held, recalled, and spoken by a single mind. If Plato hadn't recorded the wisdom of Socrates in books, it would be lost to the world today.

Books were hard to come by in medieval times, so much so that universities were given the power to regulate their production and sale in order to prevent monopoly pricing. Students generally rented books for a limited time, and since each book was hand-copied, universities employed book inspectors to spot-check for accuracy. The University of Bologna created a book supply by requiring professors to submit copies of their lectures for publication. The image of a professor reading from a lectern as a roomful of students write down the words he speaks—an experience familiar to anyone who has attended college—is rooted in this pre-Gutenberg era of higher education.

Because paper for books was scarce, scribes would omit spaces between words. Readers had to learn to recognize words in long strings of characters, a skill that was taught by reading out loud under the supervision of a master. Teachers got used to this approach and reacted with consternation when printing press technology made it obsolete. Well into the fourteenth century, professors at the University of Paris outlawed silent reading. If they didn't know what their students were reading, how could they help them learn?

The Gutenberg revolution changed and destabilized so many dimensions of society that some have wondered why it had, relatively speaking, less effect on the structure of the medieval university. Bologna and Oxford and Cambridge are still operating (the University of Paris didn't survive the French Revolution) in ways that their founders would easily recognize.

The answer is that the new technology complemented the university's established business model. While people could now read alone (if they were literate) and a few wealthy individuals could amass small libraries, books were still expensive to own. Only a few people and institutions had the means to accumulate, store, and catalogue all of the books worth reading. Then there was the question of which books to read and who to talk to about them when it was hard to find more than a vague semblance of the author's true meaning in a few characters on a page. Students also needed some kind of credential signifying what they had learned. Universities provided teachers, guidance, peers, and diplomas, things no book could offer alone.

Printed books solidified the logic of universities as scarce, expensive places. If you wanted to learn, you needed to travel to where the smart people, books, and other students were. The limitations of transportation, communication, and information storage technologies gave universities the upper hand.

HIGHER EDUCATION was very much on the minds of the Puritans who made the hard voyage to the New World in the seventeenth century. Their faith had grown out of the printing press revolution, which freed people to find their own meaning in the Word. Eight years after the Massachusetts Bay Colony was founded in 1628, its Great and General Court voted to create a "schoale or a colledge." A year later they designated Newetowne as the location, and then renamed the town Cambridge, after the university that had educated many of them, in 1638.

That was also the year that a wealthy thirty-one-year-old Cambridge alumnus named John Harvard died of tuberculosis. He left the new college half his money and his personal four-hundred-book library. In gratitude, the Great and General Court named the new college after Harvard in 1639. The Reverend Henry Dunster, another Cambridge graduate, was appointed the first president of Harvard College the following year.

Dunster duly implemented a four-year bachelor's degree program based on the residential college model at Cambridge. Of course, the college needed more than John Harvard's initial gift to keep going. A few years later the Puritans began another practice that, like many things in higher education, would endure: They sent a letter back to England hitting up friends and alumni for money.

After God has carried us safe to New England, and we had builded our houses, provided necessaries for our livelihood, reared convenient places for God's worship, and settled the civil government: One of the next things we longed for and looked after was to advance learning and perpetuate it to posterity; dreading to leave an illiterate ministry to the churches, when our present ministers shall lie in the dust.

Others followed in their footsteps. By the time the American Revolution came, there were nine colonial colleges: Harvard, Yale, Dartmouth, William and Mary, New Jersey, Rhode Island, King's, Queens, and Philadelphia. The last five are now known as Princeton, Brown, Columbia, Rutgers, and the University of Pennsylvania. The core of the present-day American higher-education aristocracy predates America itself.

Organizationally, the colonial colleges strongly resembled their English ancestors, as did those that followed them. But the American approach to starting up new colleges was different. At the time, English authorities kept tight control over the founding of colleges. Oxford, Cambridge, and the University of London were the only universities that had official government charters and the authority to grant degrees. Those places enjoyed monopoly power and government subsidies, which was good for the people who ran them and for the privileged students—all men—who were allowed inside. But it also meant there were relatively few college opportunities for the population of a literate, advanced nation on the verge of an empire.

Americans, by contrast, adopted a laissez-faire approach to college creation. The federal government played almost no role, despite vigorous attempts by James Madison, Thomas Jefferson, and George Washington to create a "national" university. Building new colleges was left to the states, which were generally happy to grant charters to a profusion of religious denominations and other organizations, with the proviso that when it came to raising money, they were on their own. The country was full of enthusiasm and open spaces. By the eve of the Civil War there were nearly

250 colleges and universities in a nation stretching from Maine to Florida and Massachusetts to California.

Those institutions were very different from colleges as we know them today. The continental model of masters and students living together remained intact. But the institutions themselves were small and inconsequential. Two hundred twenty-nine years after its establishment, Harvard graduated a class of seventy-seven students. As late as 1880, only twenty-six colleges enrolled more than two hundred people. Students were taught a standard curriculum of Greek, Latin, and mathematics, with some ancient philosophy and history thrown in. There were few lectures, laboratories, seminars, or other modern teaching methods. Instead, college learning meant *recitation,* a tedious process of students orally regurgitating large quantities of memorized text.

The teachers who supervised the recitations were of middling social status and low pay. Rather than leave colleges in the hands of the faculty, as at Oxford and Cambridge, the Puritans entrusted their academic institutions to pious old men charged with preserving their religious character. At the end of the Civil War, 90 percent of American college presidents had been recruited from the clergy.

The goal of college then was neither to create nor distribute knowledge. Instead, America's flinty Protestant founders believed that students needed to learn "mental discipline." Just as hard exercise, godliness, and deprivation would hone the body and spirit, years spent memorizing long passages of ancient Greek would sharpen the faculties of young men, even if they never had occasion to read Greek again. Educational methods were also a function of available technology. Paper remained expensive, so it was cheaper to grade students in person based on oral presentation than have them submit written work.

The 1852 catalogue for the University of Pennsylvania lists the name of every undergraduate—there were eighty-one—along with a precise course of instruction for all four years. The sophomore class, for example, would study "Plane and Spherical Trigonometry . . . with applications to

Surveying, Navigation, &c.," along with logic, rhetoric, and "Livy (Second Punic War), Demosthenes, Horace (Epistles and Art of Poetry)." The schedule could be punishing. "On each day of the week, except Saturday," the catalogue noted, "there are three recitations of one hour each for every class. On Saturday each class recites once."

But just as America eventually grew far beyond the cultural and religious beliefs of its founders, the nation's colleges and universities were poised to undergo a rapid transformation. The next three decades saw the most important debate in the long history of American higher learning, one in which three ideas battled for supremacy in defining what exactly college should be.

THE FIRST IDEA FOCUSED on how colleges could help the waking giant of the American economy. By 1862, the Southern states had seceded into the Confederacy, taking their senators and representatives with them. That altered the balance of power in Washington and created new opportunities to pass legislation. Justin Smith Morrill, a representative from Vermont, pushed through the first Morrill Land-Grant Act, which was signed into law by President Lincoln. It granted each state rights to federal land in the western territories, the income from which would be used to create

> at least one college where the leading object shall be, without excluding other scientific and classical studies, and including military tactics, to teach such branches of learning as are related to agriculture and the mechanic arts . . . in order to promote the liberal and practical education of the industrial classes in the several pursuits and professions in life.

Mechanic arts and practical education for the industrial classes were a far cry from Horace and Demosthenes, and for good reason. People were spreading out toward the frontier as the nation was beginning to be knit together by railroads, steam, and telegraph. In the three decades after the Civil War, America would use its abundant natural resources to become the biggest manufacturer in the world. It needed skilled people, and colleges seemed like natural places to train them.

The universities created in the Morrill spirit would eventually become some of the nation's largest and most productive institutions of higher learning. Some of their leaders were openly disdainful of the older colleges. In California, the robber baron Leland Stanford used a fortune made building the transcontinental railroad with exploited Chinese workers to found a university in the memory of his dead son. David Starr Jordan, the first president of Stanford, declared that colleges should not prepare students "for a holiness class which is rendered unclean by material concerns." At the University of Nebraska, the chancellor had little use for "institutions that seem to love scholarship and erudition for their own sakes; who make these ends and not means; who hug themselves with joy because they are not as other men, and especially are not as this practical fellow."

The second big idea about what college should be came from overseas. After the Civil War, American scholars who traveled to Europe began returning with stories of a new kind of institution: the German research university. While the medieval universities had continued to operate from their founding principles, the Enlightenment had brought new ways of thinking and centers of power. In 1810 the Prussian linguist and philosopher Friedrich Wilhelm Christian Karl Ferdinand von Humboldt petitioned his king to create a new university in Berlin. The Humboldtian model was built around the independent scholar, a learned man given broad freedoms to push the boundaries of human knowledge as he saw fit. Students would assist the masters and learn from their example. But the master and his research, not the student, would be the center of the institution.

This idea had obvious appeal to the professoriat. It was bolstered by the 1876 founding of Johns Hopkins, America's first research university. Hopkins made clear from the outset that, unlike the land-grant institutions, it was not in the business of training people for the trades. In a founding statement, it said, "The Johns Hopkins University provides advanced instruction, *not professional,* to properly qualified students, in various departments of literature and science." The reference to departments also signaled a new structure for colleges and universities. Professors would be organized into autonomous divisions, each focused on a particular academic discipline, with the primary goal of advancing knowledge in that field.

The third big idea was liberal arts education, a notion that many people favor and fewer can adequately explain. The man who proposed the most enduring definition of liberal education was the great British theologian John Henry Newman. Newman would eventually be elevated to the rank of cardinal and was beatified in 2010. But first he was sent on an educational mission to help found a new Catholic university in Dublin, Ireland. Shortly after arriving, he delivered a series of lectures that were collected in a book titled *The Idea of a University.*

Newman began with a definitive statement. The university, he said, "is a place of *teaching* universal *knowledge.* This implies that its object is, on the one hand, intellectual, not moral; on the other, that it is the diffusion and extension of knowledge rather than the advancement. If its object were scientific and philosophical discovery, I do not see why a University should have students."

As a man of God, Newman saw religious and liberal education as distinct. "Knowledge is one thing; virtue is another; good sense is not conscience, refinement is not humility, nor largeness and justness of view faith. . . . Quarry the granite rock with razors, or moor the vessel with a thread of silk; then may you hope with such keen and delicate instruments as human knowledge and human reason to contend against those giants, the passion and the pride of man."

Nonetheless, Newman was a great believer in those instruments. True liberal education, he believed, was not a matter of merely accumulating knowledge in a specific subject. The most important goal was to understand how all the different aspects of the world are connected. As the intellect is perfected, Newman said, "the mind never views any part of the extended subject-matter of Knowledge without recollecting that it is but a part. . . . It makes every thing in some sort lead to everything else." So educated, the student "apprehends the great outlines of knowledge, the principles on which it rests, the scale of its parts, its lights and shades, its great points and its little, as he otherwise cannot apprehend them."

Achieving this, Newman believed, takes both hard work and a well-designed educational program. "The intellect in its present state"—that is, before going to college—"does not discern truth intuitively, or as a whole." People learn "by the employment, concentration, and joint action of many faculties and exercises of mind. Such a union and concert of the intellectual powers, such an enlargement and development, such a comprehensiveness, is necessarily a matter of training."

An institution built to achieve these goals, Newman believed, needed no other justification. Liberal education was "the great ordinary means to a great but ordinary end; it aims at raising the intellectual tone of the society, at cultivating the public mind, at purifying the national taste, at supplying true principles to popular enthusiasm and fixed aims to popular aspiration, at giving enlargement and sobriety to the ideas of the age, at facilitating the exercise of political power, and refining the intercourse of private life."

There was then, and remains today, a debate at the heart of the liberal arts idea. For some, a liberal arts education meant building crucial intellectual capacities, the ability to think critically and see the lights and shades of knowledge. For others, it rested on an understanding of key texts, writers and philosophers, the wisdom of the ages. But both sides believed that universities were meant to do more than train students to become researchers in narrowly defined fields, or merely learn skills of practical value. To them, college had a higher, almost sacred purpose. It gave people the great gift of becoming more human.

Thus, America was confronted with three very different purposes for a university: practical training, research, and liberal arts education. The stakes were high. The goals of higher education would determine what the American university would look like, how it would be organized, and who would work there. Some believed there was no way to reconcile the different visions of higher learning. Newman wondered why a research university needed undergraduates at all. The founders of Johns Hopkins rejected professional education, while the land grant universities had no patience for those who loved scholarship and erudition for their own sake.

But instead of choosing, American universities decided to do all three things at once, with consequences that last to this day.

THE PERSON MOST RESPONSIBLE for that decision was Charles William Eliot, president of Harvard. Eliot was a chemist on the Harvard faculty at the beginning of the Civil War, but he left after being passed over for a promotion and went to Europe, where he studied at the continental universities. When he returned, he was hired at a brand-new, technically focused university built just a couple miles from Harvard in Cambridge: the Massachusetts Institute of Technology. In 1869 he wrote an article for the *Atlantic* that began with the question that keeps all parents awake at night: "What can I do with my boy?"

The traditional college with its years of Greek and Latin would not help his son, Eliot believed. He had seen the research universities rising in Europe and, at MIT, an example of how practical training could be accomplished in America. But unlike the absolutists in the debate between the different purposes of higher education, Eliot believed they could be reconciled. "To make a good engineer, chemist, or architect," Eliot wrote, "the only sure way is to make first, or at least simultaneously, an observant, reflecting, and sensible man, whose mind is not only well stored, but well trained also to see, compare, reason, and decide."

Eighteen sixty-nine happened to be the year that Harvard was urgently seeking a new leader. The university was at a low point, having run through three presidents, all clergymen, in the previous fifteen years. Harvard's overseers were looking for someone to lead it into the future, and were impressed by Eliot's vision. He was hired at age thirty-five, the youngest president in Harvard's history, and made the most of it, serving for the next forty years.

Eliot's greatest contributions to American higher education were less intellectual than organizational. He, more than anyone, devised a university structure built to accommodate the three competing ideas. First, Eliot made the bachelor's degree a requirement for admission to Harvard's graduate and professional schools. Previously, people who wanted to be lawyers could skip the Punic Wars and go right to contracts and torts. Eliot believed that doctors, lawyers, engineers, and architects needed their minds to be well trained before they were well stored. Other universities followed Harvard's lead, creating a large new market for undergraduate education, which they proceeded to serve.

More ingeniously, Eliot replaced the mandatory curriculum with an elective system. Instead of telling students what to learn, he let them choose from among a wide array of courses. This act of choice, he believed, was itself of great educational value. Eliot offered a challenge to incoming freshmen: "Do you want to be cogs on a wheel driven by a pinion which revolves in obedience to a force outside itself? . . . The will is the prime motive power; and you can only train your wills, in freedom."

But the elective system had another benefit: It allowed the graduate research university and the undergraduate liberal arts college to coexist at the same institution. The research university was built around specialization and scholarly freedom. Professors there pursued knowledge as they saw fit. Such people were usually interested in teaching only in their chosen field. Most of them would be useless under the old model. The entire Course of Instruction in the 1852 Penn catalogue is only three pages long. You don't need very many professors when all the students are studying the same thing.

Under the elective system, the opposite was true: The more departments a university built and scholars it employed, the more electives and choice it could offer. This was expensive, of course, just as it cost money to accumulate all of the books worth reading in a library. Only a limited number of institutions could afford to be great under this design. Once again, the structure of colleges reinforced the logic of a relatively small number of wealthy places serving as gatekeepers to higher learning.

Over the next thirty years, other universities copied Eliot's innovations. The apparatus of the modern university was built. Trustees selected presidents to hire deans who oversaw departments staffed with professors. The highest credential offered by the graduate research university, the PhD, was made a requirement for teaching undergraduates the liberal arts. Students advanced through a progression of degrees, starting with the bachelor's, and received a transcript outlining their courses and grades. Teaching methods varied by subject, with laboratories in the sciences and seminars in the humanities. But the standard method returned to the one employed by pre-Gutenberg professors reading out their books: the lecture, delivered charismatically or otherwise.

Science, research, and practical training had the advantage of being profitable and forward-reaching. They positioned the university to be supported by the government, attractive to parents and students, and indispensable for the coming age. But by themselves these purposes lacked a certain exaltedness, a grander meaning to elevate the spirits—and reputations—of colleges and their employees. Liberal arts education was nothing less than the pursuit of civilization itself, a tradition with lineage back to Socrates, Plato, and Aristotle. It became the spirituality of higher learning in America, replacing the religious convictions that secularizing universities were rapidly leaving behind.

And so the American university emerged as an institution that was designed like a research university, charged with practical training and immersed in the spirit of liberal education. It all made sense—in theory. In reality, the contradictions that Eliot had helped finesse quickly became obvious. Almost as soon as this strange hybrid university was constructed, people began pointing out the many ways in which it didn't work.

THE FIRST AMERICAN PhD wasn't granted until 1861, by Yale. Yet within three decades it had become the standard credential for academe, and remains so today. In 1903 the eminent pragmatist philosopher William James wrote an essay about the doctorate. The brother of the novelist Henry James, William began teaching at Harvard four years after Eliot's appointment and stayed there for the next forty-four years. His essay was titled "The Ph.D. Octopus."

James denounced the trend among universities to hire only PhD's as teachers. "Will any one pretend for a moment that the doctor's degree is a guarantee that its possessor will be successful as a teacher?" he asked. "Notoriously, his moral, social and personal characteristics may utterly disqualify him for success in the class-room; and of these characteristics his doctor's examination is unable to take any account whatever."

James blamed the vanity and greed of universities. "The Ph.D. degree is in point of fact already looked upon as a mere advertising resource, a manner of throwing dust in the Public's eyes." The doctorate was "a sham, a bauble, a dodge, whereby to decorate the catalogues of schools and colleges."

James was ignored. Forty years later, his cause was taken up by the historian Jacques Barzun, a prolific author and one of the most famous college teachers in American history. Along with the critic Lionel Trilling, Barzun taught Columbia's well-known freshman courses on the Great Books, including the classics of ancient philosophy. His book *Teacher in America* included a chapter titled "The Ph.D. Octopus," in homage to James.

Barzun began by repeating James's statement of the obvious. "The doctorate of course shows nothing about teaching ability." In the melding together of research, training, and liberal arts, the research university had won the critical fight over the nature of the college teaching profession. It was largely unconcerned with teaching. Scholars were paid and promoted based on the quality of their work in archives and laboratories, not classrooms. Most PhD programs included no courses in the theories and methods of education.

Under the theory of "academic freedom," which was originally advanced to shield faculty scholarship and speech from politics and administrative caprice, professors were given wide latitude to design courses however they liked. They did so largely in isolation, with little outside help or supervision. Their teaching was never evaluated by experts. Nobody checked to see how much their students learned compared to other students in similar courses. In research, college professors were highly trained experts. In teaching, they were amateurs. Some were excellent anyway, others were nightmarishly terrible, and many swam in a sea of mediocrity in between.

Colleges didn't advertise this inconvenient reality, for obvious reasons. For naïve young scholars, it could be a shock. Barzun imagined a conversation between an experienced professor and a newly initiated graduate student teaching classes while working to earn a PhD. The elder says, "Young man, you are on the wrong track. Bluff through your classes, discourage students from coming around to talk to you . . . use the time thus saved to bone up for your orals and start writing your book." The young man protests, "But why neglect my teaching? It's my chosen profession. And why injure the college, the students, and the department by rushing through an immature doctorate?"

"Because," the professor responds, "with the Ph.D. you have value, or rather a price tag. Your articles will advertise you. With luck you may be reappointed right here, *with tenure*. Whereas if you merely teach conscientiously, even brilliantly, you will not be reappointed and you will *not* have your Ph.D. to go out and bargain with." "The argument," Barzun wrote, "is as unanswerable as decapitation."

He, too, was ignored.

The underlying structure of the American university had been designed to meet the needs and desires of researchers. The German model gave them academic freedom to think, write, and teach as they pleased. As the historian Laurence Veysey recounted, "The most pronounced effect of the increasing emphasis upon specialized research was a tendency among scientifically minded professors to ignore the undergraduate college and to place a low value on their function as teachers."

Veysey's definitive account of this period, *The Emergence of the American University,* is a penetrating and at times shockingly critical description of the three-headed hybrid. Writing in the early 1960s, it was clear to Veysey that the American university was riven with problems and contradictions. Nobody had emerged from the great compromise of the late nineteenth century unscathed. Students were often taught badly, professors subject to the whims of administrators, campus leaders continually frustrated by their unruly subjects.

"The university throve, as it were, on ignorance. . . ." Veysey wrote. "The fact that students were frequently pawns of their parents' ambitions was meliorated by the romantically gregarious tone of undergraduate life. The fact that professors were rarely taken as seriously by others as they took themselves was hidden by their rationalistic belief in the power of intellectual persuasion. . . . Those at the top, in their turn, were shielded by a hypnotic mode of ritualistic idealism. . . . Tacitly obeying the need to fail to communicate, each academic group refrained from too rude or brutal an unmasking of the rest."

At first, certain realities shielded students from the structural flaws of the hybrid model. In the first years of the twentieth century, only a small fraction of unusually smart and well-off students went to college. The best and brightest had learning talents that allowed them to tolerate professors who neglected teaching. For students who were preparing for scholarly careers of their own, a professor's amateur teaching skills might be offset by his deep knowledge of the field. And while the land-grant universities and liberal arts colleges adopted the PhD along with everyone else, many stayed focused on creating coherent academic programs that trained students in practical skills and higher arts.

But as the century wore on, the balance shifted further and further against the interests of undergraduates, even as historical and economic forces sent more and more students to college. Solid evidence of the academic damage that resulted was often hard to come by. By extending the idea of academic freedom to what and how professors taught in the classroom, universities made it impossible to create any kind of common expectations for undergraduate education. There was no way for anyone other than the professor to judge the quality of his teaching, because standards of learning were, by definition, determined by the professor himself. Thus, the hybrid university defined away the possibility of creating evidence that would expose its manifest flaws.

This happened despite the fact that many of the classes being taught by different professors at scores of institutions were essentially the same. The idealized vision of a learned and engaged professor teaching a specialized humanities course to a small group of attentive students is largely a mirage. In 2012, American colleges and universities granted nearly 140,000 bachelor's degrees in business administration and four in Slavic studies. Fifty thousand students earned degrees in Accounting, thirty-five in Ancient Classical Greek. Civil engineers outnumbered students majoring in craft design, folk art, and artisanry by a ratio of 100 to 1. Meanwhile, 94,000 students earned registered nursing degrees. Almost 39,000 political science degrees were awarded by more than 1,000 different institutions. The University of Washington granted the lone degree nationwide in Danish language and literature, while UC Berkeley graduated the nation's single undergraduate specialist in Dutch. General psychology degrees came in at 103,000 strong.

But universities were so wedded to the convenience of the elective system and the prerogatives of their independent scholars that they never considered working with one another to create common expectations for teaching psychology, political science, business, and other mega-majors. They knew such sensible policies would expose the deep inadequacies of their amateur teachers and bring the whole rickety edifice crashing to the ground.

It wasn't until recently that truly damning evidence of the hybrid university's educational shortcomings became widely known. Even then, the alarming findings from the U.S. Department of Education's study of college graduate literacy—the majority of bachelor's degree holders are unable to read critically at an advanced level—so contradicted the popular image of universities as dedicated centers of learning that they seemed unable to penetrate the popular consciousness. Arum and Roksa's finding of "limited or no learning" among many college graduates gained some attention but didn't make a dent in the demand for the college experience. The standard reaction among college leaders to mounting evidence of mediocre learning, high dropout rates, and skyrocketing tuition was to throw up their hands and say that nothing, really, could be done. College is what it is, and has always been. The only thing to do is to keep paying whatever amount of money the institution requires.

This idea is wrong—profoundly wrong. There is nothing inevitable about the hybrid university model. It is a deeply flawed, irrational institution designed to be bad at the most important thing it does: educate people. This has been clear from the beginning and pointed out by every honest observer along the way. The modern American university has endured for this long only because, almost as soon as it was created, it began an epic run of good luck that is only now coming to an end.

3

The Absolut Rolex Plan

Eric Lander's lectures were the beginning of MIT 7.00x, but they were by no means the end. Often he would stop, point to a large video screen to the left of the whiteboards, and talk about electron microscope images and computer-simulated graphics showing the molecules, cells, proteins, and DNA strands that composed the building blocks of life. Sitting at home in the late hours after my daughter had gone to sleep, I was able to manipulate the same simulated models on my computer screen, rotating them around to examine proteins from different angles, zooming out to see the structure as a whole, and then zooming in to see how each atom and set of amino acids fit together.

A few days later the 7.00x course software directed me to a website containing a protein-folding simulator called Foldit. The physical shape of proteins matters a lot in biology, affecting how they function and interact with one another. The shape, in turn, is a function of how different kinds of molecules bond with one another in different ways. Switch out a single atom and the whole structure of the protein can rearrange itself as various bonds reorient into a new equilibrium.

Foldit is an online computer game that anyone in the world can play, for free. Players compete to design the most efficient way of folding unknown molecules, receiving points and high scores that are publicly displayed. A quarter million people have signed on since the game was released in 2008. In 2011 the players collectively took three weeks to solve a knotty protein structure problem that HIV researchers had been unable to crack for fifteen years. As the journal *Nature* reported, "The refined structure provides new insights for the design of antiretroviral drugs."

Foldit very much fits with Eric Lander's approach to science. In the 1990s he helped lead the Human Genome Project, a collaborative, publicly financed undertaking in which thousands of scientists from around the world worked together in sequencing all three billion base pairs in the human genome for the first time. Unlike the for-profit companies that were working on a rival sequencing effort, the Human Genome Project released all of the information it created into the public domain. The march of scientific discovery depends on the ability of this generation's scholars and thinkers to access and build on the knowledge that has come before them.

The federal government spent $2.7 billion to finance the Human Genome Project, but once that money was spent, it cost virtually nothing to store and transmit the gene sequence information to whoever needed it. The same is true for the Foldit simulator: Building it cost much more than letting additional people log on and take a turn. In both cases, the enterprise benefited from letting as many people access the information for as little expense as possible. Scientists were able to study, add to, and improve the original Human Genome Project effort. Foldit players create their own protein-folding puzzles to solve and post them on the website, adding to the depth and quality of the game.

But until the launch of 7.00x in 2013, Eric Lander's approach to teaching was almost exactly the opposite of his approach to science. While the fruits of his research were available to anyone in the world for free, the totality of his course—lectures, exercises, exams, student discussions, and some form of credit from MIT—was limited to a tiny sliver of humanity, no more than the few hundred students who could fit at one time into an MIT lecture hall. MIT rejected over 90 percent of the students who applied for the chance to be in that room, and charged those who were admitted prices that were prohibitively expensive for nearly all the smart young aspiring scientists in the world. Lander was not part of an active, global community of undergraduate genetics teachers who regularly collaborated in sharing tools, advice, and information. Like nearly all university teachers, he and his course assistants worked mostly alone.

None of this was Eric Lander's fault. As a scientist, he was free to work with colleagues across the globe and publish his findings in journals that anyone with a subscription or library card can read. As a teacher, he was confined to the students and systems established by his university. In fairness, MIT was actually among the most progressive universities in using information technology to distribute free teaching materials online prior to 2013, and was wealthy enough to offer the low-income students it enrolled generous financial aid. Unlike most universities, it had an actual undergraduate curriculum, with courses taught by tenured professors. It was more serious about student learning than most. But it was also bound by the unyielding limitations of the hybrid university model. MIT was unavoidably expensive, exclusive, and oriented toward research.

By this time many American universities had become grotesquely expensive and shamefully indifferent to undergraduate learning. This, too, was rarely a matter of bad people deliberately trying to exploit students. Rather, it was a systematic tragedy, a case of well-meaning educators making rational choices in a system they did not create and did not control, with exploitation the only possible outcome in the end.

ON A COLD MORNING in early February, just as I was beginning my months-long 7.00x journey into genetics and *The Secret of Life*, I sat down in a Starbucks in the Foggy Bottom neighborhood of Washington, D.C., with a young man named Hugh. A junior at nearby George Washington University, Hugh had a neat ginger beard and wore the standard collegiate uniform of hoodie, jeans, and sneakers. After some small talk I asked him how much money he was borrowing to go to college.

"Eighty-two thousand dollars," he said. "By the time I graduate, a hundred and ten."

The number shocked me, but not as much as the way it didn't shock him.

Hugh was born in Warwick, Rhode Island, and like generations of smart young people raised in America's decaying industrial towns, he spent his adolescence plotting to leave. That meant higher education. Hugh wanted to study international relations and get a degree from a university with a good reputation, because that's what it takes to get a job in a market where jobs are hard to find. His family didn't have any money, and tuition, fees, and room and board at GW run almost $60,000 a year. So Hugh borrowed as much as the federal government would lend him, and when that wasn't enough, he went to private lenders like Sallie Mae to borrow more, at interest rates of 10 percent and higher.

Hugh keeps meticulous track of it all on his laptop computer. He is organized and hardworking, "goal oriented" in the way that young people born into the new millennium tend to be. He has plans and aspirations, a job with a Swiss company that organizes international science conferences after graduation, then the Foreign Service exam and, he hopes, a life in diplomacy overseas.

Yet I don't think he entirely understood what it meant to have a six-figure indenture hanging around his neck when he was twenty-one years old. He assumed everything would work out, because that's the way you have to think if you're going to make the long journey from Warwick to the State Department. And besides, hadn't it worked out for all the people who had taken his path before?

The two of us got up and walked across K Street, where many D.C. lobbyists have their offices, and then Pennsylvania Avenue, which leads straight to the White House six blocks away. Entering the GW campus, I passed a bronze statue of an important-looking person who I assumed was involved in the university's founding a long time ago. In a common area outside, a young man with an unruly beard was sitting on the ground, buried to the neck in a large pile of plastic grocery bags. He appeared to be protesting something, although exactly what was not clear. Paper signs tacked onto billboards advertised for roommates and tutoring services. The campus library stood in front of me, and beyond that a basketball arena, food court, and the university bookstore. Someone had pasted Greek letters on the inside of a dormitory's fourth-floor window. Parties were afoot.

Like the University of Bologna, the iconography resonated deeply, evoking memories of my own college experience along with countless movies, books, and television shows. It was so familiar that it took a certain amount of effort to step back and notice that it wasn't exactly real.

The date on the bronze statue didn't match its historical style. It was put there in 1991. Most college campuses try to balance buildings and open space with a consistency of design. GW looked like a collection of university-like structures randomly scrunched together in an area two sizes too small. Instead of being in the middle of campus, the statue-festooned University Yard was stuck off to the side, with pathways crossing it for no particular reason. The buildings were designed in a variety of architectural styles, concrete brutalism to colonial to midcentury brick to modern stone to glass and steel, and pushed against one another with only small pockets of worn grass in between. Construction cranes rose out of multiple pits promising newer buildings to come. Everything seemed like a bad compromise between tradition and modernity, built to remind people of something old and familiar while satisfying a twenty-first-century need.

And like nearly every other college and university in America, there was no way to know what the millions of dollars spent on those buildings and the people inside them produced in terms of education. The GW website and the glossy marketing materials the university mails to high school juniors nationwide don't mention that few GW professors have been trained in teaching, or that full-time faculty are promoted based on research, not excellence in the classroom. There is no indication of how much students actually learn while they are in Foggy Bottom compared to their peers at other schools. Either the university doesn't know or it doesn't want anyone else to know.

I began talking to more of Hugh's fellow students. Many of them seemed acutely aware of what they had gotten into. A highly indebted senior who was terrified of the weak job market described GW as "the world's most expensive trade school." Another told me the university is split between serious students trying to learn something and dumb rich kids whose parents are giving them a fancy-sounding diploma the way they might a condo or a new car. Basic academic standards in the university's main arts and sciences college are almost nonexistent, he said. "You can go to GW and essentially buy a degree."

Someone must have built this place, I thought. And that person was not hard to find. In fact, he was sitting in the corner office of a building with his name on the entrance, a few blocks away.

STEPHEN JOEL TRACHTENBERG was hired as president of George Washington University in 1988. When he got there, GW was an inexpensive commuter school known for alumni like Nevada senator and Democratic Party leader Harry Reid, who got his law degree as a young man while working nights for the U.S. Capitol Police. By the time Trachtenberg was finished two decades later, GW had been transformed into a nationally recognized research university. Applications for admissions jumped. The basketball team moved to Division I, played in a new arena, and got into the NCAA tournament. Five new schools were created, in professions including health, public policy, management, and public affairs. *U.S. News & World Report* ranked the university at number fifty-three nationwide, just outside the "first tier."

It was no secret where the money had come from to pay for it all: the students and their families. Under Trachtenberg's leadership, GW became the most expensive university in America.

Following in those kinds of footsteps is never easy. Usually new leaders have the benefit of working at some remove from their predecessors. But Steven Knapp, the current president of GW, wasn't so fortunate. After vacating the president's office in 2007, Trachtenberg simply moved into the Trachtenberg School of Public Policy and Public Administration, where he writes, teaches, travels, raises money, and says whatever he likes to whomever he pleases, on a variety of topics, including the competence of the new administration.

I met Trachtenberg in his office a few weeks after my conversation with Hugh. He arrived wearing black jeans, a black sweater, and brown zip-up boots. His office was cluttered with books, papers, photographs, and mementos, including an antique radio, a Tiffany-style lamp, and a large humidor in the shape of the original U.S. Capitol Building. He settled onto a leather coach and put one leg up to rest his knee. We began to talk about his life and how the university he built came to be.

Trachtenberg's father, Oscar, emigrated to New York City from the Ukraine as a young man. He began work in a doll factory, sweeping floors. Oscar dropped out of high school and got through the Great Depression with a knack for selling insurance. When the state of New York outlawed the use of race in setting insurance rates, Oscar saw a business opportunity and developed a clientele of African-American professionals in Brooklyn. Trachtenberg's mother, Shoshana, had moved with her family from Odessa to Palestine at age ten. Life was hard there and her father eventually left to open a laundry in the Bronx, saving money to bring his family across the sea.

Stephen was their only child. His father was distant and demanding, always questioning why his son hadn't achieved more. His mother took the opposite approach, indulging him with books and taking him to experience museums, concerts, and the wealth of culture the city had to offer.

They lived in a one-bedroom apartment. Stephen slept on a pull-out couch in the living room and studied at the kitchen table. He read quickly and was often bored in school, so Shoshana made an arrangement with one of his teachers, who let him sit in the back of the class and read the *New York Times*. Another gave him extra work to do, assigning daily three-hundred-word and then five-hundred-word papers to write. Stephen went to P.S. 254 and then James Madison High School, on Bedford Avenue in Brooklyn, where he became president of the student government. Two decades later, Eric Lander would go to elementary school nearby.

When he graduated from high school, Stephen was ready to do what his parents had not done: go to college. Oscar thought the best choice was Brooklyn College, a fine local public institution that enrolled many of Stephen's neighborhood friends. But Stephen had his sights set higher, on Columbia and the Ivy League. Oscar was a businessman and a bargainer, so he offered his son a deal: Go to Brooklyn College and I'll buy you a brand-new Chevrolet. Stephen was tempted. But then he thought about car insurance premiums and gasoline and upkeep and said no, he'd go with the long-term investment. He enrolled in Columbia University in 1955.

At that moment Columbia was filling up with money and prestige, pulling students from a deep pool of talent in New York City and beyond. Jacques Barzun taught Plato and Aristotle to freshmen while world-famous scientists and philosophers populated the graduate schools. Postwar Columbia was among a constellation of elite universities that served as the template for the great expansion of higher education that was to follow, a movement to extend access to college without precedent in world history. It was a phenomenon that defined much of America's culture and economy in the second half of the twentieth century, shaping and shaped by the actions of people like Stephen Joel Trachtenberg. It was in many ways a towering success, but one built on a foundation whose flaws and inadequacies are now more apparent than ever before.

THE FLAWS of the standard university model—particularly its habitual neglect of teaching undergraduates—were obvious to anyone who was paying attention. Men like Barzun and James were particularly caustic in describing the absurdity of hiring teachers with no training in teaching and giving them jobs that actively discouraged them from teaching well. One might have reasonably predicted that such an organization would soon collapse from the internal weakness of its structural incoherence. But that didn't happen—at least, not right away. Instead, the hybrid American university survived and prospered, for many reasons—none more important than simply being in America.

A few years ago I visited Humboldt University in Berlin, named for the inventor of the research university and founded in 1810. In the early years, Humboldt was home to many of the world's greatest minds, including Hegel, Schopenhauer, and Schelling. Marx and Engels were students there, as were Albert Einstein and Max Planck. Depending on how you count, up to forty Nobel Prize winners are associated with the university.

But thirty-eight of those prizes were awarded between 1901 and 1956, all for work performed in the late nineteenth and early twentieth centuries. Today, one popular world university ranking puts Humboldt at 126th worldwide, only the seventh-best in Germany. Thirty-seven American universities rank higher.

The reason is obvious once you get there. To stand in front of Humboldt University, you have to walk east along the wide boulevard of the Unter den Linden, a few hundred yards from the Brandenburg Gate, where the Berlin Wall used to be. Humboldt was split in half by the Cold War, with the historic campus on the wrong side of the line. By then it was already badly damaged. On May 10, 1933, students and professors from the university participated in a mass book burning. Many academics fled and Jewish students and professors were forcibly expelled, or worse. Then the campus was bombed into rubble by the merciless Allied air campaign during World War II. Today, Humboldt is a large, respectable public institution serving reunified Germany. But it has never recovered the stature it once held.

American universities had the great fortune of being located safely on the North American continent, in the ascendant global power of the age. As the United States became larger and more prosperous, colleges and universities were there to meet the growing demand for education. America was the first country to move toward giving all children a high school education. That created a huge new group of potential college students. As a nation of immigrants that lacked formal class structures, Americans were on the lookout for opportunities to help their children move ahead. College degrees were a way of signaling—and achieving—upward mobility. Hybrid universities, or other institutions formed in their mold, were where you went to get those credentials.

Some people were unwilling to ignore the university's terrible educational flaws. In 1929 the University of Chicago hired Robert Maynard Hutchins as its president. Born in Brooklyn, Hutchins spent his first two undergraduate years at Oberlin College in Ohio. After leaving to fight in World War I, Hutchins finished his undergraduate career at Yale, where he graduated summa cum laude. A prodigy, he studied law, finished at the top of his class, and became dean of Yale Law School at age twenty-eight.

Hutchins was thirty years old when he assumed the presidency of the University of Chicago. Unlike most college presidents today, who ascend into the top job only after decades climbing the treacherous ladder of academic administration, Hutchins led Chicago while his undergraduate years were still fresh in his mind. He based his philosophy of governance on that experience, in the sense that he tried to make a University of Chicago education exactly the opposite of what he had received in New

Haven. Delivering the Yale commencement address as the top senior in 1921, Hutchins described his experience as "idyllic, haphazard, humanistic, without any infusion of scholarship." "The Yale of my day," he later said, "was a place where you could get excited about girls or liquor or parties or athletic contests, but it wasn't a place where you'd get excited about learning."

Upon taking the Chicago job, Hutchins set about implementing bold reforms. Six years later, in 1935, he outlined his philosophy of higher education in a series of lectures at Yale. The heart of his critique was the same observation that William James had made before him and others would make after: The many parts of the hybrid university didn't fit together, which created institutions of muddled and contradictory purpose, ill-suited to educate students well. "The most striking thing about the higher learning in America," Hutchins began, "is the confusion that besets it."

The boundless choice of Harvard president Charles Eliot's elective system had removed the responsibility of colleges to make decisions about what people needed to learn. Teaching students to apprehend the great outlines of knowledge and the principles upon which it rests required colleges to identify those principles and teach them. As Newman advised, the intellect does not discern truth intuitively. It requires education.

Many students were getting no such education at the hybrid universities, Hutchins believed. "The degree it offers seems to certify that the student has passed an uneventful period without violating any local, state, or federal law, and that he has a fair, if temporary, recollection of what his teachers have said to him. . . . [L]ittle pretense is made that many of the things said to him are of much importance."

Instead of teaching, Hutchins wrote, the bureaucrats running the hybrid university were focused on competing with one another for status and money. He foresaw the modern era of luxury dormitories and multimillion-dollar fitness centers with lazy rivers and climbing walls. "The love of money means that a university must attract students. To do this it must be attractive. This is interpreted to mean that it must go to unusual lengths to house, feed, and amuse the young. Nobody knows what these things have to do with learning."

Hutchins also tore into the bureaucratic practices that had been devised to regularize the degree production process. At the turn of the century, many college professors remained badly paid. The industrialist Andrew Carnegie was a trustee of Cornell University at the time, and decided to create a free pension system for the professoriat. Pensions were limited to those who worked full-time, which required a definition of what "full-time" meant. The nonprofit organization Carnegie founded to administer the fund (which would eventually become the pension giant TIAA-CREF) hit upon a full-time standard of twelve "credit hours," the equivalent of teaching four courses that met for three hours per week over a standard fifteen-week semester.

The creators of the credit hour didn't mean for it to be a measure of how much students learned. But colleges used it that way anyway, because it provided an easy method of adding up courses earned from uncoordinated, uncooperative departments and professors. As a result, Hutchins wrote, "the intellectual progress of the young is determined by the time they have been in attendance, the number of hours they have sat in classes, and the proportion of what they have been told that they can repeat on examinations given by the teachers who told it to them. . . . [I]t is clear that these criteria are really measures of faithfulness, docility, and memory; we cannot suppose that they are regarded as true indications of intellectual power."

Defenders of the hybrid university believed it was important to put students in the presence of brilliant scholars, with little thought to teaching methods or an educational program. As President James Garfield supposedly said of a nineteenth-century theologian named Mark Hopkins, the best education was "Mark Hopkins on one end of a log and a student on the other." Hutchins thought this was ridiculous and anti-intellectual. "Under this theory, you pay no attention to what you teach, or indeed to what you investigate. You get great men for your faculty. Their mere presence on the campus inspires, stimulates, and exalts. It matters not how inarticulate their teaching or how recondite their researches; they are, as the saying goes, an education in themselves." Hutchins believed this idea was educationally unsound and logistically impractical in a huge nation moving toward universal education. "Under any conditions that are likely to exist in this country the log is too long and there are too many people sitting on both ends of it."

Hutchins had radical ideas for reshaping the university. A true education, he believed, cultivated the intellectual virtues. It taught students the fundamental propositions and principles that shaped and connected the world. These ideas could be identified and taught, and it was the university's obligation to do so. Eliot's elective system amounted to a denial that there was content to education. "Educators cannot permit the students to dictate the course of study unless they are prepared to confess that they are nothing but chaperons, supervising an aimless, trial-and-error process which is chiefly valuable because it keeps young people from doing something worse." More than any other major university president in the twentieth century, Hutchins was Newman's heir.

With a mandate from the trustees and a confidence that bordered on arrogance and often surpassed it, Hutchins went about implementing his ideas at Chicago. He taught a Great Books seminar, heavy on the Greeks, with the philosopher Mortimer Adler, whom he had recruited from Columbia. Instead of course grades, Hutchins implemented a system of comprehensive exams that students could take whenever they were ready. If they were able to pass the exams without taking the associated courses, they received the same amount of credit.

But most of Hutchins's ideas did not outlast him. After he left the university, his step-by-step general education curriculum was dismantled along with the system of exams for credits. Today the University of Chicago is, along with Columbia, one of the few major universities that retains a semblance of a core liberal arts curriculum. But it is only a variant of the hybrid model, not a fundamentally different design. Later Hutchins wrote, "My mistake was that I thought I was a successful evangelist when actually I was the stopper in the bathtub. I thought I had convinced everybody, when all I had done was block a return to 'normalcy.'"

What was this gravitational force that brought all of Hutchins's grand plans to naught? One explanation was offered by a pair of Yale sociologists named Paul DiMaggio and Walter Powell, who developed the concept of "institutional isomorphism," which is another way of saying that organizations within a given field have a tendency to become more and more like one another over time.

Isomorphism is sometimes coercive, Powell and DiMaggio wrote. In the late nineteenth and early twentieth centuries, established colleges got together to create nonprofit "accrediting" organizations that defined what, precisely, it meant to be a college or university. In 1919 the Middle States Association of Colleges and Schools, which accredits institutions in the mid-Atlantic region, created specific standards for colleges: At least eight professors, a half-million-dollar endowment, certain required courses in the liberal arts. When state governments built universities, they wanted them to be accredited, and so they required new institutions to look like the old ones.

Isomorphism can also be mimetic. New colleges and universities needed a way to signal their legitimacy to lawmakers, students, and prospective employees. They did this by mimicking established practices and structures. It was also just a lot *easier* to adopt standard practices. True, the doctorate shows nothing about teaching ability. But if not PhDs, then who? If not departments, then what? From the university administrator's perspective, there was a lot to be said for throwing dust in the public's eyes.

The third type of isomorphism described by Powell and DiMaggio is "normative." The hybrid university created two large and influential professional classes: administrators and professors. Each had a strong interest in perpetuating itself and thus the institution that sustained them. Professors in sociology departments were loyal, first and foremost, to the sociology profession, the so-called invisible college of peers at other sociology departments in other universities. For professors, career advancement, driven entirely by scholarly success as judged by peers, often involved getting a better job at a different institution. But that meant that all the universities had to be structured in roughly the same way, so a professor or dean in University A could comfortably adapt to University B. Even institutions with different missions and cultures, like liberal arts colleges and land-grant universities, needed to be similar enough to facilitate the movement of professors and administrators between them.

None of this guaranteed the longevity of the hybrid university. Isomorphism is real and powerful, but also the reason that long-established institutions are often disrupted by new competition. Organizations become so used to the way things are, they can't conceive of another way until a new competitor springs up to take advantage of all those inefficiencies and drives the old business to extinction.

But the hybrid university managed to avoid this fate for a long time. Great forces of history kept it aloft.

As World War II drew to a close, members of Congress began worrying about what to do with veterans who would be returning home. Many congressmen remembered the days after World War I, when angry veterans led the Bonus Army march on Washington to demand jobs, after which they camped out for months in shantytowns built in front of the Capitol and White House. The movement didn't end until Douglas MacArthur assaulted the veterans with tanks, cavalry, and tear gas. With a much larger force soon returning from Europe and the Pacific, Congress didn't want a similar fiasco. So in 1944 it passed the G.I. Bill, which provided returning servicemen with money to attend college. The bill exceeded all expectations, with more than two million veterans enrolling in colleges across the country by the end of the decade.

Then, a year after the G.I. Bill was enacted, the director of the national Office of Scientific Research and Development, Vannevar Bush, sent a report to President Truman titled *Science: The Endless Frontier*. Bush had a doctorate in electrical engineering from MIT, where he had served as a scientist and administrator. He and his colleagues had made important contributions to the emerging development of computer science; his student Claude Shannon helped develop the information theory that sits at the heart of modern computing.

Science, Bush said, was a source of great good for humanity. Penicillin and other medical advances had saved countless lives. "In 1939 millions of people were employed in industries which did not even exist at the close of the last war—radio, air conditioning, rayon and other synthetic fibers, and plastics. . . . But these things do not mark the end of progress—they are but the beginning if we make full use of our scientific resources." Bush called for a huge new federal investment in science through competitive grants administered by the National Institutes of Health and what would become the National Science Foundation.

Who should get the government's funding? Universities. "The publicly and privately supported colleges, universities, and research institutes are the centers of basic research," Bush declared. "They are the wellsprings of knowledge and understanding. As long as they are vigorous and healthy and their scientists are free to pursue the truth wherever it may lead, there will be a flow of new scientific knowledge to those who can apply it to practical problems in Government, in industry, or elsewhere."

Bush saw that even as the war against the Axis was ending, a new conflict was emerging with the Soviet Union. "In this war it has become clear beyond all doubt that scientific research is absolutely essential to national security. The bitter and dangerous battle against the U-boat was a battle of scientific techniques—and our margin of success was dangerously small. The new eyes which radar supplied to our fighting forces quickly evoked the development of scientific countermeasures which could often blind them." The radar technology had been built at the Radiation Laboratory at MIT.

"War is increasingly total war," he wrote, "in which the armed services must be supplemented by active participation of every element of civilian population." So rivers of federal research money began flowing into universities. State College, Pennsylvania, for example, is located nearly two hundred miles from the nearest deepwater port, yet Penn State maintains to this day a thriving research program in hydroacoustics, hydrodynamics, navigation, and propulsion, the legacy of decades building better torpedoes for the United States Navy's Naval Sea Systems Command.

The federal government didn't care whether the research scientists it funded were any good at teaching undergraduates. It probably preferred they didn't teach them at all. There was a global economic, scientific, and ideological war to be fought, and the world's biggest economy had money to spend. In response, universities nationwide invested billions expanding their capacity for research. The concerns of men like Hutchins were swept aside.

At the same time, the nation's middle class was growing, *Brown v. Board of Education* and other crucial legal precedents opened the doors of college to minority students, and the economic and social liberation of women was well under way. Many colleges, particularly the elite private institutions on the East Coast, had spent the previous decades blatantly discriminating against women, minorities, Jews, and anyone else who didn't fit the male WASP mold. But they gradually bowed to social pressure and the changing legal environment, creating new customers and demand for their education.

Bright students like Stephen Joel Trachtenberg who grew up near established colleges and universities could now find someplace to enroll. But for everyone else, particularly those in the fast-growing Sun Belt states, there was no Ivy League to attend. The land-grant schools weren't enough: States would have to build new colleges and universities to accommodate the surge of new students. The question was: What kind of universities should they be?

The man who did the most to answer that question was the president of the University of California, Clark Kerr.

Kerr was an economist who graduated from Swarthmore before going west to graduate school at Stanford and UC Berkeley. Like Hutchins before him, he took the opportunity of speaking in the heart of elite higher education to lay bare the inadequacies of the hybrid model. In April 1963, he delivered a series of lectures at Harvard, which were collected in a book titled *The Uses of the University.*

Kerr, too, saw confusion in the modern university. It is, he said, "so many things to so many different people that it must, of necessity, be partially at war with itself." Eliot's elective system had produced "a kind of bizarre version of academic laissez-faire," one that "came more to serve the professors than the students for whom it was first intended." The resulting organization was less a coherent organism than "a mechanism held together by administrative rules and powered by money." Or, to put it another way, "a series of individual faculty entrepreneurs held together by a common grievance over parking."

Kerr had watched the Cold War billions from the federal government transform Stanford, Berkeley, and other California universities in ways that often came at the expense of students. Liberal arts education had always been the weakest part of the hybrid, an exalted but abstract doctrine that people would periodically bow down to at formal ceremonies before returning to their daily lives. The overwhelming force of government research money made these gestures even more perfunctory. At the time of Kerr's lectures, a recent Brookings Institution study had found that federal research money had "accelerated the long-standing depreciation of undergraduate education at large universities." It was, Kerr said, a "cruel paradox that a superior faculty results in an inferior concern for undergraduate teaching."

But Kerr also knew that the universities had reached a point of no return. "Hutchins was the last of the giants," he said, "in the sense that he was the last of the university presidents who really tried to change his institution and higher education in any fundamental way."

Meanwhile, millions of new students, the products of the baby boom and the too-gradual emancipation of women and minorities, needed somewhere to go to college. Kerr knew he couldn't build a different university model. Instead, he used public policy to give similar universities different things to do.

The result was the California Master Plan for Higher Education, the most influential piece of state higher-education policy in the twentieth century. Kerr's blueprint for the Golden State called for a three-tier design. At the top would be the University of California system, which would enroll the best of the state's high school graduates and concentrate on research. In the middle would be the California State University system. They would have deans, departments, electives, PhDs, and all the rest. But the Cal State campuses would operate in the job-focused land-grant tradition, training teachers, nurses, and other middle-class professionals. Faculty there would teach more and research less.

And the bottom half of students—over a million people per year—would start in community colleges, a uniquely American institution that grew out of junior colleges that had often been run by local public school systems. Community colleges would be inexpensive and open to everyone. Students who completed a two-year degree would, in theory, be eligible to transfer up into the UC or CSU systems. This had the great advantage of keeping the unwashed masses out of elite institutions and, since community colleges were run on the cheap, saving taxpayers a lot of money.

Kerr's Master Plan was copied by states nationwide. Hundreds of new public universities were built after World War II using the standard hybrid design combined with mission designation. Many had compass points and localities in their names (University of Northern Iowa, Indiana University Kokomo) along with a not-so-subtle implication of subservience and derivation from the elite ideal. So-called normal schools that had been created to train teachers in the mid-nineteenth century were converted to colleges and then regional public universities.

Meanwhile, the federal government was preparing its next big foray into higher education. In 1965, Lyndon Johnson went to Texas State University in San Marcos and signed the federal Higher Education Act into law as a major plank of the Great Society. It established a new system of helping students pay for college through subsidized student loans. A few years later Congress enacted what would become known as the Federal Pell Grant Program, providing millions of low-income undergraduates money for tuition.

To administer the new program and implement the ongoing integration of K–12 schools, President Johnson appointed Harold "Doc" Howe as U.S. commissioner of education, the most important education position in the federal government before the U.S. Department of Education was created and granted cabinet status in 1979. The son of a college president, Howe was a World War II veteran with degrees from Columbia and Yale. He needed people to help build the new education federalism. He called around and ended up offering a position to a younger man with a similar background: a Columbia graduate with a Yale law degree who had just entered a PhD program at Harvard. "You have enough degrees to sustain a man," Howe told him. Stephen Joel Trachtenberg took the job, moved to Washington, D.C., and never looked back.

Yet all the money and students America had to offer couldn't change the fact that the hybrid university was a strange and inefficient institution, conflicted against itself and disinclined to do the hard work of educating undergraduates well. The student protest movement of the 1960s had turned large swaths of the electorate against the universities. Ronald Reagan used antistudent outrage as a springboard to the California governor's mansion and promptly ousted Kerr. In 1971 the government-sponsored Newman Report (no relation to John Henry Newman) found "disturbing trends toward uniformity in our institutions, growing bureaucracy, overemphasis on academic credentials, isolation of students and faculty from the world."

Worse, there were ominous signs that the great expansion of higher education had gone too far, too fast. In 1976 a Harvard labor economist named Richard B. Freeman published a book called *The Overeducated American*, which predicted that a surplus of diplomas would push the long-term wages of college graduates down. The *New York Times* ran a front-page story about the book that began: "After generations during which going to college was assumed to be a sure route to the better life, college-educated Americans are losing their economic advantage." *People* magazine framed its coverage of Freeman's book with a provocative question: "Is a college degree still a passport to white collar success?"

The answer, it turned out, was unequivocally "Yes." Just as Freeman's book made the rounds, the labor market embarked upon a decades-long run-up in the value of college degrees. The great manufacturing economy that sustained American prosperity through the middle of the twentieth century was becoming increasingly battered by foreign competition. Mills, plants, and factories began disappearing and blue-collar jobs along with them. Those jobs were replaced by a new white-collar workforce in banking, finance, insurance, consulting, and technology services. The parts of the economy that didn't suffer from foreign competition were local and professional, particularly the massive fields of education and health care.

What all of those burgeoning sectors had in common was college. To get your foot in the door at the bank or corporate headquarters, you needed a college degree. Students responded. The number of young adults with a bachelor's degree, which was less than 10 percent of the population in 1960, passed 20 percent in the 1970s, 25 percent in the 1990s, and stands at over 33 percent today. Yet, despite the increase in supply of college graduates, the price that employers were willing to pay for those people went up, not down. Technology had made advanced skills more valuable. Jobs involving simple, repetitive tasks were rendered obsolete by machines. The jobs that remained required increasingly sophisticated skills. A steel mill that once employed twenty low-skill laborers per unit of production might now employ one person manipulating complex equipment instead. Economists call this "skill-biased technological change." When this happens, people with the most sophisticated skills prosper while those with the fewest skills get left further and further behind.

As a result, the gap widened between college haves and have-nots. In

1977, people with bachelor's degrees earned 40 percent more per hour than people with only a high school diploma. By 2005, the college advantage had doubled to 80 percent. People with graduate and professional degrees earned even more. Workers needed college more than ever, and flocked to established institutions. Once again larger forces had bailed out the flawed hybrid university model.

This was also the point when the great American college building spree came to an end. States had opened an average of almost one new community college *per week* for the entire decade of the 1960s, along with scores of new universities. But once there was an accessible institution within driving distance of most people, the expansion stopped. Colleges also enlisted the government to stymie new competitors. Accreditors, which are independent associations of existing colleges, were allowed to decide which colleges would be allowed to enroll students flush with billions of new dollars in federal financial aid. To compete on a level financial playing field, new colleges would have to adopt the expensive, inefficient hybrid model. Thus, colleges isolated themselves from the same competitive forces that were driving more students to their doors.

That meant that colleges were principally competing with one another. Because most were nonprofit, they weren't fighting over money for its own sake. They had their eyes on a more precious commodity: status. Both public and private colleges were driven to constantly one-up one another, buying more famous scholars on the job market, building fancier buildings, and passing the cost along to students and parents. When you're in the status business, nothing is ever enough if your competitor has more.

Meanwhile, the federal government was in the process of deregulating the airline and telecommunications industries. As it became cheaper to fly across the country for college and call home to Mom when you ran out of money, more high school students began attending colleges farther from home. But which college to choose? In 1983, *U.S. News & World Report* had the novel idea of ranking the nation's colleges and universities. Copies featuring "Best Colleges" rankings flew off the newsstand shelves. The rankings ultimately outlasted the magazine itself. Increasingly, students were behaving like consumers, consulting guidebooks to find the best the market had to offer as determined by magazine journalists.

This created a fertile environment for a new kind of college president, one more attuned to the times. *U.S. News* ranked colleges based on the number of students with high SAT scores and the percentage of scholars with PhDs. The more students who applied to your college and were rejected, the more exclusive and higher-ranked you became. While the old guard of colleges retained a huge built-in advantage because of their reputations and histories—and continue to dominate the very top of the rankings today—there was a lot of room for mobility just below. The right kind of leader could bootstrap his university to fame and fortune. The gentleman scholar as president was disappearing. The empire builder was upon us.

One such man was John Silber of Boston University. BU had been founded in 1869, at the birth of the modern American university. It sits on the banks of the Charles River, right across from MIT, Cambridge, and the higher education promised land. When Silber took over as president in 1971, BU was already trying to catch up with its famous neighbors. Silber threw the process into higher gear, embarking on a huge building campaign while bringing luminaries like Saul Bellow and Elie Wiesel on board to teach.

Silber was brash and outspoken and had little patience for those faculty members who called him authoritarian and worse. By the time he retired in 1996, BU had climbed the *U.S. News* ranks, becoming a bigger, more famous, and much more costly institution. (Tuition and room and board at BU now run over $60,000 per year. It's more expensive than Harvard.) Silber and college administrators like him had written a game plan for the aspiring college president. One of those people was among Silber's inner circle: his vice president, Stephen Joel Trachtenberg.

Of course, most colleges and universities couldn't aim as high as BU. The small liberal arts colleges, community colleges, and compass-point universities weren't able to lure Nobel Prize winners or get away with charging Harvard tuition. But they remained hugely influenced by the hybrid university model. Graduate programs churned out many more PhDs than the academy could hire, creating a brutal job market for academic labor and ensuring that most university professors would teach at institutions less prestigious than the ones at which they trained. The members of the elite college diaspora remembered where they came from and wanted their new homes to resemble the ideal as much as possible.

There was only one model of what higher-education greatness looked like. Even though they had little or no research to conduct, the regional universities and community colleges adopted the forms and trappings of the hybrid research institution: deans and departments, tenure, academic freedom, and PhDs. At some institutions, the lurid spectacle of quasi-professional intercollegiate athletics was thrown into the mix, further driving up costs and distracting from the business of undergraduate education.

All of this made colleges much more expensive than they needed to be. (The point when college prices began to rise quickly came in the early 1980s, just as the *U.S. News* rankings first hit the newsstands.) Worse, the hybrid model's deep indifference to student learning was applied to students who had little tolerance for educational malpractice. Selective schools can afford to put students in courses taught by untrained doctoral students, because they only enroll those most likely to succeed. Not so an open-access community college or regional university. States made matters worse by giving two-year community colleges much less public money per student than four-year institutions. On average, public research universities spend 79 percent more per student on education—not research—than community colleges. To add insult to injury, the community college path to a bachelor's degree was often blocked by four-year universities that refused to accept credits earned at "lesser" institutions.

Despite this, students poured into community colleges, because they had nowhere else to go. The master plans dictated that as many as two-thirds of freshmen in a given state would start at local two-year schools.

These were often students who were the least prepared for college, many juggling jobs and families. They found themselves shunted into colleges with the fewest resources to serve them, and most of them failed to progress. Today, only 10 percent of all students who enroll in community college with the goal of earning a bachelor's degree actually get one within six years. Others earn associate's degrees or remain enrolled in school, but nearly half simply drop out. Open-access four-year universities that serve the same purpose as community colleges often have equally bad graduation rates.

Students at less prestigious institutions tended not to leave college with $100,000 or more in debt, like Hugh from Warwick, Rhode Island, or even the average debt of $29,400 among those who borrow. Instead, they left with a deficit that was even worse: no degree in an economy that increasingly required credentials to grab even the bottom rung of opportunity's ladder. Or they had a degree but little in the way of useful knowledge, leaving college with the kinds of marginal skills that result from being educated at a cash-poor public university built in a hybrid mold that was never designed to be good at undergraduate teaching.

JOHN SILBER was a difficult man to work for. Stephen Joel Trachtenberg had left the federal government after the Johnson presidency ended and taken an administrative position at BU while still in his twenties. He was the only top official who survived the transition after Silber arrived, and the two men formed a professional bond. "I learned my craft from John Silber," Trachtenberg told me. "He died last year, may he rest in peace." Trachtenberg's voice caught for a moment and he shifted on his couch. "I got sentimental there for a second and my mind went back. Forgive me."

Eventually even Trachtenberg, the thick-skinned son of Brooklyn, reached his limits. His wife told him that if he stayed at BU, either he would kill Silber or Silber would kill him. Other universities were eager to hire administrators who could execute the BU game plan and climb the ranks of higher-education fame and fortune. The University of Hartford came calling, and in 1977 Trachtenberg became its president.

He spent eleven years there, always building. Trachtenberg understood the centrality of the university as a physical place. New structures were a visceral sign of progress. They told visitors, donors, and civic leaders that the institution was, like beams and scaffolding rising from the earth, ascending. He added new programs, recruited more students, and followed the dictate of constant expansion.

In 1987 the George Washington University presidency became available and Trachtenberg moved back to D.C. He inherited a university with some assets, most important a prime location in Foggy Bottom just a few blocks from the White House. No university in America was physically closer to the political centers of power. But it had little money and suffered from an inferiority complex. "I was given an institution and told, 'Make this place better,'" Trachtenberg told me. "And by the way, be embarrassed that you're not Georgetown." Everyone wanted something from him: better facilities, better colleagues, better students—and all of those things cost money. He had no base of rich alumni like the centuries-old Ivies or Georgetown did. GW is a private institution, so government funding wasn't an option. Fund-raising was a chicken-and-egg problem: Rich people wanted to support something that was already excellent, but excellence as they understood it required millions of dollars to buy.

However, Trachtenberg understood something crucial about the hybrid university. It had come to inhabit a market for luxury goods. Colleges weren't selling education anymore, if they ever had. They were selling the signs and signals of success. People don't buy Gucci bags merely for their beauty and functionality. They buy them because owning a Gucci bag makes them feel luxurious, and so other people know they can afford the price of purchase. The great virtue of a luxury good, from the manufacturer's standpoint, isn't just that people will pay extra money for the feeling associated with a name brand. It's that the high price is, in and of itself, a crucial part of what people are buying. The price and the product are one and the same.

In other words, Trachtenberg convinced people GW was worth a lot more money by simply charging a lot more money. Unlike most college presidents, Trachtenberg was surprisingly candid about his strategy. College is like vodka, he liked to explain. Vodka is by definition a flavorless beverage. It all tastes the same. But people will spend $30 for a bottle of Absolut vodka because of the brand. A Timex watch costs $20, a Rolex $10,000. They both tell the same time. An expensive degree "serves as a trophy, a symbol," he told one interviewer. For the buyer, "it's a sort of token of who they think they are."

The Absolut Rolex plan worked. Over the next twenty years, George Washington University went from having below-average tuition to becoming, with a $37,820 bill in 2007 for tuition alone, the most expensive university in America. By 2014, GW tuition was past $47,000, plus another $11,000 for room and board.

In the looking-glass world of college economics, demand for services goes up as prices rise, not down. Trachtenberg bought as much Foggy Bottom real estate as he could find and filled it with new buildings. The number of applicants surged and the average SAT score of its students rose.

It wasn't easy, because Trachtenberg wasn't the only college president who played the game this way. The other schools GW was competing with in the national market for students, scholars, and money weren't standing still. "We built a new building, they built two new buildings. It was like those gangster movies where they say, 'You kill one of my guys, I kill two of your guys.' That's what was going on all the time." He looked for opportunities to paint the luxury school picture. Someone realized that only seven colleges in America had varsity squash programs for men and women, and they were all in the Ivy League. GW started the eighth.

The university became a magnet for the children of new money, young men and women who didn't quite have the SATs or family connections required for admission to Stanford or Yale. It also aggressively recruited international students, rich families from Asia and the Middle East who believed, as nearly everyone did, that American universities were the best in the world and that Washington was a good place to attend college. There were also scholarship students who received financial aid. But the average debt for GW graduates flew above the national average, surpassing $33,000 per borrower in 2012.

The campus culture became tinged with consumption. Blogs published pictures of undergrads toting Louis Vuitton bags. A luxury apartment building that opened near campus in 2011 quickly filled with students whose parents paid $3,900 a month in rent. On weekends they gathered in nearby nightclubs to pay $1,000 for reserved tables and bottles of premium vodka and champagne.

GW was hardly alone in this. The empire builders prospered in reviving urban centers. In New York, John Sexton turned NYU into a global higher-education player by selling the dream of downtown living to students raised on *Sex and the City.* In Boston, Northeastern followed BU up the ladder, while Silber's legacy continued to expand along the Charles. In Los Angeles, Steven Sample turned USC from the "University of Spoiled Children" into a *U.S. News* top 25 university. In St. Louis, Washington University did the same.

And in hundreds of regional universities, community colleges, and erstwhile normal schools, presidents and deans and department chairs watched this spectacle of ascension and said to themselves, "That could be me." The restrictions created by the Master Plans began to buckle under the pressures of ambition. The agricultural schools and technical institutes lobbied for tuition increases and PhD programs, fitness centers, and arenas for sport. Even the community colleges got into the act. In south Florida, the sprawling Miami-Dade Community College added bachelor's degree programs and dropped the "community" (and the hyphen) from its name. Dozens of two-year schools followed. State governors and lawmakers would complain about rising tuition and university efforts to climb the status ladder instead of staying in their Master Plan–approved place. But states were also in the middle of a decades-long fit of tax cutting, prison building, and structural adjustment to exploding health care costs for an aging population. Public colleges and universities saw their funding decline relative to other public services and asked for freedom to define their academic missions, student bodies, and pricing structures in exchange. They all wanted to go in one direction—up!—and they all moved with a single vision of what they wanted to be.

I asked Trachtenberg if it was morally defensible to let students borrow tens of thousands of dollars for a service that he himself had compared to a valueless luxury good. He is not, by nature, one for apologies and second-guessing. The *Atlantic,* still writing about higher education a century and a half after launching the career of Harvard president Charles Eliot, had recently published an article describing Trachtenberg as "the high priest of runaway college inflation." I didn't mention it for fear he'd be insulted. Trachtenberg made a point of handing me a photocopy before I left.

"I'm not embarrassed by what we did," he said. "It's not as if it's some kind of a bait and switch here. It's not as if the faculty weren't good. It's not as if the opportunities to get a good degree weren't there. There's no misrepresentation here." He seemed unbowed but also aware that his legacy was bound up in the larger dramas and crises of American higher education. "I'm in favor of a perfect world." he said. "I didn't get to be a president in a perfect world. I got to be president in a world in which I was living."

In the end, Stephen Joel Trachtenberg did no more or less than what every other successful, ambitious administrator in his position had done in the hundred years since the hybrid university had been invented. "Most of us," he said, "unless we have a greater intelligence and a greater imagination than I claim to, we build what we know, what we saw." He had seen the university from the Olympian vantages of Cambridge, New Haven, and Morningside Heights, watched it grow with students and federal money during the great expansion, and lived in the cauldron of administrative ambition. And so he built the perfect representation of what, for good and for ill, American higher education has become.

IN 2007, Stephen Joel Trachtenberg turned seventy years old. His father had died at that age, and he wondered how many years he had left. He still loved being a university president. The endless meetings and decisions and controversies continued to thrill him, in their way. But twenty years in one job is a long time, and the trustees had begun talking about who was next. So he stepped down, settled into his office in the Trachtenberg School, and continued to travel, write, speak, raise money for the university, and not apologize for raising tuition. When I noted that some other college had recently passed GW in having the highest price, he said that wouldn't have happened on his watch: He would have kept it going.

But he also began to realize that the time for men like him was coming to an end. One of his sons had moved across the country, to Silicon Valley, where he landed a job with the business networking firm LinkedIn. Like his father before him, Trachtenberg had opinions about his son's future and was inclined to share them. Get a PhD, he urged, the degree he had never gone back to complete himself.

"But, Dad," his son replied, "if I get a PhD in my line of work, I'll be looked down upon."

That was strange. So Trachtenberg visited this place where the traditional markers of status had somehow been reversed. At Stanford, one of the great modern research universities, he saw technologies that made him believe that the university model he had perfected was about to be torn down.

Trachtenberg didn't know it yet, but the University of Everywhere was already beginning to rise from a foundation of ideas that had been steadily building at the best hybrid universities. Some of the smartest people in the world had been unraveling the deepest mysteries of human cognition, while others had launched an information technology revolution that was rapidly leveling and rebuilding whole fields of human endeavor. Finally, those forces together had grown powerful enough to shatter the hybrid model and forge something new.

4

Cathedrals

If education were only a matter of presenting information to students, the Gutenberg revolution would have destroyed the university five hundred years ago. Offering *The Secret of Life* online would involve nothing more than taping Eric Lander's lectures and posting them on YouTube. But teaching and learning are much more complicated than mere presentation. The brain is not a passive receptacle for knowledge. Rather, people actively build knowledge and understanding by integrating new facts and ideas into all of the concepts, memories, and information that already exist inside their minds.

This requires hard and unavoidable work, which is why every standard MIT course includes a large number of problem sets, or "p-sets" as the students call them. You don't really know whether you've learned something until you have to apply the lessons of the lectures to complicated tasks designed to test your ability to use abstract concepts in solving concrete problems. Completing those problems strengthens and deepens your understanding of the ideas and information. For example, one 7.00x p-set opened up a little window on my computer that showed a diagram of a molecule and a menu of buttons that let me change the molecule by adding different kinds of atoms to other atoms at different points, thus forming different kinds of bonds. It then presented this question:

> *Dopamine is a neurotransmitter—a chemical released by nerve cells to send signals to other nerve cells. Activities like sex and gambling increase the levels of dopamine released within the brain. The highly addictive drugs cocaine and methamphetamine mimic the effects of dopamine. Loss of dopamine-releasing cells in parts of the brain can lead to Parkinson's disease, a condition characterized by tremors and motor impairment. The dopamine molecule in the window below is capable of making strong hydrogen bonds. Edit the dopamine molecule so it can no longer make strong hydrogen bonds.*

I got it wrong the first couple of times, went back to my notes, watched a portion of the lecture again, and finally nailed down the underlying principles of molecular bonding in my mind. Later in the course, we learned how the amino acids in DNA molecules fit together, and how Linus Pauling raced with Crick and Watson to discover the double helix, along with the intricate dance of transcription and translation, mismatch detection and repair. The p-sets in this part of the course used another computer program, called the "Integrative Genome Viewer," which allowed me to see what happens when mutations alter single base pairs in a DNA sequence that can run hundreds of millions of pairs long, resulting in a new set of instructions for protein creation and sometimes disastrous consequences for the organism in question. In another p-set, we had to breed multiple generations of fruit flies in a computer simulator and submit "cages" containing, say, 1,000 virtual drosophila showing a particular statistical distribution of characteristics—this many wings of this shape, this many eyes of that color—as evidence of the underlying genetic inheritance patterns.

It was taxing work. As one of the MIT students taking the course later told me, "Learning science is about spending hours banging away at something until you get it right." The p-sets were designed for the 9 percent of top high school applicants who are accepted by MIT. As the course progressed, I could feel a new part of my brain being partitioned off to hold all the new ideas and information. Accessing the partition was always a struggle; every time I sat down in the evening to watch a new lecture or work on a p-set it was like slowly pushing open a heavy set of doors.

The biological nature of this process—the complex interaction of sensory information with neural networks and mental constructs—was a mystery to the founders of traditional colleges. So were many modern ideas about how people think and learn. Those discoveries were made over the course of the twentieth century, often at hybrid universities that made phenomenal contributions to the understanding of human cognition even as they steadfastly refused to apply those insights to their own philosophies and practices of teaching.

At a few universities, however, the learning scientists and computer engineers came together to build educational tools that could be far more effective—and far less expensive—than the mediocre, bankruptcy-inducing classes being taught at the hybrid universities. So I went to one of the universities on the cutting edge of learning technology—a place that is also, in a sense, where my own educational journey began.

A LOVELY PEDESTRIAN BRIDGE connects the fine arts and computer science buildings at Carnegie Mellon University in Pittsburgh, Pennsylvania. It's made of steel punched with empty silhouettes of penguins. The bridge was built in honor of Professor Randy Pausch, whose "last lecture" of life's wisdom, delivered with the certain knowledge of his imminent death from cancer, inspired millions. In his lecture, Pausch described the "First Penguin Award" that he would bestow on the team of students that took the biggest gamble while not meeting its goals. Pausch liked to observe that when a group of penguins jump in water that might have predators, one of them has to be first. Pausch's field was human-computer interaction, the exploration of ideas that connect what it means to be human with humanity's ever more powerful machines.

I walked across the penguin bridge early one Saturday morning in spring, on my way to meet with the university's provost, Mark Kamlet. As Kamlet and I talked about Carnegie Mellon's past, present, and future, he couldn't help but boast. Of all the great American research universities, CMU is by far the youngest, birthed through the 1967 merger of the Carnegie Institute of Technology and the Mellon Institute of Industrial Research. CMU had taken full advantage of Vannevar Bush's grand plan for federally financed university-based research, building world-class research centers in robotics, information systems, and design. The computer science building, named after its primary benefactor, Bill Gates, includes an actual lunar lander in the late stages of manufacture in the basement. At the same time, CMU is highly invested in the arts, boasting one of the nation's finest drama departments. To an unusual extent, Carnegie Mellon is focused on truth, beauty, and what connects the two.

But despite all of that, Provost Kamlet seemed worried. We spoke in his office, which is on the top floor of the CMU administration building and has a commanding view of downtown Pittsburgh. "We're on the razor's edge here," he told me. Of the thousands of colleges and universities that had ridden the great wave of twentieth-century higher-education expansion, he believed that only fifteen of them were poised to survive what he saw coming in the future. Or maybe twenty-five, or fifty, but not many, and he was not as sure as he wanted to be that Carnegie Mellon would be one of them.

Three buildings stood out in the view below us. There was a red fortress-like structure in the right foreground, just past the end of campus, called Central Catholic High School. Saint Paul Cathedral stood farther up the street, framed by two Gothic spires. And to the left and behind them was a single five-hundred-foot tower, built to skyscraper proportions, but with architectural echoes of Chartres, Reims, and Notre Dame.

It was the Cathedral of Learning, the iconic academic building of the city's other famous research institution, the University of Pittsburgh.

I pointed at the Cathedral of Learning and asked Kamlet, of the fifteen or maybe twenty-five or fifty survivors, is that going to be one of them?

He shook his head. Because Mark Kamlet knew that even as universities like his had both embodied and exploited the hybrid model, they had also, through their intellectual endeavors, been nurturing the seeds of their own destruction. The scholars in all of those federally funded labs had been thinking very hard about two of the intellectual questions that would define the age: the nature of human cognition and the uses of information technology. Now those ideas and technologies had reached a crucial point of maturity. The world was poised on the brink of a massive shift in how education works and how people learn—the emergence of the University of Everywhere. People across the globe would be able to enter learning environments that were far superior to anything they had access to before. Organizational models like the hybrid university that had been built prior to the information technology revolution were highly vulnerable. Whether they knew it or not, every university in America and beyond was in a race with the onrushing future, and history suggested that most old organizations in that predicament tend to get trampled into dust.

It was clear to Kamlet that the new education technologies being developed at Carnegie Mellon and elsewhere would radically change the underlying economics of higher education as well as the broader narrative of American opportunity in which colleges and universities had long played a central role. That story was at the front of my mind as Kamlet and I were speaking. Because the three standout buildings in the view below us weren't just emblematic of Pittsburgh's educational past: They also defined the first twenty-one years of my father's life.

BERNARD CAREY JR. was born in Pittsburgh in 1941, the grandson of Irish immigrants who had come to work in the steel mills. He spent nearly his entire childhood in a four-square-mile area encompassing the neighborhoods of Oakland and Bloomfield. The second of five children, Bernard and his older brother, Michael, attended the local Catholic grammar school, where the teachers were nuns with a stern sense of discipline. The sisters were suspicious of information technology. Every term, Bernard's mother was required to indicate on his report card the number of "times a week child attends movies" and "hours a night spent with radio or television." At the bottom of the card, where the parents had to sign, it said, "Be interested in your child's work. Ask him about it; do not do it for him. Praise his success; encourage him when he fails. *Be a good parent.*"

Bernard and Michael served as altar boys at Saint Paul Cathedral, trudging through the snow in winter to serve at early Saturday morning Mass. Afterward, Bernard liked to tag along with his brother and visit the mammoth Carnegie Library of Pittsburgh across the street, looking for new books to check out. Or he would wander through the stately Carnegie Museums nearby. It made him wonder about the world beyond.

When Bernard turned thirteen, he enrolled in the all-boys Central Catholic High School, which was run by the Christian Brothers order. The Brothers weren't averse to using their fists to keep their charges on the road toward salvation. Boys wore suits and ties to school and interaction with girls was limited to Saturday night dances where close contact was prohibited. "Leave room in between you for the Holy Ghost," said the watchful nuns from the girls' schools.

Classes were segregated by ability and Bernard consistently got top marks. When he graduated, it was clear he would have to find money on his own if he wanted to go to college. So he got a scholarship to the University of Pittsburgh, his mother's alma mater, a then private research university with roots dating back to colonial times. That, along with jobs, loans, and living at home, was enough to pay the bills. The university had moved to the Oakland neighborhood in 1908, just as the hybrid university model had become firmly set in stone.

Pitt's tenth chancellor, John Gabbert Bowman, had caught the fever of institution-building and made plans for the greatest university edifice ever conceived. He eventually had to scale back his designs for what remains the tallest educational building in the western hemisphere: the Cathedral of Learning. Built forty-two stories high in the late Gothic Revival style, the Cathedral is clad in gray Indiana limestone over a steel frame donated by the local industrial magnates. The Common Room in the center soars fifty feet to the ceiling under load-bearing gothic arches. Described by a critic as "one of the great architectural fantasies of the twentieth century," the room strongly resembles the Hogwarts Great Hall in the *Harry Potter* films.

Bernard was nervous as he began school at Pitt. He attended freshman orientation in a lecture hall with hundreds of classmates where they were told, "Look to your left, and look to your right. Only one of the three of you will graduate from college."

Bernard wanted to study electrical engineering, where the expected attrition rate was even more extreme. A family connection gave him an important advantage: His aunt Helen arranged a job as a laboratory technician at the nearby Mellon Institute of Science. He worked twenty hours a week during the semester and full-time during breaks for a group doing ceramics research sponsored by the Hanley Brick Company. The older scientists served as mentors, teaching him the discipline and art of working in the lab.

Bernard joined a fraternity and enjoyed being a young man on a campus with many women and no nuns. He spent hours hanging out in the campus coffee shop, where he was drawn into intense discussions about the meaning of life and was challenged to logically defend the Catholic belief system. He found that he couldn't, and by his sophomore year had withdrawn from the Church, never to return.

Nineteen sixty-two was a good year to leave an American university with an engineering degree. Bernard had six job offers upon graduation. One of them was from Litton Industries, an aerospace firm in California. He had two weeks between commencement and his first day on the job. Aunt Helen lent him $200 and bought him an American Tourister luggage set. He went west to see what life would bring.

MY FATHER FITS NEATLY in the story Americans like to tell themselves about education and opportunity. An immigrant goes to work in the factory, his children get an education, their children go to college. All five Carey brothers and sisters earned bachelor's degrees or better. They went to work as naval officers, teachers, engineers, and businessmen, married people of similar station, and had children who all went to college, too.

The twentieth-century American higher-education system was undoubtedly better than any other that existed—or had ever existed—for lifting up people like my family. Such successes resonate so deeply that it can be easy to forget how unusual they really are.

Bernard Carey worked hard for everything he achieved. He also grew up in a part of Pittsburgh that contained two major research universities, a huge library, a world-class museum, a concert hall, and a highly organized parochial school system. At a time when children couldn't travel farther than they could walk, he lived within walking distance of all the books in the world. He had a mother who graduated from college at age nineteen despite deep societal sexism and loved to read to her son. Bernard was a white man in a white man's world. He was never poor, hungry, legally discriminated against, or threatened with existential harm.

The engineering program at Pitt didn't hold with Charles Eliot's laissez-faire elective approach. Unlike the legions of business and political science majors wandering through college today, Bernard had to take a prescribed curriculum. The job his aunt found for him at the Mellon Institute put him into an Oxfordian master/student relationship that only a small fraction of undergraduates ever experience. College was cheap enough to afford with prudence, part-time and summer work, and reasonable loans. He happened to be born twenty-one years before a time when the economy really needed engineers.

What about all the people who weren't so lucky? The one sitting to the right and the one to the left? The other children who happened to be born elsewhere in Pittsburgh or in the surrounding hills and countryside, or in a different state or nation altogether? Most of them never graduated from college. They never came close.

On the day my father hit the road for California, 42 percent of Americans between the ages of twenty-five and thirty-four hadn't even graduated from high school. Only 11 percent had a bachelor's degree. Even now, after a massive investment in building a community college system and stamping out hundreds of copies of the hybrid university, most Americans have not graduated from college.

Educational opportunities in my father's days were, then as now, largely a function of place. If you were close enough to the cathedrals of learning, you lived one kind of life. If you weren't, you lived another. Even if you were in the right place at the right time, there was still the risk of being the one on the left or the one on the right.

For a long time, America got away with ignoring this kind of unequal opportunity because we were so big and so rich and so far ahead of everyone else. But as the hybrid model inevitably became more decadent and expensive, its cost to society became harder to bear.

The problem was that there didn't seem to be any viable alternatives. The American college system had already been built and the people who ran it were disinclined to change. So society learned to live with the hybrid university, and over time we came to accept its many weird and maddening qualities as the best—indeed, only possible—way for college to be.

The only way, that is, until scientists and researchers in the oldest and richest universities began unlocking the secrets of the human mind and building the technologies that would define the age to come.

ROBERT MAYNARD HUTCHINS's grand plans for the University of Chicago ultimately faded into the mass of university conformity. But while he was there, a remarkable generation of students came through the university's campus in Hyde Park. Milton Friedman and Saul Bellow studied there in the 1930s, as did *Washington Post* publisher Katharine Graham. Two Hutchins-era Chicago graduates in particular would have an outsized influence on the convergence of technology and education. One was a Milwaukee native named Herbert Simon, who would make his home at Carnegie Mellon. The other was Patrick Suppes, a brilliant philosopher and mathematician who went on teach at the iconic Cold War research institution, Stanford University.

Simon's father earned an engineering degree in Germany, then emigrated to Milwaukee, where Herbert was born. His home was full of books and music and as a child Herbert liked to explore the science section in the local public library. It was another big city close enough to higher education for an immigrant's son to make the leap to college, and Simon enrolled in Chicago in 1932, shortly after Hutchins's arrival. He went on to earn a PhD in political science there, taking full advantage of the breadth of departments by studying mathematics, logic, and graduate physics on the side. Simon became fascinated with human organizations. Why did they act the way they did? He wrote a seminal book, *Administrative Behavior*, exploring those questions.

Simon challenged the classic Economics 101 model of people using perfect information to make choices that maximize their expected outcomes. He understood that the world is enormously complicated and that people are faced with constant choice restricted by finite time and limited knowledge. Simon called this "bounded rationality," and the resulting search for a good enough result "satisficing." Thirty years later, the work would win him the Nobel Prize in economics.

Simon was a rigorous thinker who wanted to test and improve his theories at the mathematical and theoretical levels. But it's hard to experiment on organizations: You can't create two identical General Motors Companies just to fiddle with the management structure of one of them to see what happens. He needed a way to simulate dynamics and probabilities, some kind of machine that could calculate faster than any human. A computer, in other words. In the mid-1950s, Simon had settled in Pittsburgh at Carnegie Tech, where he would think and teach until his death in 2001. During the winter break from classes in 1955, he and a computer science colleague developed a computer program that was able to solve complex mathematical and geometric theorems. The next month Simon returned to class and told his students, "Over the Christmas holiday, Al Newell and I invented a thinking machine."

Six months later, Simon attended a conference at Dartmouth College, where he and a small group of scientists gave a name to this new field of research: artificial intelligence. The study of the human mind and the exploding power of information technology were coming together, and the smartest people in the world were in the middle of the action.

Among the Dartmouth participants was Claude Shannon, a former student of Vannevar Bush at MIT and one of the fathers of modern information theory. In addition to creating the blueprint for the Cold War university, Bush had also seen the future technological revolution. In a 1945 *Atlantic* article titled "As We May Think," Bush observed that various fields of manufacturing and computing were on trajectories of improvement that would soon lead to changes that, although they might be unknowable in the specific, were highly predictable in general. "The world has arrived at an age of cheap complex devices of great reliability," he said, "and something is bound to come of it."

Like Simon, Bush understood that the great challenge of the modern world was not accessing information but organizing and making sense of it. "There may be millions of fine thoughts," Bush wrote, "all encased within stone walls of acceptable architectural form; but if the scholar can get at only one a week by diligent search, his syntheses are not likely to keep up with the current scene." In his essay, Bush proposed the "Memex," a system of structured, interconnected information that laid theoretical foundations for hypertext, digital media, and the World Wide Web.

Over the next seventy years, researchers would tackle a host of fundamental questions and create whole new fields of inquiry. Neuro-scientists studied how the brain works. Cognitive psychologists asked: How do people think and learn? As neuroscience and information theory developed in parallel, the connections between them were obvious to polymath thinkers like Simon. Whether it was neurons and axes in the brain or integrated circuits in a computer, people were trying to understand the structures and theories of information being transmitted via electricity through vast and complicated networks. Something was bound to come of it.

What they discovered had important implications for human learning and education. Your brain is a fantastically complex network. It contains between eighty billion and one hundred billion neurons, each of which can form tens of thousands of individual connections with other neurons. These thousands of trillions of connections can be arranged in an unimaginably large number of ways. Every new thought and memory produces a physical change in your neural network. Education is a deliberate process of rewiring your brain.

The cerebral cortex matters most for thinking and learning. It's the folded layer of gray matter that envelops the brain, regulating sensation, memory, language, and consciousness. The back part of the cerebral cortex receives information from your senses. Different parts receive different kinds of information, working in parallel. Parts of your eyes sense color, for example, while other parts sense lines, edges, and forms. This information is routed to different parts of your visual cortex, which then integrates the data into coherent shapes. The same is true for variations of sound, taste, smell, and touch. Just by living, you are constantly awash in new information.

This creates a biological version of the problem that Herbert Simon won a Nobel Prize for studying in organizations, and that Vannevar Bush's Memex was designed to solve for the growing mass of research: too much information. Your brain solves this problem with *patterns*. Consider the sentence "My mother bought an encyclopedia." When you read the word "encyclopedia," it required very little time and mental effort for you to understand what it meant. You did not consider the shape of each letter in turn, as a small child might, carefully relating each to a specific sound and then linking them together to form a word: "en-sigh-klo-pee-dee-ah." That's because before you read that sentence, a pattern had already been created in your brain, involving a specific set of neurons linked together by axons, dendrites, and synapses, representing the word "encyclopedia."

Because you have spent thousands of hours reading over years of your life, that pattern is very well established, and the connections between the neurons are quite strong. So your brain required only a brief glance at that combination of letters to understand that it meant "encyclopedia" and all the word implies. The process was largely automatic, just as you don't consciously think "that broad, flat surface located approximately three feet below me is the floor, which will support my weight" when you climb out of bed in the morning.

The brain's capacity for pattern recognition is adaptable, flexible, and strong. If the word in that sentence had been spelled "encylopedia," you would not have been utterly baffled, even though it is missing the second letter *c*. You might not have even noticed the mistake at all. If, on the other hand, I had written "iderēbagon," you probably would have been confused, unless you happen to be fluent in the verb forms of High Valyrian, a language spoken by certain characters on the HBO television series *Game of Thrones*.

The use of patterns extends far beyond tasks like reading words or walking around your home. Some patterns relate to the physical world: Throw an object up in the air and the force of gravity will slow and then reverse that acceleration. We know the pattern: What goes up must come down. Other patterns are interpersonal: A smiling face usually indicates a happy emotional state in another person; tears and scowling suggest anger and frustration.

While some mental patterns are largely universal—everyone understands gravity—many others are not. Different cultures and creeds offer different ways of understanding and interpreting the world. The ways that we receive new information, the sense we make of it and the meanings we ascribe, are a function of the patterns that already exist in our brains. Exactly the same sequence of words could trigger very different neural patterns in different people, and thus come to mean, for each of them, very different things.

All of this has huge implications for the practice of teaching and the design of educational organizations. It helps explain why so many college graduates learn so little in their four years on campus. Education, it turns out, is far more complicated than anyone realized, and standard hybrid universities aren't equipped or motivated to do the extremely difficult work of helping students with vastly different individual neural patterns to achieve the same rigorous learning goals.

In 1973, Herbert Simon and a Carnegie Mellon psychologist named William Chase published a study of human memory. The study participants had varying levels of chess expertise, ranging from novice to master. In one part of the experiment, each participant was shown a chessboard for five seconds on which the pieces were arranged in a random pattern. Then they were asked to remember where the pieces had been. All of the participants performed about the same, and badly: They could remember only about four of the correct positions.

Then the same participants were shown another chessboard, this time arranged in a position consistent with the rules of chess. The novice players performed no better than they had with the random board. The master players, by contrast, did far better. They were able to remember the positions of as many as twenty pieces after the same brief glance. Why? Because those positions fit neural patterns that had been built through years of study and practice. For the masters, it was the difference between reading the letter sequences "iderēbagon" and "encyclopedia."

Using the word "pattern" this way can be too simplistic. It means far more than just a physical arrangement of things. Psychologically and neurologically, patterns are complex combinations of associations and principles. In 1982, Simon's coauthor, William Chase, published a study with a young Swedish psychologist named K. Anders Ericsson. They found that people were much more likely to remember words arranged in coherent sentences than the same words rearranged in random order. Ericsson went on to devote much of his career to the idea of expertise. He found that extraordinary achievers like chess masters and concert pianists had, through thousands of hours of practice, neurologically inscribed sophisticated principles of their professions into patterns that operated at almost automatic levels. While a beginning chess player will waste precious time thinking through specific possible sequences of moves without considering the big picture, a master will quickly consider a position from strategic principles: Keep the pieces active and mobile, be mindful of the tempo of the game, control the center of the board. An expert football quarterback can run, scramble, and throw while simultaneously looking for patterns in the dance of receivers and defenders in front of him, while a normal person put on the same field would stumble and collapse in total confusion.

Experts also learn differently. They are able to filter the noise of sensation, locate relevant new data, and integrate it into sophisticated structures of information. It's not that experts can remember more; it's that they know what to remember. Hard-won expertise is incredibly powerful, allowing people to perform in ways that are beyond the understanding of everyone else.

Indeed, to be human is to be constantly searching for patterns that ease the ache of awareness and incomprehension. This explains the great power of story and metaphor in human thinking. We are always looking for meaning, for patterns that are both familiar and revelatory, that give us some small understanding of ourselves and the universe around us.

THE COMPLEXITY of human thinking and importance of patterns and expertise meant that education needed to be considered in new ways. By the middle of the twentieth century, scholars such as the Soviet psychologist Lev Vygotsky and the Swiss psychologist Jean Piaget were developing theories of learning and cognition that would ultimately complement the emerging field of neuroscience.

Vygotsky coined the phrase "zone of proximal development" to describe the difference between what a child can learn on her own and what she can learn with the help of a teacher. Potential learning proceeds from each individual and his or her particular neural patterns. Vygotsky died in Moscow of tuberculosis in 1934, when he was thirty-seven years old. Those who continued to develop his ideas used the metaphorical pattern of "scaffolding" to describe the implications of his work. We can see in the mind's eye the image of a worker building a platform ten feet off the ground, and then standing on that platform to build another ten-foot platform above. The ascension proceeds in stages, each new level depending on the progress made below. The worker could never scale a tall building in one leap. But with the right tools and carefully constructed scaffolds, he can reach great heights.

Similarly, Piaget believed that children used "schemas"—what we now think of as neural patterns—to interact with and interpret information, and that these schemas grow more sophisticated and powerful as we age. If you've heard someone say this or that activity is "developmentally appropriate" for a child, you're hearing the legacy of Piaget. He believed that learning happens when students actively engage with the world around them, building knowledge and meaning by applying schemas to challenges and experience.

Neuroscience would eventually underscore the wisdom of Vygotsky, Piaget, and others like them. The brain doesn't get information just from the five senses. It also gets information from *itself*, through the product of abstract thought, active learning, and higher-order cognition. There are connections from the temporal lobe back to the parts of the brain that process and interpret new information, an unending loop of neural pattern making in continuous formation.

This, ultimately, is why the problem sets are such an important part of the MIT core curriculum. As a novice student of genetics and molecular biology, I didn't have well-established patterns of scientific theory with which to efficiently process new information. I had to *build* those patterns, piece by piece, in my mind. The problem sets forced me to take various newly introduced facts and ideas and connect them to one another in the right way. That feeling of pushing open a heavy door every night was physical and neurological: After spending the day in the comfort zone of my expertise in education policy, I had to light up new, often fragile neural constructs of biological science that required far more effort to strengthen and expand.

Designing courses and problem sets that stimulate that kind of work isn't easy. Neither is motivating students to persist and persevere. But that's the difference between an encyclopedia and a college—or Wikipedia and the University of Everywhere. As Jacques Barzun and many others have observed, the hybrid university perversely *penalizes* scholars who spend too much time trying to be good teachers. Professors are given strong reasons to shirk a difficult task, and react accordingly. What results is a kind of mutual disarmament pact among college professors and students: Neither is asked to work very hard, the professors get to focus on the research they care about, and the students all get good grades. This was among the most depressing findings in Arum and Roksa's *Academically Adrift*. College students from impoverished backgrounds were given less challenging work to do—fewer opportunities to actively engage in learning—and learned much less as a result.

As modern society has become more complicated, the negative consequences of this for students have become much worse. The kinds of jobs that pay a decent salary require far more from workers than they used to. People with the expertise and skill to perform complex tasks using machines powered by ever-improving information technology can thrive and prosper. People without that kind of education are being left in the cold. And as college becomes more expensive, the have-nots are increasingly students from low-income backgrounds. Colleges are taking existing inequality and making it worse.

But with the powerful hybrid universities entrenched by law and custom, nothing could change until some kind of breakthrough occurred: a way to provide a much better educational experience for far *less* money than the current model allowed, even while accounting for each learner's individuality. Some kind of technology, in other words, that could be applied to education.

As it happened, there were smart people at the great research universities thinking about this problem, too.

5

Learning Like Alexander

As the weeks and months of 7.00x unfolded, I thought back to my own undergraduate days. I had arrived on campus with a personal computer that had no hard drive: The MS-DOS operating system had to be loaded into memory every time I turned the computer on, using 5¼-inch floppy disks. My PC wasn't connected to the Internet because there was no Internet for anyone other than a small number of scientists. My research was accomplished with card catalogues stored in the university's biggest building, the library, along with copies of the *Reader's Guide to Periodical Literature,* bound in green hardcover on shelves near the reference desk. When the library closed, I had to find something else to do.

Fast-forward twenty-five years to my dining room table, with all the world's knowledge a Web browser away. Lander's lectures streamed over a fast broadband connection into a brilliant, high-definition display. If I needed to understand more about a particular concept or term, I didn't have to buy a $300 textbook that the campus bookstore would buy back from me later for pennies on the dollar and then resell at huge profit to someone else. The 7.00x course materials included a free, searchable molecular biology textbook with hundreds of pages of charts, graphs, and explanations. Wikipedia helped, too. The 3-D models, fruit fly simulator, and interactive gene viewer with millions of DNA and RNA base pairs to manipulate were easily handled by laptop computer hardware that anyone can buy for a few hundred dollars.

I also had thousands of other students to talk to if I needed help. The MIT learning management system included forums and message boards where students could pose questions and help their who were stuck on a particular problem set or idea. A 7.00x Facebook group appeared almost instantaneously as the class began, including students from over a hundred countries. Scrolling through the members, I saw names and faces from familiar places like Rotterdam, Lisbon, Brasília, Tehran, and Berlin, along with scores of students from places I had never heard of before: Omdurman Islamic University in Sudan, the Xinzhuang district of Taipei, the Indian district of Tiruchirappalli, and the city of Chennai. It was remarkable to see how far and fast information technology had spread, and how many people around the world were driven to learn.

MIT teaching assistants moderated the official edX forums and occasionally answered questions. But there was no way to provide thousands of online students working around the clock with the same kind of personalized feedback that the one hundred students taking the same course in Cambridge received. Sometimes this forced me to redouble my mental efforts, banging away until I got it right. But at other times, it was simply frustrating. I would get stuck at some juncture on the path toward molecular biology enlightenment, unable to find a way forward. Chemistry, in particular, was vexing. Well into the course, I looked up the academic prerequisites for the terrestrial version of Introduction to Biology—*The Secret of Life*. It said:

CHEMISTRY PREPARATION FOR BIOLOGY

You will need some chemistry background to be successful in 7.01x. Before enrolling in one of the Biology classes, you should either have a strong high school chemistry background (e.g., score of 5 on AP

Chemistry), or you should complete one of the MIT core chemistry subjects (5.111 or 5.112 or 3.091) before enrolling in Introductory Biology.

The last time I took chemistry was in 1986, when I was a sophomore in high school. I got a B minus and never studied it again. The 7.00x course had been designed, quite sensibly, for the typical MIT undergraduate. I was able to overcome my general lack of MIT-caliber science aptitude by spending more time reviewing the lectures and working on the problem sets than, I suspect, a typical eighteen-year-old prodigy requires. But my lack of chemistry knowledge was a different kind of barrier to learning. The 7.00x course lectures were first-rate, the problem sets challenging, and the online forums welcoming. But the educational software was not designed to diagnose my particular strengths and weaknesses nor offer any kind of specific, personalized educational experience in response. It had not overcome the basic dilemma of mass higher education: how to give individuals with unique experiences and neural patterns exactly what they need.

Solving that problem will be a key step toward building the University of Everywhere. As expensive and indifferent to student learning as the old hybrid universities are, at least they still offer the potential for one-on-one attention. To break through and compete with traditional colleges, new learning organizations will need to use technology to provide something markedly better than what traditional schools offer.

Efforts to reach that milestone began further back in history than I realized, before the age of modern computing itself.

PATRICK SUPPES was born in Tulsa, Oklahoma, in 1922 and raised in a family of oilmen. His stepmother was a devout Christian Scientist, and young Patrick found himself taking the side of empiricism in Sunday school arguments about the bacterial theory of disease. A student growing up in the Dust Bowl during the Great Depression was very far from the traditional cathedrals of learning.

But Patrick Suppes was lucky. In 1930 a group of progressive education reformers came together in Washington, D.C., to talk about the nation's high schools. Curricula had become too rigid and narrow, they believed, too focused on the mechanical accumulation of credits needed for acceptance to college. High school students needed an education that was more flexible, rigorous, and focused on the underlying principles of science, math, language, and other academic fields rather than mere facts and figures.

To test these theories, the reformers chose thirty high schools from among tens of thousands nationwide to participate in what became known as "The Eight-Year Study." Many of the high schools were elite private institutions, including Horace Mann in New York City and the University of Chicago High School. But they also included a few more prosaic institutions, including Tulsa Senior and Junior High Schools.

To identify students for the program, the Tulsa school district administered a standardized aptitude test to students who happened to be in the sixth grade that year. Patrick Suppes got a very high score. He was enrolled in a special program within his high school, in which the teachers taught a curriculum designed by the administrators of the Eight-Year Study. He would later describe those classes as among the most competitive he ever attended.

The special curriculum was enough to get Suppes into the University of Oklahoma, which he found to be academically unchallenging. After a year, he transferred to the University of Chicago, where he dug into Aristotle as part of Hutchins's focus on teaching the Great Books.

By then, the world was in flames. Suppes was called up into the Army Reserve in 1942 and studied physics at Chicago during the day while nights and weekends were spent preparing for war. He graduated with a BS focusing on meteorology. The Army sent him to the South Pacific to monitor the weather as Nimitz and MacArthur drove titanic fleets across the ocean toward the final confrontation with imperial Japan. Suppes was stationed in the Solomon Islands and found their solitude and serenity to his liking. He played poker with his U.S. Army Air Force buddies, read more Aristotle, and took correspondence courses in mathematics and French. When the war ended, he worked in the Oklahoma oil fields for most of a year and then enrolled in the graduate philosophy department at Columbia, where he earned his PhD. In 1950 he landed a teaching position at Stanford University. He taught there for nearly five decades and still lives on the campus today.

The traditional critique of the hybrid university as a research institution is that it forces scholars to burrow into increasingly specialized fields while remaining ignorant of other ways of thinking. But for a certain kind of scholar, the twentieth-century American research university was an intellectual wonderland. Suppes formed close partnerships with scholars in a huge range of fields, publishing on quantum mechanics, the philosophy of science, theories of measurement, probability and decision theory, distributive justice, the principles of causality, psycholinguistics, cognitive psychology, and the philosophy of language.

Shortly after arriving at Stanford, Suppes and his wife had a daughter. She entered kindergarten in 1956 and her father became very interested in how children learn mathematics. Other professors with young children had similar interests, but Suppes quickly realized that most weren't inclined to tackle such questions with the rigor they gave to their own research. "They had no desire," he later wrote, "to know anything about prior scholarship in education." Suppes threw himself into learning science and was amazed by its depth. His experience, he wrote, was that "even a subject as relatively simple as elementary-school mathematics is of unbounded complexity in terms of understanding the underlying psychological theory of learning and performance." To study learning was to study the human mind, a subject that daunted even the most formidable interdisciplinary thinkers.

In addition to being a city of intellect, Stanford sat at a nexus of commerce and information technology. Suppes was interested in how computers could help improve education. In 1963 he received a grant from the nonprofit Carnegie Corporation of New York to set up an educational computing laboratory at Stanford where elementary school students would take math courses on computers. Three years later he published a landmark article in *Scientific American* titled "The Uses of Computers in Education."

Suppes began with a grand prediction. Soon, he said, "millions of schoolchildren will have access to what Philip of Macedon's son Alexander enjoyed as a royal prerogative: the personal services of a tutor as well-informed and responsive as Aristotle." The ancient Greeks had understood what modern cognitive psychology and neuroscience would confirm: Because every person's learning proceeds in the unique context of his or her neural patterns, every person needs to be taught in an individualized way. That's why they used the tutorial teaching method, and why Oxford and Cambridge did the same. The challenge in an age of universal education was to simulate the adaptability of the tutorial without having to hire a personal Aristotle for every student.

This is what Suppes had been working on in his education lab. "The computer makes the individualization of instruction easier because it can be programmed to follow each student's history of learning successes and failures and to use his past performance as a basis for selecting the new problems and new concepts to which he should be exposed next." Suppes also understood that deliberate practice was integral to education, something that would later become a key part of Ericsson's theory of expertise. Learning is *work,* a deliberate process of strengthening neural connections to the point where they operated automatically, creating a framework for understanding new information and freeing up mental capacity for learning more. The challenge, then, was giving each individual student the right kind of practice, work that would help him move from where he was to where he needed to be.

The math and language programs on the Stanford computers contained questions and problems of escalating difficulty. Students who got the easier questions right would ascend quickly, while those who got them wrong would get more problems of an appropriate difficulty to solve. Suppes found that the learning variation among elementary school students of the same age was enormous: Some progressed through the curriculum five or ten times faster than their peers.

All of this was accomplished with early 1960s technology. The computer posed problems with a Teletype machine—essentially, a typewriter hooked up to a computer, with the words and numbers typed out on spools of paper. Soon, Suppes noted, they might adopt an exciting new technology: "the cathode ray tube; messages can be generated directly by the computer on the face of the tube, which resembles a television screen." But that didn't really interest him, because people can read words on paper well enough. There is more computing power in your cell phone today than existed on the entire Stanford University campus in the early 1960s. That didn't bother Suppes, either. "With modern information-storage devices it is possible to store both a large body of curriculum material and the past histories of many students working in the curriculum. Such storage is well within the capacity of current technology, whether the subject is primary school mathematics, secondary school French or elementary statistics at the college level." This was in 1966.

The real challenge, he understood, was "not technological, but pedagogical." Suppes, a man who would explore and reveal some of the deepest problems of science and philosophy, marveled at the intricacies of human learning throughout his career. "The magnitude of the problem of evolving curriculum sequences is difficult to overestimate: the number of possible sequences of concepts and subject matter in elementary school mathematics alone is in excess of 10^{100}, a number larger than even generous estimates of the total number of elementary particles in the universe."

He also knew that information technology could help find meaning in that complexity. There is a concept in psychology called "response latency"—the elapsed time between stimulus and response. For certain kinds of activities that have benefited from thousands of hours of deliberate practice, your neural connections are so strong that response latency is almost zero, such as when you see and recognize the word "encyclopedia." When students answer questions on a computer, the machine can measure response latency down to the millisecond. It can tell whether you understand something automatically or have to devote precious mental energy to figuring it out.

A great many aspects of human-computer interaction can be recorded and saved digitally, for tens or hundreds or thousands of students simultaneously, with perfect accuracy. This much data is beyond the ability of even the smartest people to fully absorb. Most teachers, whether in elementary schools or college classrooms, have little training or experience in translating large amounts of data into ways to improve their instruction. As education inevitably moves into the digital world and more information is generated, this problem will become more acute. "The millions of observational records that computers now process in the field of nuclear physics," Suppes wrote, "will be rivaled in quantity and complexity by the information generated by computers in the field of instruction."

If that information could be fully utilized and understood, it would help solve the fundamental education policy dilemma of the modern world: how to systematically teach millions of people when each of them learns and progresses and understands information in different ways. "Whatever we may think about the desirability of having a diverse curriculum for children of different cognitive styles," he wrote, "such diversity is not possible because of the expense." With computers, "it will indeed be possible to offer a highly diversified body of curriculum material. When this occurs, we shall for the first time be faced with the practical problem of deciding how much diversity we want to have. That is the challenge for which we should be prepared."

THIS WASN'T THE FIRST TIME people had used information technology to improve education. In 1639, the same year that the College at Newetowne was named after John Harvard, Massachusetts officials named Richard Fairbanks's tavern in Boston as the official repository for mail coming in and out of the British colonies. The makings of a North American postal system—the state-of-the-art information network of its day—were established by the British in 1692. By 1728, readers of the *Boston Gazette* were told via advertisement that "Persons in the Country desirous to Learn the Art [of shorthand] may by having the several Lessons sent Weekly to them, be as perfectly instructed as those that live in Boston." One hundred and fifty years later, the land-grant universities established postal correspondence courses as part of their mission to spread useful knowledge to the masses. Postal courses eventually reached the farthest points of the globe—even a young meteorologist who wanted to learn French and math along with his Aristotle on a remote outpost in the Solomon Islands.

But it was *electronic* technology that truly excited the minds of education futurists. When radio was widely adopted in the 1920s, a number of universities invested in courses that were broadcast over the airwaves to listeners in nearby regions. Yet, as the radio historian Douglas B. Craig later wrote, these programs "soon faltered as broadcasting costs increased, audiences diminished, and professors demonstrated that lecture-hall brilliance did not always translate into good radio technique. These problems were quickly reflected in an unfavorable allocation of frequency or broadcast times, sending many of these stations into a downward spiral to oblivion." The University of Chicago was more successful than most, producing a roundtable discussion among professors that was broadcast nationally until 1955. But radio did not transform higher education.

Television was next, and there were high hopes that the addition of pictures would make the courses good enough to bring high-quality education to the general public. In 1922, Thomas Edison said, "I believe that the motion picture is destined to revolutionize our educational system and that in a few years it will supplant largely, if not entirely, the use of textbooks in our schools. Books are clumsy methods of instruction at best. . . . [T]he education of the future, as I see it, will be conducted through the medium of the motion picture, a visualized education, where it should be possible to obtain a one-hundred-percent efficiency." In 1938, several hundred students put on suit jackets and ties and gathered to watch a New York University professor named C. C. Clark explain the principles of photoelectricity on a bank of television screens in the RCA Building in Manhattan. Among those watching the proceedings was James Rowland Angell, the former president of Yale, who had been hired by NBC to oversee and promote their educational program. "We regard the possible uses of television in connection with educational work as literally unlimited," Angell said.

Televised education would be a significant part of the effort to educate students at a distance for the remainder of the century. Public access television channels, first on broadcast and then on cable, would regularly air taped university lectures, usually sandwiched between channels showing endless infomercial reruns and the local equivalent of *Wayne's World*. In the late 1990s, when the Internet boom was well under way, I visited local community centers in rural Indiana with rooms dedicated to the simultaneous televised broadcasting of classes from Indiana and Purdue Universities.

Yet none of this altered the hybrid university in any fundamental way. Most people still traveled to the cathedrals of learning to earn their degree. Almost everyone who made a confident prediction about how technology would change higher education in the twentieth century was wrong. Why?

The answer is that people were confused about what, exactly, technology could change.

There is a commonly used term for education conducted via mail, radio, television, or other media: "distance education." It is meant to differentiate these methods from traditional place-bound learning, which is not, by implication, conducted at a distance.

But this is less true than it seems. *All* education is distance education. An educational process or environment is something designed by people *other than you,* in a way that is meant to instigate learning that would not have happened had you been left to your own devices. Whatever that process might be, it happens at some remove from your mind and is mediated by your senses in some way. Hopkins might be at the end of a log, or at the front of a class, or on a television screen. He might also exist at some distance of time, sitting at his desk, writing words that you don't read until months or years later. But in all cases he is somewhere else, manipulating symbols in order to imperfectly connect the neural patterns in his mind to the neural patterns in yours.

The technologies developed up until the middle of the twentieth century were primarily useful for increasing the speed and cost-effectiveness of moving information from one place to another. Once most people could send and receive letters, the correspondence course was born. Radio made the transmission of voices instantaneous. Television added images to sounds, increasing the number of senses that could be engaged in absorbing and integrating information.

But while broadcasting the sights and sounds of college lectures increased the number of people who could watch and listen to college lectures, it didn't change the lecture itself. The whole point was to change it as little as possible, to replicate the experience of being in class. Lecture watching is a passive and standardized experience. And no matter where you are—in the front of the lecture hall or the back, in a community center or in your living room or sitting in front of your computer—it is distance education.

The last information technology to truly change the nature of education itself was the written word. Reading a book allows you to engage with the mind of the author in a very specific way, a different way than talking with or listening to her, regardless of how skilled in dialogue she may be. Written words have their limitations, just as Socrates said in the *Phaedrus* long ago. But they have great virtues of depth, breadth, and organization. People can read and reread words in their own time and pace, which is crucial given the vast differences among our neural patterns. A radio broadcast of spoken words is no better than a book in many ways and substantially worse in others.

All of this was clear to people who stopped to think about it as the new technologies emerged and traversed the cycle of hype and disappointment.

The United States armed forces are, collectively, one of the biggest teaching and learning organizations in the world. War fighting requires people with specific and highly defined skills. Teaching those skills effectively is a matter of life and death. Military organizations are also unusually sensitive to changing technology. History is full of great armies that were defeated because they failed to adapt their strategies and tactics to new killing machines. Henry V's English longbows defeated a fourfold larger force of armored French knights at Agincourt. Six hundred years later, the British Army sacrificed almost one hundred thousand men to the machine guns of the Somme. Armies that don't adapt and evolve eventually succumb to more lethal forces.

In 1947, the U.S. Army conducted an education technology experiment. First, they wrote a script explaining how to operate a micrometer, which is a device used to measure small distances in the precision components of modern war-making machines. Then they randomly assigned a group of soldiers to one of three classes. In the first, students sat in a classroom and listened to an instructor read the script, followed by a demonstration using an actual micrometer and visual diagrams. The second group read paper copies of the script, along with the same diagrams. The third watched a film of an instructor reading the script and demonstrating how to use a micrometer. The Army then tested the groups to see how well they could use a micrometer. All three groups performed exactly the same.

The technologies of printing and film gave the Army important ways to increase the number of people it could train to use micrometers at a reasonable cost. It could print scripts and mail them as far as the Solomon Islands. It could play the film over and over again for rooms full of soldiers. It could offer the same education to more people for less money. But what technology did *not* do was change the fundamental nature of the educational *design*. That was embodied in the script and the choice of diagrams and charts. Comparatively, everything else amounted to small variations in the media of the same distance education.

In the decades that followed, these results were repeated hundreds of times over with a wide variety of subjects and technologies. In fact, there is a whole website devoted to such research, called, in case people are tempted to miss the point, www.nosignificantdifference.org. The U.S. Department of Education has examined scores of online learning studies and found similar results. In fact, the study found, "on average, students in online learning conditions performed modestly better than those receiving face-to-face instruction."

In education, the medium is not the message. *Design* is what matters: how curricula are created and how students are engaged to do the necessary work that results in learning that lasts. The difference between watching a lecture live or on film is like the difference between reading *Anna Karenina* in two different fonts. You may prefer Garamond to Times New Roman, but either way, all happy families are alike and Anna jumps in front of the train.

That's why nothing in Patrick Suppes's experiments had anything to do with education at a distance. His students were right there on the Stanford campus and in the surrounding schools. They were closer to the Teletype machine than they were to their teachers, who were right nearby. The difference was the design of the education itself.

That distinction sprang from the fundamental difference between computers and every other kind of information technology that came before them. Written words, printed books, and reels of film were ways to *store* information. The postal service, radio, and television were ways to *move* information. Computers were very good at those things, too—exponentially better, in fact—and would become more so over time, to the point where digital storage is now well-nigh infinite and oceans of data can be flashed around the globe at the speed of light.

But the crucial difference was that computers could also *process* information, analyze it, and act on it. There are patterns embedded in the rules and algorithms governing the actions of all those ones and zeros cycling through electronic memory, links between different kinds of information, connections that are altered by various kinds of mechanical stimuli and by the inner workings of the computer itself. The neural patterns of Suppes's elementary math students became entangled with the electronic patterns inside the Stanford machines, and unlike every other information technology ever invented before, both were changed by the experience.

That's what Herbert Simon meant by "thinking machine." That's why Patrick Suppes was moved to recall Alexander of Macedon. And that's why Suppes didn't hesitate to apply the same principles that worked for young children learning math to men and women studying philosophy at one of the greatest universities in the world.

SUPPES'S BRANCH OF PHILOSOPHY tended toward the formal and mathematical, so he was a natural choice to teach Introduction to Logic at Stanford. In 1972, he created a wholly automated, computerized version of his course. Suppes showed up on the first day of class as a kind of master of ceremonies, but from that point forward there were no lectures. Students did their work in the educational laboratory, crafting logical proofs based on questions posed by the computer and submitting them for electronic evaluation. Teaching assistants would answer questions when people needed help. A couple of years later, Suppes created a computerized version of his Axiomatic Set Theory course, too.

Soon he had the heaviest teaching load in the department—perhaps the whole university—as measured by the number of students and courses he was teaching. He accomplished this uncommon productivity by translating the highly developed neural patterns of philosophy within his own mind into the rules and programs that governed the class computers. In the meantime Carnegie Mellon was continuing to push the boundaries of computer science and human cognition. Along with Herbert Simon, CMU was home to a psychologist named John R. Anderson, who had finished his Stanford PhD in 1972. At the original Dartmouth conference on artificial intelligence back in 1955, the participants conjectured that "every aspect of learning or any other feature of intelligence can in principle be so precisely described that a machine can be made to simulate it." Anderson devoted his career to making good on this promise by creating a working model of human cognition that could be broken down into rules and patterns and component parts that could then be simulated on a computer. He called it the Adaptive Control of Thought—Rational, or ACT-R.

ACT-R breaks knowledge into "chunks" that are "declarative" and "procedural." Declarative chunks are facts, such as "The sky is blue." Procedural chunks are knowledge of how to do things and how things work, like "Press Ctrl-Alt-Delete to reset your computer" or "To add 25 and 25, first add 5 and 5, get 10, carry the 1, and then add it to 2 plus 2."

In the ACT-R model, learners work toward goals that can be broken down into subgoals that involve taking in new information and acting on it in different ways. Sometimes new declarative chunks are simply added to memory; for example, "It rained this morning." Other times, however, the mind does something more complicated. It looks for procedural chunks that are analogous to a problem it is trying to solve. For example, say the mind wants to figure out how to add 26 and 26. It finds the procedure for adding 25 and 25 and follows the same rules. It does this because both questions are embedded in a similar set of neural patterns associated with ideas like "addition" and "math." This is a narrow example of a large and incredibly important concept in learning science called "transfer," which is the process by which people apply patterns and concepts learned in one context to another.

Transfer is the basis of teaching by analogy. It is the reason that human thinking is so powerfully driven by metaphor. It's why we believe that life is a journey and you shouldn't judge a book by its cover. Strengthening transfer is the goal of all good education programs. We learn relatively few of the specific facts we know—the declarative chunks—in school. But if our schools are doing their job, they teach us broad patterns and principles that transfer to new environments and help us make sense of new information.

The use of the ACT-R theory in clinical research has helped confirm the findings of cognitive psychologists, including the crucial role of practice and work in human learning. Although we like to think of learning as arriving in flashes of insight that may be divinely inspired, this just reflects how imperfectly aware we are of our own minds. In fact, human learning tends to proceed along a logarithmic scale, with the first rounds of practice producing meager results that eventually accelerate and result in gains that are orders of magnitude more powerful. This, too, is crucial for education, because it means that people who successfully get to the end of a process of learning have far more knowledge and skill than those who quit halfway. It's like compound interest on an investment, where you make most of your money in the last few years.

There are competing theories of artificial intelligence, and ACT-R, which is built around the computation of symbols, is only one of them. Many of the heady predictions made by the original AI theorists have fallen short, because the human mind has proved to be more complex than almost anyone imagined. But the long-term trend in the field is clear: AI theories continue to get better, and the computational models based on them continue to improve.

All of which leads to the last piece in the puzzle of how information technology is poised to transform higher education and power the University of Everywhere. We can already, today, replicate much of what colleges are charging a great deal of money for and distribute that information electronically at almost no marginal cost. Books don't need to be stored in libraries anymore. Lectures can be recorded with perfect fidelity and broadcast to anyone with a computer, on demand. The underlying design of courses—the selection of books and assignments and course materials—can be replicated with ease. The kinds of virtual problem sets I worked on in 7.00x are superior to anything that could be done without computers. Instead of taking weeks to messily breed actual fruit flies, as I did in high school, I can breed multiple generations of virtual flies in seconds. And no paper-and-pencil exercise or conversation with a teaching assistant can replace being able to use an Integrative Genome Viewer to manipulate a genetic sequence billions of base pairs long.

The final element is customization and personalization, the product of artificial intelligence, the ability to create digital learning environments where the educational design *changes* based on the learner himself. So if I arrive at a 7.00x course with a serious deficit in chemistry knowledge, the computer figures that out and changes the lectures I watch and problems I solve accordingly, or puts me in a discussion group with other students who can help me learn. If I get stuck at a certain point in a problem set because I don't understand a key concept, the computer figures that out, too. Instead of just marking me "Wrong," it reroutes the learning process like a car GPS that calculates a new route to your destination after you've made a wrong turn.

Learning scientists at Carnegie Mellon are using the ACT-R model to make this dream a reality by developing "cognitive tutors" that use artificial intelligence to help people learn. Every tutor is built around a cognitive model of a particular subject. For example, any basic introductory genetics class will teach you how Gregor Mendel crossbred different kinds of pea plants and discovered that certain traits are inherited through genes. Which genes you inherit depend on a pair of 50/50 coin flips, one each from your father and mother, for each gene. Some genes, like blue eyes and blond hair, are recessive, expressing themselves only when both coin flips go the right way at the same time. This explains why certain traits run in families but can remain hidden, surfacing in some generations but not in others.

But this is only the basic theory. Human genetic interaction and inheritance turn out to be far more complicated in the specifics than in Mendel's elegant experiments with round and wrinkled peas. Despite the Human Genome Project and great advances in gene sequencing technology, it is still not possible to analyze every element of a person's genetic makeup in the same way we might X-ray a broken bone. Knowing the exact sequence of base pairs in a person's genome doesn't automatically tell you what all those letters mean.

Part of learning genetics involves looking at certain kinds of evidence and figuring out the underlying genetic dynamics. If a certain rare disease shows up three times among forty people in five generations of a single family and all of them are men, what might that mean? Is the disease dominant or recessive? Is it passed along on the X-chromosome that helps determine gender? These can be life-and-death questions for people considering medical treatment or whether to have children.

Solving a problem like this involves the application of facts, processes, and ideas—declarative and procedural chunks, in ACT-R terms. When the Carnegie Mellon learning engineers create a cognitive tutor for genetics, they map all of those things out and use them to build an artificial intelligence model. They program a computer to solve genetics problems by taking the same information and theories that students are given and using them in a way that mimics the processes of the human brain. When a student sits down at a computer and starts working on a genetics problem, the AI model is working on the same problem right along with her. That way, if the student gets stuck, the computer knows what kind of advice to give. It knows what the student is thinking, because it is, in its own way, thinking the same thing.

In other words, the computer is doing what a good human tutor does: It's paying close attention to an individual person's learning, and teaching accordingly.

This is a much more sophisticated application of the principles Patrick Suppes was applying to elementary math students back in the early 1960s.

Back then, the computer could only give more difficult questions to students who got answers right and easier questions to those who got them wrong. The Carnegie Mellon cognitive tutors, which have been built in a range of subjects, are based on a complex AI-based model of continually interacting knowledge and theory. They're even programmed with certain kinds of *incorrect* theories that many students have, like "Heavier objects fall to the ground faster than lighter objects." That allows the computer to recognize human mistakes that proceed from flawed ideas. These strongly established neural patterns need to be carefully dismantled and rebuilt based on a correct understanding of the world.

At the same time that the cognitive scientists were refining their models of human cognition, other researchers were changing the way humans interact with machines. In 1967, Herbert Simon and his Christmas break coauthor, Albert Newell, helped found the CMU department of computer science. In addition to studying the inner architecture of computers, the researchers there were interested in how computers were designed to work for and with their Homo sapiens masters. Today, Carnegie Mellon's Human-Computer Interaction Institute hosts a cadre of scientists and graduate students developing tools and design principles that go far beyond the mere typing and reading of text.

We now use computers to see digital pictures and graphics, hear chimes and instructions, read words, and give instructions via gestures and touch. Studies have found that people learn more from coordinated words, diagrams, and sounds than from text alone. The human-computer interaction experts came to understand that the best designs carefully engaged multiple human senses, which are neurologically designed to receive and integrate information in parallel. Other researchers focused on how computers allow people to connect with one another, and how people connect with information about themselves that we increasingly store in digital form.

All of this greatly increased the potential for using computers to help students learn. Yet despite those decades of technological progress and mounting evidence that students learned perfectly well in a variety of technology-aided and mediated environments, it did not change the nature of the hybrid university in any important way.

Until the 1990s, the most important reason for this lay in the limitations of the technology itself. Computers made many new things possible in the decades after World War II. But at first they failed to alter the economic logic of the hybrid university as a scarce, expensive place.

Television and radio extended the university classroom to anywhere a broadcast could reach. But that came at a steep price in terms of personalization and interactivity. Students flipping through the educational access channels on UHF or gathering in a community center in rural Indiana to watch a TV screen couldn't raise their hands to ask questions. They also had to be in a certain place at a certain time, adjusting their schedules around a fixed broadcast.

Correspondence courses offered more scheduling flexibility and the chance for grades and feedback from an instructor. But this method stretched out the distance of *time.* It could take weeks for papers and feedback to travel back and forth through the mail, meaning that a student's learning and the teacher's understanding of that learning were always badly out of sync. Distance-learning classes were better than nothing. But they weren't better than what was being offered within the cathedrals of learning.

Even the kinds of interactive AI-driven learning environments being developed at Stanford, Carnegie Mellon, and elsewhere were tied down to specific places. The children taking Patrick Suppes's advanced math classes were working on terminals directly wired to Stanford computers a few miles away. So were the philosophy students on the Stanford campus. For most people, information only moved in one direction through the airwaves—broadcast *out*—and the same was true for the growing network of coaxial cable. The only common way to exchange information in real time at a distance was over the copper wire telephone network, and that was designed for voice interaction. This happened to be one of the tasks computers couldn't do very well. Although many advances have been made in electronic speech recognition, nobody has invented a computer that can listen and talk to you with the speed and facility of a person.

When the Internet became available to ordinary people in the mid-1990s, many of these barriers began to fall. Connections to both powerful computers and to other people that had been limited to small populations in the defense and research sectors were suddenly available to millions and then billions worldwide.

As always, this produced a convulsion of hype, greed, and prognostication connected imperfectly with the evolution of law, culture, and human organizations. Smart people opined that this really would change higher education as we knew it. In 1997 the well-known management guru Peter Drucker predicted that "thirty years from now the big university campuses will be relics. Universities won't survive. It's as large a change as when we first got the printed book." In 1999 the CEO of Cisco Systems told the *New York Times* that "the next big killer application for the Internet is going to be education. Education over the Internet is going to be so big, it's going to make e-mail usage look like a rounding error."

At the time, Cisco was about to become the most valuable company in the world. The dot-com boom dominated the popular press, with stories of overnight billionaires thrilling the masses. In 1998, Columbia University began working on an ambitious plan called "Fathom" to sell college courses over the World Wide Web. Launched in 2000, Fathom.com was an attempt to gain first-mover advantage in what Columbia believed would be a multibillion-dollar market for higher education. At the time, Columbia was making more money from patent royalties than any other research university in America. This, university administrators believed, was an opportunity to similarly monetize Columbia's prestigious brand and intellectual resources.

MIT took a different approach, creating a nonprofit endeavor called MIT OpenCourseWare in 2001. The university put course syllabi, reading lists, video lectures, homework assignments, and other materials from hundreds of MIT courses online for anyone to use. The effort garnered front-page coverage in the *Times* and was likened by some to Gutenberg's printing press and the Great Library of Alexandria. The CEO of IBM said it would send "shivers" throughout the higher-education system.

Other universities used technology to improve what they offered to their enrolled students. Virginia Tech, a land-grant university with a sterling reputation for science and engineering, had been one of the first campuses to equip all of its students with networked PCs and laptops. In 1997 the math department found itself seriously short of the money and staff needed to teach big introductory classes like calculus and linear algebra to hundreds of freshman engineering students. The department noticed that the gated university design created a strange discontinuity in the value of physical space: It was scarce and expensive within the campus walls, cheap and plentiful without. So the math department rented out 60,000 square feet of empty space in a down-on-its-heels shopping mall a few blocks away from campus, and filled it with hundreds of iMac computers.

The Virginia Tech Math Emporium opened up twenty-four hours a day, seven days a week, offering seven full college math classes that involved no lectures or professors in the traditional sense of the words. Teaching assistants were on hand from 10:00 a.m. to 10:00 p.m. to give individualized instruction as students worked through videos, texts, and problem sets on the iMacs. According to the department's analysis of students' math test scores, the students learned as much or more at the Emporium than they did when the course was taught on campus, with a 75 percent reduction in the cost to the university. Dozens of colleges followed Virginia Tech's lead and built emporiums of their own.

At Carnegie Mellon, the ideas of people like Simon, Newell, and Anderson were embodied in the university's Open Learning Initiative (OLI). The science and theory of learning were married to ever more powerful computers attached to a worldwide computer network. Rather than merely broadcast or publish course materials, OLI built digital learning environments that were responsive to the distinct actions and neural patterns of individual students. They began by developing four courses, in economics, statistics, causal reasoning, and logic. To develop the logic course, they turned to the preeminent logician on campus, a man who had had been steadily experimenting with computers and education ever since taking his first online class with Patrick Suppes at Stanford back in the early 1970s.

WILFRIED SIEG'S OFFICE at Carnegie Mellon University is framed by tall windows that face directly onto the university's central lawn, where undergraduates with backpacks walk back and forth among old brick buildings and modernist centers of science and research. The extensive and carefully arranged collection of books on his office shelves is just the right combination of number and age that it seems plausible Sieg has actually read them all over the course of a long and distinguished career. Behind Sieg's desk, there is a large framed black-and-white photograph of his intellectual hero, the great nineteenth- and twentieth-century German mathematician David Hilbert. The room is a kind of monument to the genius of the elite research university as a center of scholarship, to how much intellectual work a person can achieve given a lifetime and a place dedicated to that purpose.

A crucial aspect of logic is constructing proofs. You can read about logic and listen to someone explain logic, but you can't really learn logic until you actively apply logical principles to philosophical work. This kind of active learning strengthens neural patterns, allowing you to transfer logical principles to other areas of philosophy and intellectual pursuit.

Most college logic classes involve students writing proofs and turning them in to be graded by a person. This has the advantage of making students' thought processes visible to teachers so they can give students personalized advice. But it has the disadvantage of extending the distance of time. Students may not know what they got wrong for days or weeks, inhibiting their ability to learn in the meantime. A proof may involve a large number of distinct steps, and if a student makes even a trivial mistake early on in the process, it ruins everything that comes after. Grading proofs is also drudgery for philosophy professors (or, more accurately, philosophy teaching assistants).

To solve this problem, Sieg developed a computer program with the vaguely steampunk name "automated theorem prover." It uses artificial intelligence to solve proofs entirely on its own. That means that as a student is working through a proof on the computer, the automatic theorem prover is clanking along in cyberspace right alongside her, thinking as she thinks, ready to give feedback not in days or weeks but instantaneously. Instead of giving students an imperfect copy of what college teachers give college students, it gives them something better, something that *only* a computer can provide: a perfect evaluation of their logic, based on insight into their individual thinking processes, instantaneously, at any time of day or night.

The automated theorem prover allowed Sieg to design a complete online logic course that any computer-enabled student in the world can take, for free, on the OLI website. It also changed the way he educated students at CMU. Sieg teaches an advanced class at CMU called Logical Argumentation, mostly to computer science majors. Rather than make Introductory Logic a prerequisite, requiring a whole semester and tuition to match, he has them go through the entire OLI logic class in four weeks. These students have the intellect and wherewithal to learn quickly. But before the automatic theorem prover there was no way to grade all the proofs fast enough.

Introductory Logic itself is offered to a broader array of CMU undergraduates. Sieg had taught it for a number of years and he noticed a clear pattern of student achievement. Invariably, there would be sharp divisions of grades within the course. The science and math students would sail through while the humanities students would do poorly. But once the course was redesigned around the automatic theorem prover, the arts-versus-sciences grade split disappeared. To find out why, Sieg pored through the volumes of data the computer had been collecting about how students were learning—diagnostic information that had never been available to him before. He discovered that the humanities students were spending much more time working through the proofs and problems—ten times longer than the science students, in some cases. But they eventually learned what they need to know.

College classes had become routinized over time in order to serve the bureaucratic interests of the hybrid university, holding the amount of learning time constant at three instructional hours per week over a standard fifteen-week semester. Different students got the same educational experience over the same amount of time, while their learning was allowed to vary. The automatic theorem prover allowed Sieg to let the amount of instructional time expand to meet students' needs, because the additional cost of providing ten times as much attention from the computer was essentially zero.

The OLI course software also included a course "dashboard" that showed Sieg how students were progressing through class in real time. This kind of information had been lost to teachers ever since education evolved, for technological and economic reasons, away from the one-on-one tutorial model. Professors would learn about their students' learning only after the fact, when the tests were taken and papers submitted and it was too late to help those who couldn't keep up. The OLI dashboard opened up a window onto the minds of individual students, showing what they were like upon arrival in the course and how they changed over time.

Wilfried Sieg had combined his lifetime of scholarship with information technology to build a better logic and proofs course. It wasn't a trivial matter: The up-front cost to Carnegie Mellon ran into the hundreds of thousands of dollars, plus hundreds of hours of his time. But once the course was built, it didn't require a lot of updating. Logic has been taught since Aristotle, and the proof that the square root of two is an irrational number is what it is. The cost to Carnegie Mellon of allowing an individual to take the class online was virtually zero—nothing but a tiny fraction of electricity and digital storage. Plus OLI was a nonprofit organization. So it gave away the course to individual students online and charged colleges that wanted to adopt it for their own courses a nominal fee.

Sieg assumed that other universities would adopt his course en masse. After all, the automated theorem prover was a major advance in teaching logic and the course was available for next to nothing. In a time of rising college costs and student debt, courses that were better and cheaper were exactly what higher education needed. He had built a better mousetrap, a Logic 101 for the University of Everywhere, and now the world would come knocking on his door.

He was wrong.

Ten years after being given to the world, Sieg's logic course has been used by thousands of students online and at a smattering of institutions, including the University of Nevada, Las Vegas; Indiana University–Purdue University Indianapolis; and a public university in Guatemala City. This is far more than the number who ever could have sat in Sieg's classroom in Pittsburgh. But it is far fewer than the number who study logic and proofs worldwide. Most of higher education proceeded as if the course simply didn't exist.

In different ways, the same was true for every heralded new use of information technology in higher education.

Other professors at Carnegie Mellon had also developed sophisticated new OLI courses. In 2013, William G. Bowen, the noted economist and former president of Princeton, published a study comparing the learning outcomes of two randomly assigned groups of students. One group took an interactive OLI statistics class, plus an hour of face-to-face instruction. The other took the same course in a traditional on-campus format, with three to four hours of instruction. When Bowen and his coauthors compared how the two groups fared in terms of "course completion rates, scores on common final exam questions, and results of a national test of statistical literacy," they found no statistically significant differences.

Bowen had previously been skeptical of the idea that technology could fundamentally change higher learning. Based on his new research, he wrote, "I am today a convert. I have come to believe that now is the time."

For cash-strapped colleges looking to keep tuition prices down, this would seem like a golden opportunity to charge students less money without sacrificing the quality of instruction. Such technology-driven increases in productivity are the lifeblood of modern organizations. Yet, in response to Bowen's research, the vast majority of all colleges teaching statistics did . . . nothing. They continued to teach statistics as they always had.

At Virginia Tech, the Math Emporium is going strong. But it is still limited mostly to math classes, not physics or computer science or subjects taught by other departments that don't have a budget crisis to solve. In the ten years after the Math Emporium opened its doors in 1997, tuition at Virginia Tech doubled. The university saved millions of dollars over those years teaching with computers. But none of those savings were passed on to students and parents in the form of lower prices.

Fathom.com went belly-up in 2003, taking millions of Columbia's dollars along with it. Desperate for revenue, Fathom had moved down-market into business training courses and pleaded with its partner institutions for revenue to prop up the enterprise, to no avail. Despite the fanfare and Ivy League pedigree, the venture simply couldn't get customers to pay for online courses.

By 2013, MIT OpenCourseWare had put materials from more than 2,000 courses online for anyone to use. Since the service was created in 2001, more than 125 million people from around the world have logged on. Arguably the greatest science and engineering university in the world took the bulk of its teaching-related intellectual property and simply gave it away. Yale University started a similar project on a smaller scale, limiting the number of courses but including complete, professionally produced videos of course lectures. They, too, were free.

Yet the shivers in the higher-education system never appeared. Colleges quickly adopted technologies for routine administrative and communications tasks. Syllabi, course grades, and reserved readings were posted online. You could e-mail your professor and submit your term paper as a pdf or Word document. The library was still a place for quiet study, but the microfilm machines and card catalogues faded into memory.

Some professors and departments delved deeply into the possibilities of teaching better with technology. And a much larger number of colleges tried to teach the same with technology, to more people, at a lower cost to the institution. Cash-strapped community colleges, for example, began offering online courses to students with jobs and families—people who didn't want to commute to campus every night. Meanwhile, a lucrative industry in for-profit higher education sprang up in a startlingly short amount of time. By selling inexpensive online courses at large profit margins, for-profit colleges generated millions of dollars that were poured back into marketing and recruitment, bidding up the share prices of the companies that owned them and putting tens of millions of dollars into the pockets of investors and CEOs.

By 2012 there were fifteen publicly traded higher-education corporations listed on U.S. stock exchanges, with a total market value in the billions of dollars. Some of these companies gave working and adult students access to convenient, job-focused education and training. Many others simply replicated the traditional classroom experience with video lectures and online discussion groups. And as a series of congressional investigations revealed in 2011 and 2012, some lured students into taking out large loans for largely worthless courses, leaving students with few job prospects and debt they couldn't afford to repay. By then, the single biggest college in America was the University of Phoenix online, with more than 300,000 students enrolled in the United States alone.

But for most students in most classes at most colleges, the information technology revolution had almost no effect on the two most important aspects of college: how much it cost and how students learned. When the bell rang and the college classroom door closed, education for most college students proceeded as it had since Bologna: professors talking and sometimes listening while students took notes.

And unlike nearly every other information-focused industry, the price of higher education was not driven down by the liberating, disruptive forces of technology. Instead, the opposite happened: Many colleges added "technology fees" on top of regular tuition. The dot-com era officially commenced in August 1995 with the $2.9 billion initial public offering of Netscape, the pioneering Web browser firm. By the time children born that year entered college, in 2013, the average sticker price of attending a public four-year university increased by roughly 80 percent after adjusting for inflation, to $18,391 per year. Some private colleges charged a quarter of a million dollars for four years of tuition and room and board. During the same period the amount of outstanding student loan debt increased nearly ten times over. Borrowing for college went from the exception to the norm.

In part, this was because the first technologies were immature. Taking a class online is a lot more complicated than downloading an MP3 file of a three-minute song. When Fathom.com was launched, a lot of people were still surfing the Web with slow dial-up connections. Online videos were small, balky, and blurred. Part of college was learning with other students, and the online experience was more solitary then. The social network had yet to be built.

But the colleges also made mistakes more fundamental than simply getting too far ahead of the technological adoption curve. The promotional language from Fathom.com betrayed a simplistic conception of education. The company's managers said their goal was to take Columbia's knowledge and "project it" to the public at large, to "put Columbia out there" on the World Wide Web. The university's provost said the goal was to "re-create in virtual space the kind of possibilities that one can usually get only from being at a great university or a great museum."

But knowledge and education are not the same thing. Knowledge can be represented in symbols, stored, copied, and broadcast. The Internet made that process cheaper, but the process itself had been in place since Gutenberg. Being at a great university is almost nothing like visiting a great museum. There is only one place in the world where you can stand in front of Vermeer's *Woman Holding a Balance*, and the experience is essentially brief, solitary, and unmediated. Education is structured, interactive, and lengthy. It can also take place almost anywhere, not just where the hybrid universities happen to have been founded long ago.

The Internet had a profound and immediate impact on the conduct and distribution of university *research,* allowing scholars to share data and knowledge instantaneously. But education is more than that, too. It involves sustained, organized interaction with the educational designs of experts, either in person or as represented in words and computer code. Fathom described itself as a "global e-learning company" that "works with leading educational and cultural institutions to project their teaching and research to an international audience," as if both teaching and research could be flung along the information superhighway in the same way. The hybrid universities had neglected teaching in favor of research for so long that they forgot that the two aren't the same thing.

They were also blind to the economic and regulatory forces that sustained modern higher education. Competition from new technologies can destroy jobs and organizations, sometimes whole professions and industries. The hybrid university left decisions about teaching—and thus teaching with technology—in the hands of autonomous academic departments and individual professors who operated from the principle of keeping themselves employed. If a professor adopted free curricula, teaching materials, and lectures from MIT or Yale, then what exactly was the university paying him for? If a university department used technology to teach the same number of students with fewer professors, then it had fewer professors. Departments want *more* professors, to produce more research and prestige, the currencies of the scholarly marketplace. In 1992, Patrick Suppes retired from regular teaching duties at Stanford after supervising and improving upon his automated logic course for twenty years. The university promptly handed it to another professor, who shut the automated part down. When it comes to teaching, colleges and universities *do not want to be more productive*, and will do whatever they can to avoid such a fate.

The question is why, unlike newspapers, travel agencies, record labels, and countless other industries, they were able to get away with it. The answer lies with public subsidies and regulations. The higher-education industry receives hundreds of billions of government dollars every year in the form of direct appropriations, tax preferences (Harvard pays no taxes on its $33 billion endowment), and subsidies for their customers in the form of government scholarships and guaranteed student loans. The only way to get that money is to be an accredited college. And the accreditation system is controlled by the existing colleges themselves, who set the standards for which organizations are eligible for public funds. Those standards typically include things like hiring faculty who have degrees from an existing college and constructing a library full of books. It's like a world where Craigslist needs the local newspaper's permission to give online classified ads away for free, or Honda has to build cars exactly like GM.

Colleges also benefited from the fact that people become used to certain ways of doing things—what DiMaggio and Powell called "normative isomorphism." Routines and assumptions are just another way we manage the constant onslaught of information, limiting the number of problems we have to solve and choices we have to make. In the case of higher education, society has invested a great deal in the meaning of traditional higher-education credentials and the credits that constitute them. Whole structures of regulation and human resource practice are built around associate's degrees, bachelor's degrees, master's degrees, and PhDs. You can't be a teacher at a public school in America without a bachelor's degree from an accredited college or university; it's the law. If your higher education includes courses taken at more than one institution, as is true for the majority of all undergraduates today, only credits earned at accredited colleges count toward a degree.

It was the monopoly over the sale of recognized credits and credentials more than anything else that allowed the hybrid university to ignore the possibilities of technology-based efficiency and continue to increase prices without mercy. The first wave of higher-education technology companies completely failed to understand this. A Columbia diploma signifies a number of things, including "I earned passing grades in the Columbia curriculum," "I lived with a bunch of smart people in Morningside Heights for four years," and "When I was seventeen years old, I was smart enough to be admitted to Columbia." Fathom.com couldn't give standard Columbia diplomas to people who took its classes because they didn't satisfy the second or third criteria. So it inadvertently conducted an experiment to determine the market price of online Columbia courses based only on their educational value. The answer turned out to be: almost nothing.

The gates around higher education were more than just physical barriers to entry. There was a wall of regulation, money, habit, and social capital surrounding the industry, keeping competitors at bay. Even as technology wrought profound changes in society around them, hybrid universities grew richer and more expensive than they had ever been.

6

Thunder Lizards

As *The Secret of Life* progressed from the basics of how proteins are structured and genes are inherited to the inner workings of human DNA, it was hard not to wonder at the elegance of it all. Even the simplest biological and chemical processes involved a highly choreographed interaction of molecules, structures, and energy states. How did all the pieces fit together so well?

The answer, Lander explained, was mathematical. Over hundreds of millions of years, untold trillions of bacteria and other organisms had been competing to survive and replicate. It was evolution at a level of frequency and complexity far beyond the capacity of the human mind to fully understand, with each small improvement ultimately adding up to something miraculous. The biological systems worked because only working systems could have survived for so long.

The DNA sequencing techniques developed by the Human Genome Project and others gave scientists new insight into the nature of the evolutionary tree. By comparing the DNA of different species to one another and identifying which genes were common among them, scientists could pinpoint the moments in history when different kinds of living things branched off in new directions. The environments in which evolutionary competition took place had a profound effect on which ways the branches ultimately grew. A species evolving in a small, isolated valley with few competitors might develop over millennia into something strange and wonderful but also fragile and vulnerable to predation. And some environmental changes were intolerable: The dinosaurs evolved for over 150 million years until an asteroid strike changed their environment so quickly and drastically that they could not adapt and survive.

Human organizations exist in a kind of partially controlled evolutionary environment. Societies make judgments about whether to let them compete, fail, thrive, and change in something resembling a free market, or to use the power of regulation and public subsidy to shelter them in valleys. Traditional hybrid universities have spent the last century in a highly protected place. To be sure, this had many benefits. If colleges were left entirely vulnerable to unpredictable business cycles, mismanagement, and bad luck, society couldn't ensure that each new class of high school graduates would have someplace to enroll. Institutions that create knowledge on behalf of all humanity can't rely exclusively on the funding that private markets provide.

But those benefits also had a cost. Traditional colleges were not forced by the threat of competitive extinction to make the kinds of painful organizational changes the adoption of new technologies often requires. Becoming more efficient in a labor-intensive industry like higher education means doing more with the same amount of labor or doing the same with less labor, i.e., firing people. Nobody in a nonprofit university wants to fire people. They want *more* people, because people are the currency of prestige.

The hybrid university endured in its protected valley but also stagnated there, becoming stranger and more expensive and increasingly vulnerable to its inherent structural incoherence. The more information technology created opportunities to educate more people for less money, the greater the lost opportunity of failing to adopt that technology became. As the Internet era neared the end of its second decade, it was clear that traditional universities were never going to change fast enough on their own. Only when a new competitor found a way into the valley would the march of evolution begin again and the University of Everywhere emerge.

It wasn't hard to guess where those competitors would come from: Silicon Valley, a place with enough money, smart people, and cultural prestige to compete head-to-head with the hybrid universities, using a profoundly different philosophy about what to do with information technology and what the future should bring.

IT WAS FOUR in the afternoon on a gorgeous spring day in the Mission District of San Francisco. I was standing on a sidewalk with Michael Staton, waiting for an Uber to arrive.

Michael came to the Bay Area in the early 2000s to launch an Internet start-up company that builds social networks for incoming college freshmen. He had recently switched to the investment side of the deal-making table and become a partner in a venture capital firm specializing in technology and education.

I wanted to get a better sense of the competitive forces on the horizon that people in traditional academia should be scared of. And I wanted to get a glimpse of the future, the new approaches to education technology that people like me would be adjusting to, and that people like my daughter would take for granted as the only way the world could be. So I asked Michael to introduce me to some of the start-ups that he found most exciting—those that, in the minds of the people trying to change higher education forever, made the strongest argument for how and why it would happen.

At that moment he was trying to get us to our next appointment. He fiddled with his iPhone and frowned as cars rushed by. He was using an app on his iPhone that was supposed to summon another person with the same app to drive us, but the first guy flaked, so he switched to the popular limousine-summoning service Uber. The GPS chip in Michael's phone told the Uber driver's phone where to pick us up, and the fare was automatically charged to Michael's credit card.

This was a year or so before Uber and competitors like Lyft became ubiquitous in major cities worldwide. We were running behind schedule and I asked Michael if we should just take a regular taxi. He is by nature laid-back, so I was surprised to see him scowl. He didn't take taxis, he said. You have to stand out in the street and wave your hand to find one but half the time they drive right by you and you don't even know why. Then it's random whether they have a credit card machine, and if they do, they hassle you to pay cash even though he never carries cash with him, or they run his credit card through some kind of mechanical impression machine that must have been invented in the nineteenth century. He's not putting up with it. We're going with Uber.

The Uber showed up a few minutes later, and as we bumped along the downtown streets, dodging cable cars and oncoming traffic, it occurred to me that I, too, was annoyed by every single aspect of the standard taxi experience that Michael had described. But I had simply learned to live with it, because it hadn't occurred to me that things could be different. In Silicon Valley, people are unusually disposed to think otherwise. They see every inconvenience, inefficiency, and injustice as a problem technology can solve.

As I met the people trying to remake the whole world of education, I ran into variations on this ethos over and over again. It is hardwired into an enormous generator of business development and technological innovation, a machine fueled by money, ambition, idealism, and the iron laws of physics. That machine was created, beginning in the crucial period following World War II, to search for old, expensive institutions and burn them to the ground. And in the last several years it has turned its gaze toward the cathedrals of learning.

DOUGLAS ENGELBART grew up during the Great Depression on a farm outside Portland and studied at the nearby land-grant university, Oregon

State. He was drafted into the Navy and found himself working as a radar technician on a small island in the Philippines, where he came across an article that had recently been published in the *Atlantic*: "As We May Think," by Vannevar Bush. He spent the rest of his life making Bush's prophecies come true.

After the war, Engelbart returned to the West Coast, completed his degree, and enrolled at the University of California, Berkeley, where he finished a PhD in electrical engineering with a specialization in computers in 1955. Berkeley hired him as an assistant professor the following year. He was on track to have the paradigmatic research university career, comfortably writing and thinking and teaching for as long as his mind and spirit could sustain him.

But that's not what happened. Instead, Douglas Engelbart walked away from academia, into a life that was similar in some respects and profoundly different in others. In 1957 he went to work at a company that shared the name and purpose of the Cold War university but not its nineteenth-century peculiarities: the Stanford Research Institute.

The United States government acted on Vannevar Bush's recommendations for scientific investment on a gargantuan scale. Enormous amounts of money came to California. Some of it went to the research universities, but much of it went to defense contractors and scientific facilities that had begun growing as the military managed points of its global communications and aeronautical networks in and around the San Francisco Bay.

Like other universities, Stanford experienced an influx of students after the war. One of Vannevar Bush's MIT graduate students was appointed dean of engineering. His name was Frederick Terman, and he saw opportunity in symbiosis between business, technology, and academe. In 1951 he helped convert some nearby university land into the Stanford Industrial Park. Among the tenants were two of Terman's students, William Hewlett and David Packard, who would turn their eponymous company into the biggest personal computer manufacturer in the world.

At the time, Bell Labs in New Jersey was the center of the computing universe. But that began to change when William Shockley left the lab, went west, and founded Shockley Semiconductor in Mountain View, just a few miles up the road from Stanford. In 1957, Shockley begat Fairchild Semiconductor, which in turn produced Intel. The valley filled with factories churning out the hardware that would power the twentieth-century information technology revolution. Shockley and Fairchild built their increasingly powerful integrated circuits in silicon. Thus the valley's name.

The industrial genius of the circuit builders was to constantly fit more powerful arrays of computing architecture on smaller and smaller surfaces. To those who lived and worked in the thick of the industry, it was clear that exponentially increasing computing power would have to be matched by new means of human-computer interaction. In May 1961, Engelbart delivered a paper at the Western Joint Computer Conference titled "Augmented Man, and a Search for Perspective." In handwritten notes summarizing his speech, he wrote that the computer "must be viewed as but one component in the system of techniques, procedures, and artifacts that our culture can provide to augment the minds of its complex problem solvers." The relationship between human neurons and silicon circuits would become ever closer over time.

Engelbart also understood that computers would steadily replace human jobs of greater and greater intellectual complexity, and that people would be forced to adapt in order to survive. "When the day comes that intelligent machines begin to usurp his role," he wrote, "our individual would hardly still be human if he didn't want to continue developing his augmentation system to extend to the limit his ability to pursue comprehension in the wake of the more intelligent machines."

If people could better interact with computers, they could harness computers' power and avoid or mitigate displacement. Engelbart and his partners developed a suite of tools that would define human-computer interaction for billions of people around the globe: electronic monitors with images and words separated by windows, manipulated with a cursor controlled on the screen. Files organized in folders and subfolders. Text with links you could click on to reach more text. Words that could be processed with newly invented commands like "Delete," "Insert," "Replace," "Move," and "Copy." People in different places talking simultaneously on video. The team used the tools they developed as they built them, collaborating across distances. Their system was called NLS/Augment, with the *NL* standing for two words that had not yet been combined in the popular mind: "oNLine."

For people to get online and use—or compete with—the intelligent machines, there needed to be a lot of lines networked together. In 1968, Engelbart presented the revolutionary NLS to a thousand fellow computer experts at a conference in the San Francisco Convention Center. The following year NLS was integrated into a new network being developed by the Department of Defense. The copper wire phone network had been designed to create two direct circuits between people simultaneously sending analog voice signals—that is, talking—in two different places. But computers exchanged digital information, ones and zeros, that could be far more efficiently broken into small chunks, or "packets," routed electronically along the most efficient path and reassembled in another computer.

In 1969 the Pentagon's Advanced Research Project Agency Network, or ARPANET, was built to connect computers in four locations. One was the Stanford Research Institute, home of Engelbart and his team. The other three were research universities: the University of California, Los Angeles; the University of Utah; and the University of California, Santa Barbara, where my father was completing his PhD in computer science.

Bernard had married a Peace Corps volunteer and schoolteacher from Burbank and made extra money working as a research assistant in the university's labs. They hired him to design, build, and install equipment connecting the electrical engineering and computer science department's computers to the new ARPANET node. While working there one day, he was introduced to some Stanford graduate students who were members of Engelbart's team. They had built a small wooden box with rollers attached to a wire that was connected to computers. Moving the box back and forth on a table made the cursor on the screen move in the same direction. Bernard had never seen such a thing before and thought this was a nifty way to interact with computers, much better than doing everything with a keyboard. SRI's oNLine system would run the new world of networked computers. The wooden box was called a "mouse."

DOUGLAS ENGELBART never made much money from his inventions. The oNLine system migrated to Xerox's Palo Alto Research Center, which didn't quite know what to do with it. But two other people did: Bill Gates and Steve Jobs, who used windows, word processing, and the mouse, among other things, to become the defining IT businessmen of their time. Apple's initial public offering in 1980 valued the company at over $1 billion, making instant millionaires of hundreds of employees and investors and establishing Silicon Valley as the source of not just innovation but dramatic wealth. Venture capitalists looking for the next Apple began setting up shop on a winding stretch of asphalt a few miles from Stanford University called Sand Hill Road.

Meanwhile, ARPANET continued to expand. By 1995 it had been replaced by the Internet, which was no longer restricted to academic and military uses. That was the year that a recent graduate of the University of Illinois at Urbana-Champaign named Marc Andreessen founded the Web browser company Netscape, based on the Mosaic software program he had helped develop. Netscape's IPO created a $2.9 billion company and launched the dot-com boom that would consume financial imaginations for the next six years.

The Internet big bang lit fuses on bombs sitting beneath the economic foundations of scores of long-established information-centered industries. The only uncertainty was how long they would take to explode. Back in 1995, people said the Internet would kill the print newspaper, yet the industry became more and more profitable for another decade until it fell to pieces in the late 2000s. People said electronic books and Amazon.com would kill the brick-and-mortar bookstore industry, which kept chugging along for another fifteen years before Borders imploded in 2011.

Yet the high-profile failure of Fathom.com and similar ventures lulled most higher-education leaders into believing that they were immune from the disruptive forces of innovation—or, more cynically, that the day of reckoning would probably arrive after they retired. So the industry settled into another decade of punitive tuition hikes, administrative bloat, and perpetuation of the nineteenth-century hybrid model's greater glory.

But while the dot-com crash of 2001 cost a lot of people a lot of money, it left the mechanisms of Silicon Valley largely unchanged. Computer chips continued to get smaller and faster and cheaper at an exponential rate. Much of the developed world wired itself to the Internet, with the developing world following closely behind.

Three post-crash developments in particular stood out. Mobile communications networks grew in scope and density like a web of fast-firing neurons on a global scale. The computer memory and processing power that had sat on desktop computers for the previous two decades migrated onto remote, Internet-connected servers called, collectively, the "cloud." And computing devices evolved into more than tools left on the office desktop at quitting time. They became an essential part of how people interacted with one another in everyday life—a social network. Mobile, social, and cloud, each driven by venture-backed technology companies in Silicon Valley.

Decades of increasingly powerful technology married to capital and the best minds of the research university had created a distinct and powerful culture in the converted industrial buildings south of Market Street in San Francisco and the storefronts and garages around the academic and industrial giants of Silicon Valley. It was a belief system in which people were not just augmented but liberated by technology—a place where people could discard the compromises and confusions of human living and build something more rational and enlightened in their place.

NETSCAPE WAS QUICKLY overwhelmed by Microsoft, and Andreessen went from entrepreneur to venture capitalist, setting up shop on Sand Hill Road. It was clear to him and the other VCs where the next great fortunes would be made. "Software," Andreessen wrote in a 2011 *Wall Street Journal* op-ed, "is eating the world." By allowing people to purchase computer processing and storage services remotely, over the Internet, instead of investing in expensive hardware, the "cloud" had made it incredibly cheap to start new software businesses. The growth of mobile computing on inexpensive commodity hardware was rapidly putting the number of potential customers for software on a growth path toward every man, woman, and child on earth. Business after business would succumb. All that is solid melts into air.

But for investors to make money, they needed more than this broad insight, which was already deeply ingrained in Silicon Valley. They needed to get the timing right. Software might eat everything in the long run, but in the long run we're all dead. The crucial question was: What's *next*? Which industries had the shortest fuses on the bombs in their basements? Who was making billions of dollars using an ancient business model? Where was the complacence, the bloat, the irrationality and waste so deeply ingrained into the way of things that people simply couldn't see how close they were to the abyss? Andreessen saw two clear answers: health care and education.

I got a more detailed version of this argument when Michael Staton and I walked into the offices of a venture capital firm called Floodgate, on the second floor of a building located about a half mile from the Stanford campus, in downtown Palo Alto. We were there to talk to Mike Maples Jr., Floodgate's cofounder. Mike has an engineering degree from Stanford and began his career at Silicon Graphics, the multibillion-dollar manufacturer of high-end computer workstations built by Netscape cofounder Jim Clark. Floodgate, one of the first investors in Twitter, is deeply enmeshed in the web of financial, cultural, geographic, and personal connections between business and academia that make Silicon Valley what it is.

The receptionist brought us to a conference room with typically spare and modern décor: glossy brown conference table, white leather and stainless steel chairs, and modern art. In the middle of the desk was, incongruously, a six-inch-high toy model of Godzilla with pieces of candy stuck in his teeth and claws.

Mike told us he is a big fan of Harvard Business School professor Clayton M. Christensen's work, which was not surprising. Christensen's theory of "disruptive innovation" holds that change comes when start-up companies use technology to sell low-value products and services to the fringes of a given market. The dominant players in the market ignore this, because they're fat and happy selling highly profitable products to the richest customers. A favorite example is Toyota selling cheap cars in the 1960s while Ford and General Motors built Lincolns and Cadillacs. Over time, the start-ups get better and better at what they do, climbing the ladder of value and profit. By the time the incumbents are truly threatened, it is much too late for them to change. The consonance with the theory and culture of Silicon Valley is obvious, which is why Christensen was cited ad nauseam by everyone we met.

Companies built for such disruption, Maples said, are like thunder lizards. They lay radioactive eggs, breathe fire, pick up and consume trains. They also grow at a terrifying rate. Silicon Valley is a breeding ground for thunder lizards, companies that go from $0 to incredibly valuable, in the many billions of dollars, in very short periods of time. That's why Godzilla was sitting on the conference table.

It's also a good example of how Silicon Valley is dominated by metaphor. Having good instincts about the onrushing future is only part of what it takes to make it big. Successful investors have to process an onslaught of new information about inflows and outflows of money, burn rates and stock prices, the comings and goings of key engineers and technologists at different firms, other companies proceeding from similar insights, broader economic trends, and the disruptive progress of other thunder lizards that are changing the same landscape—sometimes for good and sometimes not—that your thunder lizards are planning to traverse. Managing a hybrid university is largely a matter of executing a well-understood game plan under rules and assumptions that were established a long time ago. The investment and entrepreneurial games are much more contingent and fluid. It can be a fantastic rush, but it's also a hard game to win.

Metaphors and aphorisms help people transfer important ideas from one context to another. That's why, along with Christensen, another book you'll find on many Silicon Valley shelves is called *Blue Ocean Strategy*, a guide to finding and creating markets that, like open water, stretch to the horizon and are devoid of competitor boats. It's why common wisdom in Palo Alto holds that customers are most likely to break out of their routine patterns of living and purchasing when strongly motivated, and the most immediate and powerful human impulse is the cessation of physical pain. Thus, businesses are built to address customer "pain points" and "it's better to be a painkiller than a vitamin."

In arguments about whether higher education or anything else is disruptable, Maples believes, the burden of proof is on those with a negative view. Maples said that he likes to "invest in the laws of physics," that people like him use Moore's law—the famous observation that the number of circuits that can be fit on a silicon chip doubles about every two years—to "crush incumbents." He believes that no incumbent organization or regime of public subsidy and cultural habit is strong enough to withstand the power of a Moore's law–type exponential curve forever. "What I do is identify major technology shifts"—the moment when the future suddenly becomes tomorrow—"and use that technology to arm thunder lizards."

Staton made a similar argument in the offices of Learn Capital, using a series of graphs and charts. The first chart featured four circles. In the upper left corner there was a small circle that said "Enterprise Software, $0.3 trillion." Next was a bigger circle that said "eCommerce, $0.8 trillion." Then "Media & Entertainment, $1.6 trillion." Then a big yellow circle taking up more than half the screen that said "Education, $4.6 trillion." Each circle represented the size of a global market. Staton explained that Enterprise Software and eCommerce were fully converted to a digital marketplace and Media & Entertainment was about half-converted. Yet, while education dwarfed them all in size, it is still, in terms of how money is spent, almost entirely an analog business.

Now the moneymen in Silicon Valley were looking at the big yellow circle and seeing a tremendous business opportunity. Venture capital investment in education technology companies increased from less than $200 million in 2008 to over $1.2 billion in 2013.

There is, of course, a great deal of complexity sitting inside of the big yellow $4.6 trillion circle—thousands of potential business models and strategies for getting a piece of the pie. As Staton and I drove around Silicon Valley from one new business to another, certain broad categories of start-up became clear. Some of the companies we visited were going after parts of the big yellow circle. They weren't really trying to "disrupt" the hybrid university all at once in a world-changing, fire-breathing kind of way. They were just looking for opportunities to pick off certain pieces of the market.

One example was Chegg, a company that rents college textbooks through the mail in the same way that Netflix got its start renting DVDs. This turned out to be a very profitable business, enough to pay for hundreds of people working in a playfully designed office on the top floor of a building in Santa Clara, eating catered lunches on the company dime. But while Chegg was trying to beat the old-line textbook publishers that have long made outsized profits by selling expensive textbooks that college professors force students to buy, other companies were trying to beat Chegg by getting rid of textbooks altogether.

One of them was called Rafter, which works from the premise that there's going to be a big change in the type of content students use to learn. The Rafter theory is that electronic textbooks will become less and less like paper textbooks. They will transform into software, flexible, interactive, and responsive to individual students, like the courses being developed by Carnegie Mellon and MIT. Both the book publishers and hybrid universities are large, old, profitable, and in danger of seeing the important parts of their respective businesses dissolve and meld together into software that can be copied and sold for tiny amounts of money.

This kind of radical change in business cost structure is important to understanding the likely economic impact of technology on higher education. Often, new technology businesses don't *capture* parts of an existing market. They *destroy* them. Craigslist, for example, didn't steal away the profits that newspapers were making from selling classified advertisements. It simply made the profits disappear by giving away nearly all of its ads for free. Charging for a few services while keeping costs low is enough to keep Craigslist profitable—and drive newspapers into bankruptcy. In this sense, Mike Maples's favorite metaphor is apt. The thunder lizards don't mind destroying large buildings and setting everything around them on fire as long as they get enough to eat.

Other start-ups were building new services designed specifically to support online higher education. One, called Piazza, creates online study rooms where students can ask teaching assistants and other students questions about homework problems and academic work. When I visited Piazza's Palo Alto headquarters, I saw bunk beds in a room next to the standard workspace of MacBooks and ergonomically designed black chairs, perfect for the all-night bouts of coding that are typical in the fast-paced world of thunder lizard care and breeding.

A company called InsideTrack offered coaching services over the Internet, giving students personalized attention and improving their chances of beating the terrifyingly low odds of graduation at some colleges and universities. A four-person start-up called USEED was trying to change the way universities raise money. Instead of script-reading undergraduates interrupting your dinner to beg for donations to the university general fund, USEED was helping individual students create specific experiential learning projects that alumni can choose to support, in the same way that people fund new comic books and food trucks through Kickstarter, or lend money to impoverished Kenyan farmers through Kiva. A company called Course Hero had amassed a seven-million-document archive of study materials from thousands of college courses by creating a way for undergraduates to upload and share materials online. Quizlet, which was created by a high school student in his bedroom, had millions of users creating and sharing flash cards and learning games—all for free.

Textbooks, study rooms, coaching, fund-raising, learning aids, and much more—what I saw was the steady unbundling of the hybrid university into pieces that can be reassembled into the University of Everywhere. It was a virtual hive of Silicon Valley start-ups, each working to specialize in providing a specific kind of service that students have traditionally been forced to buy all at once from colleges, whether they needed or wanted them or not. Each start-up was taking advantage of the enormous economies of scale now available to software businesses by serving huge numbers of students at prices that were radically different from what undergraduates were indenturing themselves to pay. Some were attacking the college degree, developing ways for students to signal their knowledge and skill to the labor market other than "I have a bachelor's degree from XYZ University." Others were homing in on the job training mission that has historically been the main justification for public subsidies to higher education. Still others were going directly after the core business of teaching itself. One of them was our destination as we rode in the Uber that Staton had called after his taxicab denunciation.

The company is called the Minerva Project, the brainchild of a man named Ben Nelson, whom I had first met a year earlier at an education technology start-up company barbecue that Staton had thrown at a friend's house in San Francisco. At least half of the companies I met that day have since gone out of business: The attrition rate in Silicon Valley is incredibly rapid, and that's entirely the point. With cheap computing power and ubiquitous broadband making the cost of creating a company close to nothing, it makes perfect sense to shoot for the moon with bold ideas and, if they don't work, simply close up shop and start something new. One company I visited, headquartered in a Palo Alto building owned by the dying tech behemoth AOL, was dedicated to incubating new start-ups at a cost in the low tens of thousands of dollars per firm, taking a small percentage of equity in exchange under the theory that only a few needed to pan out to make money in the long run.

Ben Nelson, by contrast, had just landed a $25 million round of seed funding, an almost unheard-of sum for an education start-up. Seed funding is purely speculative: When I first met Nelson, Minerva consisted of nothing more than Ben and the ideas he could confidently present in PowerPoint, on a tablet of paper, or in a ten-minute conversation over glasses of whiskey at a barbecue. Since the seed round is usually followed by further rounds of investment, the initial dollars buy only a fraction of the entire company, which means Minerva was implicitly being valued in the hundreds of millions of dollars before it even existed in tangible form.

Nelson's pitch was that he was going to make enough money to justify that valuation by serving the huge, pent-up demand for elite American universities. People in Silicon Valley talk about "first-mover advantage," in which the first business entering a new market gains so many customers that competitors can never catch up. Elite American research universities experienced first-mover advantage on a historical scale. Harvard, Princeton, and Yale were on top of the heap in 1790, 1890, and 1990, and they're still there today. As time went by and their alumni moved into positions of wealth and power, their endowments of reputation, social capital, and hard money grew. In a good year Harvard earns more money in interest on its $33 billion cash hoard than all but a few dozen universities have in their entire endowments. At the same time, the top schools have experienced a kind of parallel accumulation of compounding reputational interest. The more everyone wants to go to Harvard, the more everyone wants to go to Harvard.

But the hybrid model also has severe limitations. It is place-bound, and places are expensive to expand, particularly when they're surrounded by cities. Yale recently decided to increase the size of its undergraduate class by a modest 15 percent, or eight hundred students. This required building two new "colleges," the rectangular stone Gothic-style buildings with courtyards that Yale originally built in the 1930s in imitation of Oxford and Cambridge. They will cost $600 million, equivalent to the total venture capital investment in education technology in 2011.

Even this kind of small expansion is rare. Harvard hasn't increased the size of its undergraduate class by a single student in over two decades, even as the number of students applying for those spots has risen dramatically. The university's reputational capital is tied to exclusivity. The thing that makes its services so valuable also prevents the university from selling those services to the vast majority of people willing to pay for them.

What if that weren't true? How much money would Harvard be worth if it were a for-profit company willing and able to serve 20,000 or 200,000 smart people around the world, instead of just 2,000 who currently get in? Ben Nelson created the Minerva Project as an answer to that question.

As he first described it to me over Chinese food in a restaurant in San Francisco, Minerva is designed to soak up the excess demand for elite American higher education, and provide a better education to boot. Admissions will be based strictly on academics with none of the inherited privilege that corrupts the admissions process at established schools. In the spirit of Hutchins-era University of Chicago, there will be a rigorous, mandatory undergraduate curriculum. Minerva won't offer courses like Economics 101, which is taught everywhere. Students will be admitted as early as the end of their junior year in high school and will be expected to get up to speed on the basics before they enroll. Grading policies will be strict, and students who don't measure up will experience something that hardly ever happens at the Ivies: They'll flunk out.

Minerva's undergraduates will study together in San Francisco for the first year, then spend each of the next six semesters living in a different global city, like Shanghai, Mumbai, São Paulo, or Jerusalem. While students will live together in the different cities, the instruction itself will take place through online seminars, allowing students around the world to engage in a common academic experience. That also means there's no theoretical limit on how many students Minerva can enroll, and marginal costs will decline as classes grow. That's why Minerva's tuition will be only $10,000 per year, 75 percent cheaper than the standard Ivy League rate.

Nelson is essentially going back in time to the creation of the hybrid university and striking a different organizational bargain, one that places much more emphasis on liberal education; avoids the legacy expenses of football teams, comprehensive academic departments, and large buildings full of books; and takes advantage of a century's progress in information technology.

Stephen Kosslyn, Minerva's founding dean, spent his career immersed in the revolutions of cognitive psychology and neuroscience. He was a year behind Carnegie Mellon AI guru John Anderson in graduate school at Stanford and went on to chair the psychology department at Harvard before returning to Stanford as director of the university's world-renowned Center for Advanced Study in the Behavioral Sciences.

Like a lot of people who make a career of studying learning science in academia, Kosslyn couldn't help but notice that most of the insights he and his colleagues discovered failed to have any effect on teaching practices at research universities. Minerva is a chance for him to take a lifetime of knowledge and apply it to the rarest of organizations: a well-resourced, elite American university built from scratch.

Minerva will not try to recruit well-rounded students with great SAT scores, Kosslyn told me. Instead, they want students who are "uneven," meaning really good at one thing. All Minerva courses will be organized as online seminars that combine students from different cities meeting in virtual space via video. That, Kosslyn says, will allow Minerva's professors to do things that can't be done by a single professor sitting with students in a room. Because students will be learning in a digital environment, Minerva will have up-to-minute data on their progress in various courses—the kind of information that traditional universities, fractured into autonomous departments and lacking any kind of coherent educational program, never gather or use. Detailed information about student learning will allow Kosslyn and his colleagues to custom-build seminar groups in which students will be best able to help and support one another given their relative strengths and weaknesses. Minerva will also be able to mix and match students over the course of a single class period as the subject matter changes.

During the seminars, Minerva students will be given problems to solve based on ideas like the "concept tests" developed by Harvard physicist Eric Mazur. These short problems are designed to quickly reveal a student's understanding of basic ideas like the meaning of "force" in physics and to allow students to collaborate and help one another learn. Because students will take the concept tests online, Minerva professors will see what students know, what they don't, and how they are improving, in real time. From Socrates's misgivings about writing to the silent-reading controversy at the University of Paris to postal correspondence courses and college over the radio, the consistent effect of information technology on education throughout history has been to make education cheaper and more accessible but also more removed from the individual teacher. Now technology is finally bringing the teacher and student back together.

Minerva's courses will be designed in terms of defined learning objectives. This sounds obvious—yet most college courses have no such things. Typical course syllabi tell you when the class meets, broad topics to be covered, sometimes day by day, and the work students must perform to get a passing grade. But in most courses, none of that is articulated in terms of the actual academic goals students must achieve. That's because defining and sequencing detailed learning outcomes is a lot of work. It takes the course designers at the Carnegie Mellon Open Learning Initiative months of labor and hundreds of thousands of dollars to do it in a way that can be applied to their AI-based cognitive tutors. It is almost impossible for a solitary university professor to accomplish the same thing on her own for multiple classes per semester. And why would she? That kind of work does nothing to get you tenure or a raise.

The learning objectives in Minerva courses will also be coordinated, so the concepts, ideas, and skills learned in different courses support one another. This, too, is commonsensical and impossible to achieve in a hybrid university built around Charles Eliot's elective scheme, in which students pick from a menu of thousands of courses, each controlled by individual faculty within autonomous, uncooperative academic departments.

At Minerva, by contrast, all freshmen will take the same four courses, and only those courses: one each from the university's colleges of social sciences, natural sciences, computational sciences, and arts and humanities. Each course will focus on the essential investigative and analytic methods of the particular discipline. This will also allow Minerva to do something else traditional hybrid universities almost never do with their undergraduate programs: experiment. Because the learning environment will be digital, Minerva will be able to create randomized trials of different teaching methods, improving and refining over time.

Minerva's first students enrolled in the fall of 2014. Seventy students were accepted from nearly 2,500 applications, a 2.8 percent acceptance rate that bested Harvard and Stanford in selectivity. A number of the students Minerva turned down enrolled in the Ivy League instead. It will be a great experiment to see if an institution designed to meet or exceed the highest existing academic standards in every way, for much less money, can overcome the blinding aura of privilege that sustains America's oldest institutions of learning.

A FEW DAYS AFTER my first meeting with Ben Nelson, Staton and I walked to the part of Market Street in San Francisco where the city makes a hard transition from tourists and opulent shopping malls to strip clubs and liquor stores. We came to a metal garage-door-style grate that was shut and spray-painted gray. Staton smiled, pointed to a small unmarked door to the right that looked like the entrance to an ultra-exclusive nightclub and/or heroin den, and said, "This is where the revolution is happening." He hit the buzzer, the door opened, and we were greeted by Shereef Bishay, founder of a company called Dev Bootcamp.

Bishay was born in Egypt, sold a company to Microsoft at age twenty-three, launched some start-ups, and now runs a company that provides an intensive nine-week course to become a Web developer, one of the computer programming code jockeys who are building the virtual world. At the end of it, Dev Bootcamp sets you up on interviews with various employers who are looking for programming talent. It's a practical education for the twenty-first-century industrial classes.

I wandered around the second floor of Dev Bootcamp for a little while. There was a quote from Yoda stenciled on the wall: "Do, or do not. There is no try." Then Staton, Bishay, a man named Dale Stephens, and I sprawled out on couches and talked about the future of education. I didn't recognize Stephens at first but eventually realized that he's the UnCollege Guy—the subject of a bunch of stories in the *New York Times* and most of the major news networks. Stephens dropped out of school in the fifth grade, taught himself at home, went to Hendrix College in Arkansas for seven months, dropped out, and is now trying to lead an UnCollege Movement, "a social movement designed to help you hack your education." According to a manifesto posted on its web site, UnCollege "will show you how to gain the passion, hustle, and contrarianism requisite for success— all without setting foot inside a classroom." Stephens is one of the most well-known "Thiel Fellows," a program named for the billionaire Silicon

Valley libertarian entrepreneur Peter Thiel, who gave a small group of smart young men and women each a "a no-strings-attached grant of $100,000 to skip college" and do something useful instead, like start a technology company.

Within a year, both Stephens and Bishay would be well on their way to building new higher-education enterprises existing completely outside of the established system. When I returned to San Francisco the following spring, Dev Bootcamp had moved into a bigger hip start-up space in order to handle pent-up demand. I talked to a group of freshly minted Web developers who included a disillusioned former financial trader, a Spanish ophthalmologist who had come all the way from Madrid to start a new career, a botany major from the University of Florida, and recent graduate of Duke University who said the last two months had been his first experience attending a school that was actually focused on teaching and required hard work. Dev Bootcamp has opened up branches in other cities, while a rash of copycat companies have launched using the same model.

The theory of Dev Bootcamp proceeds directly from the logic of preparing people for work. While there are plenty of jobs that people simply can't start before undergoing some kind of formal training, it remains the case that people acquire most of their valuable knowledge and skills *on the job,* while working. The more complicated and better-paying the job, the more true this is. The best practical training program, therefore, isn't designed to teach people everything they need to know to be good at a profession. It's designed to teach them just enough to successfully *start* a profession.

Hybrid universities simply assert that the appropriate time period for such preparation is four years for everyone, regardless of the profession. This is fantastically illogical—Marines don't spend four years on Parris Island—yet everyone goes along with it because they don't have much choice, or any other way of conceiving what higher education could be, and because hybrid universities have an enormous financial incentive to convince people that it is so. Community colleges are somewhat better, offering short-duration programs designed for specific jobs, including computer programming. But most community college students still get degrees defined by time, not skills: two-year associate's degrees or one-year certificates.

Dev Bootcamp was designed to keep people in a formal educational environment for no longer than they need to be. That turns out to be nine weeks, less time than universities take off for summer vacation. Dale Stephens, meanwhile, used his Thiel money to write a book about the UnCollege movement and then founded an UnCollege program called Gap Year. His idea is that most of the important things young people learn in college have nothing to do with time spent in the classroom. Instead, it's the shared experience of growth with peers, the internships that provide real-world experience, travel abroad, and the larger process of transformation into adulthood. You don't necessarily need academic libraries and a faculty full of PhDs to have those experiences. Gap Year students spend three months living together in San Francisco, taking seminars and workshops; three months living in a foreign country where they don't speak the native language; three months in an internship; and three months working on an independent project. The first class of students enrolled in fall 2013 and hundreds of students applied for spots in the subsequent winter and spring.

IN DEV BOOTCAMP and UnCollege Gap Year, I saw two more examples of Silicon Valley start-up companies picking the hybrid university to pieces by serving discrete parts of the higher-education market. In Minerva, I saw a university with the financial, technological, and intellectual resources to exploit the weakness of the hybrid model and the various inefficiencies and absurdities that universities have allowed to fester within their cocoon of wealth and privilege. Minerva showed something crucial about how information technology will enable the University of Everywhere: It won't create a future of *no* higher-education institutions, where everyone learns alone. Students will still need organizations built around educational expertise: places that create curricula, employ experts and teachers, and assess what students know. Rather, information technology will allow for the creation of many new and *different* higher-education institutions that offer a much better education for a much lower price.

Meanwhile, another group of start-up companies was aiming for a full-scale Godzilla-style higher-education disruption, with the burning cities and charred carcasses of advancing tank brigades.

7

Anything for
Anyone, Anywhere

Putting *The Secret of Life* online wasn't Eric Lander's idea. The course was offered through a nonprofit organization called edX located a block away from the MIT Brain and Cognitive Science Complex in Cambridge. EdX began as an MIT initiative and was quickly joined by Harvard in 2012. A host of other elite research universities from around the world soon followed. By 2014, edX was offering hundreds of free online courses in subjects including the Poetry of Walt Whitman, the History of Early Christianity, Computational Neuroscience, Flight Vehicle Aerodynamics, Shakespeare, Dante's *Divine Comedy,* Bioethics, Contemporary India, Historical Relic Treasures and Cultural China, Linear Algebra, Autonomous Mobile Robots, Electricity and Magnetism, Discrete Time Signals and Systems, Introduction to Global Sociology, Behavioral Economics, Fundamentals of Immunology, Computational Thinking and Data Science, and an astrophysics course titled Greatest Unsolved Mysteries of the Universe.

Doing this seemed to contradict five hundred years of higher-education economics in which the wealthiest and most sought-after colleges enforced a rigid scarcity over their products and services. The emerging University of Everywhere threatened institutions that depended on the privilege of being scarce, expensive places. Why would the world's greatest universities spend millions of dollars developing courses only to give them away?

The answer was that they were jostling for a dominant position on the next great stage of higher learning. And that they had been spurred to do so by the threat of mortal competition from a group of highly capitalized technology start-up companies that were bound and determined to get there first.

SILICON VALLEY was built on manufacturing. Some of the companies there are still in that business, including Apple and Intel. But making physical things is a tough financial row to hoe. Even with patent protection, you can get ground down by competitors that are better at optimizing supply chains and buying inexpensive labor. There are enormous downward pressures on prices, which is why every year stores sell bigger, nicer flat-screen televisions for less money. And if you come out on top, that means managing a large organization with tens of thousands of employees, plus factories, trucks, equipment, warehouses, etc. It doesn't leave much time for your yacht.

Software, on the other hand, is a different game. It's intellectual property. With ubiquitous broadband, cheap computers, and the cloud, the only physical thing you need to make software is a bunch of ergonomically designed black office chairs for your programmers to sit on and tables where they can rest their MacBooks and empty pizza boxes. It doesn't take tens of thousands of programmers to make great software; in fact, once you add too many cooks to the development kitchen, software tends to get worse. Michael Staton and his buddies speak with awe about coders like David Heinemeier Hansson, a thirty-four-year-old Danish wunderkind, the "Elvis of software engineers," who created the popular Ruby on Rails Web development framework, races sports cars in his spare time, and is, they say, worth one hundred ordinary men.

The cost of reproducing software is essentially zero, which means large profit margins on every copy you sell or every customer you add after the first one. And unlike hardware, which is always on the precipice of commodification, software becomes more valuable as more people adopt it—the first mover's advantage. That's why a decade after IBM PCs running Microsoft operating systems transformed the modern workplace, IBM quit the PC business entirely and Bill Gates was the world's richest man.

Microsoft employs nearly 100,000 people around the world to continually update and refine its suite of operating systems and applications and to sell them to the businesses and government offices that provide most of the company's revenue. But what if these expenses, too, could be avoided? What if *someone else* did most of the work that makes your business valuable and you didn't have to pay them? What if customers just showed up on your doorstep and deposited piles of money without you having to spend much on marketing or sales to get them there?

It sounds like a fantasy, but it's actually the business model underlying modern Silicon Valley's most heralded entrepreneurs: platforms. The platform makers are the new emperors of the digital world.

The idea isn't new. Walmart, the world's largest private employer, builds actual, physical platforms, made of concrete, with walls around them and a roof overhead. It connects those platforms to networks of transportation, telecommunication, and commerce, matching tens of thousands of companies that make things with hundreds of millions of people who want to buy things, and Walmart takes a small percentage of every sale.

Internet platforms work the same way—except, instead of building thousands of them, you only have to build one. eBay is a platform for auctions and person-to-person sales. Amazon started as a platform for selling books and expanded into all the other things people buy at Walmart. Craigslist is a platform for selling products and services that are inherently local, like apartment rentals, used stereo equipment, and prostitution. Netflix is a platform for movies and television shows. Facebook is a platform for social interactions like wishing your friends happy birthday or sharing videos of your cat.

The beautiful thing about owning an Internet platform is that other people pay for all the expensive parts of your business. The hardware and software are developed by Apple, Intel, Apache, Samsung, and Microsoft. The telecommunications networks are maintained by Comcast, Verizon, and AT&T. Pez makes the Pez dispensers, Pixar makes the cute cartoons, Penguin Random House publishes the books, and the nation's aunts make the cat videos. You sit in the middle and take a small percentage of every sale, or charge advertisers for the privilege of marketing their low-profit commodity products to your customers. The key is getting there first, because a platform's value increases exponentially as the number of buyers and sellers grows. The more everyone wants to be on a platform, the more everyone wants to be on a platform.

And what is the hybrid university if not the original higher-education platform? Students need knowledge and skills and credentials. Scholars need a way to make a living while pursuing their research. Under the elective system, the university doesn't need to concern itself with how exactly those transactions are conducted, which courses are offered, or whether they're any good. That's up to the buyer and seller. The hybrid university just used the best available technology—printed books and air-conditioned lecture halls with microphones—to build a platform, and took a percentage of every sale.

The money guys out on Sand Hill Road understood all of this. The hard part was bypassing all of the regulatory and public subsidy barriers that had been built around the cathedrals of learning, and overcoming the ingrained cultural belief that only colleges and universities as we know them today can provide a true higher education. They could see the blue ocean shimmering with the possibilities of a multitrillion-dollar market. The challenge was getting people to jump in.

The first splash came when a Stanford professor made the oddly radical choice to take his computer science course and put it online.

———

By 2011, Stanford University had evolved into an almost perfect symbiosis with the venture capitalists, entrepreneurs, and technology giants in Silicon Valley. The money was ten minutes away up on Sand Hill Road, while the jobs were a short trip down the 101 to Apple's headquarters in Cupertino, or Intel's office in Santa Clara, or in one of the legions of start-up companies percolating in storefronts and garages around town. Walking down Palo Alto's tree-lined streets of neat two-story buildings, Michael Staton pointed to a second-story office over a cell phone store— that's where Google had its first office—and nearby another space that was Facebook's early home.

All of it is a few blocks from Stanford's graceful collection of yellow brick buildings under red tile rooftops, which sit in a kind of perfect chromatic harmony with immaculate green lawns and a cloudless blue sky. The university kept the borders between scholarship and commerce deliberately porous. Professors and students would form start-up companies and do for-profit consulting gigs with the tech giants while working on their courses and dissertations. Everything about this arrangement was good for Stanford: It attracted fame and money and the smartest people from all over the world. The university relished becoming a breeding ground for thunder lizards because those unruly beasts always left their nest unscathed.

Until, that is, the summer of 2011, when a computer science professor named Sebastian Thrun had a kind of inspiration. Thrun was born in Germany and trained in computer science and statistics at the University of Bonn. His specialty was artificial intelligence, continuing the project first outlined at the Dartmouth conference by Herbert Simon, Claude Shannon, and others back in 1956. Carnegie Mellon hired Thrun as a professor in 1995, and he spent most of the next decade in Pittsburgh working at the intersection of computer science, statistics, and machines.

Artificial intelligence had come in and out of fashion over the years.

Initial hopes for replicating the human mind in silicon had proved highly optimistic as the parallel march of neuroscience and cognitive psychology revealed how fantastically complicated human cognition truly was. Thrun's generation of researchers were part of a minirenaissance in the field. By combining ever-growing computing power with advanced statistical methods, they were able to build computers that could sense and react probabilistically, comparing incoming data to patterns stored in memory and making statistical judgments about the likelihood of a match. Thrun and others built computers that could make smart decisions given limited time, information, and processing power—or, to use Herbert Simon's term for organizational behavior, satisfice.

In 2003, Stanford lured Thrun to Palo Alto and put him in charge of the university's artificial intelligence laboratory. Two years later the Pentagon's Advanced Research Projects Agency (DARPA)—the people who built ARPANET back in the 1960s—held a contest to see who could build a car that used AI to drive itself across treacherous desert terrain with no humans at the wheel. Thrun was part of a team that built the winning Volkswagen SUV. Google hired him to work in its research laboratory while he continued to teach AI as a tenured professor at Stanford.

By 2011, Sebastian Thrun was something of a Silicon Valley rock star, a certified genius and visionary maker of very cool things. He dressed in jeans and stylish T-shirts and married a beautiful professor of comparative literature who liked to tease him about his techno-utopian ways. In March of that year, Thrun was invited to TED (Technology, Education, Design), the annual festival of technologist self-congratulation, where he stood before a rapt audience and described how he and his colleagues at Google had built a self-driving car.

Afterward, Thrun hung around the conference to watch the other presenters, including an energetic former hedge fund analyst named Salman Khan. Khan had computer science degrees from MIT and an MBA from Harvard, and had become recently famous for creating a series of instructional videos for elementary, middle, and high school children that had attracted millions of views on YouTube. The videos became the basis for Khan's hugely popular education web site, Khan Academy. Thrun is a logical person and he saw no reason why someone couldn't do the same for college.

So he returned to Stanford and talked with Peter Norvig, who was both Google's research director and Thrun's co-professor for an upcoming graduate course at Stanford called CS221: Introduction to Artificial Intelligence: Principles and Techniques. The course consisted of what most college courses consist of: Thrun and Norvig giving lectures and assigning texts to read, followed by a series of problems to solve, followed by exams to certify what students had learned. All of those things, Thrun and Norvig knew, could be provided via computer at zero marginal cost. So they put together the videos and problem sets and e-mailed members of the global AI community to let them know that anyone who was interested could take CS221 online for free, alongside the regular Stanford students in Palo Alto. They expected a few hundred people to sign up. Within two weeks, there were 58,000.

As journalist Steven Leckart would later report in *Wired* magazine, this was the point where the Stanford administration caught wind of what was going on. That the university would have no idea what was happening inside one of its classrooms is not surprising: The hybrid university leaves mundane matters like teaching to professors, because that's the point of being a platform. Often this leads to a lot of uninspired instruction conducted in blissful ignorance of the principles of learning science. But in this case it gave Thrun and Norvig a crucial head start. While they were shuttling through a series of meetings with university lawyers and bureaucrats, CS221 online enrollment continued to grow. Then a *New York Times* reporter wrote a story about the course, and suddenly word shot around the world. Enrollment reached six figures and continued to climb.

Sebastian Thrun had done nothing particularly interesting from an educational or technological perspective. He did not invent the college equivalent of a self-driving car. There were already thousands of lecture videos on YouTube and iTunes by 2011 and millions of students enrolled in online courses offered by accredited colleges and universities. Because it was huge and free, CS221 was soon described as a "massive open online course," or MOOC. But Thrun hadn't invented MOOCs, either; the term had first been used three years earlier to describe a course on the nature of learning taught at the University of Manitoba by a pair of Canadian professors named George Siemens and Stephen Downes.

So why the enthusiasm for CS221? To start, Thrun called his online course a "course," because that was clearly what it was. There were no caveats like at MIT OpenCourseWare, which insisted that it was only offering course "materials." The conceit of the hybrid university had always been that there was something special about taking the course in a particular place that made the learning experience greater than its component parts. Thrun observed that his on-campus Stanford students soon began taking CS221 just like everyone else—on their computers—and got better grades than when they had attended live lectures in a hall.

But the most important aspect of CS221 was not the lecture or curriculum or Web interface or series of tests. The one characteristic that distinguished it from the many online courses and MOOCs that had come before it—the single quality that created a virtuous cycle of publicity and enrollment and more publicity—was its association with Stanford University and AI rock star Sebastian Thrun. The cash hoards accumulated by the great American research universities (Stanford's $17 billion endowment is third behind Harvard's and Yale's) were tiny compared to their vast reputational endowments. Stanford had promised the world that it was the best of everything higher education had to offer, plus a healthy dose of Silicon Valley cool. Now Thrun was drawing on that deep pool of global goodwill to attract non-Stanford students to his course. He was disrupting the one thing about Stanford that mattered above all else: its name.

Because CS221 was a course, Thrun naturally told his students that he would give them a test to certify how much they had learned. This is what

made Stanford's administrative hairs stand on end. Knowledge and learning were all well and good—everyone was in favor of advancing the cause
of human learning and bringing inspiration to the masses and so on and
so forth—but *credits*? That was Stanford's *business*. Now Thrun wanted to
give away something that students in Palo Alto were buying for $50,000 a
year?

Stanford had reached a point in its business life cycle that has been
well documented by people who study the kinds of technology-driven
entrepreneurial firms that litter the landscape in and around Palo Alto.
Someone was offering a product that was basically the same as what the
university was selling (or perhaps not quite as good), and giving it away for
free. Standard Clay Christensen–inspired business school doctrine (Stanford has the number one ranked business school in America, including an
entire Center for Entrepreneurial Studies) holds that at this point the only
long-term survival path is to bite the bullet and start shutting down the
highly profitable business you've spent decades building before the thunder
lizards burn it to the ground. It also holds that most firms never manage
to pull this off, which is why the business dead pool is wide and deep and
contains many corpses of once-mighty firms.

Predictably, Stanford chose not to take the leap. The school's administrators decided they could live with the lecture videos but asked Thrun to
stop offering problem set assignments, i.e., the part of the course where
students work actively to ingrain their learning. Thrun refused. So they
settled: Thrun could keep giving away the lectures and problem sets, but
he could only give the students who passed the tests a "statement of accomplishment," not a "certificate" or, God forbid, a "credit." And the statement
had to include various caveats declaring that the person who had just
watched all the Stanford lectures and finished all the Stanford problem
sets and passed the Stanford exams could *not* in any way use his or her not-
Stanford statement of accomplishment in pursuit of a Stanford degree.

Normally, administrators have a lot of leverage in negotiations with
faculty. In most academic disciplines, the fabulous university life of the

mind can only be led at a university, and Stanford sits at the very top of the ladder of prestige. But here again, Stanford's fabulously successful postwar policy of open borders between scholarship and commerce proved to be a liability, as did its location in the heart of Silicon Valley. Unlike a professor of comparative literature, Sebastian Thrun had another organization he could work for that was just as wealthy and famous and prestigious in its way: Google. Also unlike a professor of comparative literature, Thrun had money from his various tech-related activities. Before CS221 even launched, he had withdrawn $300,000 from his bank account and created a start-up company to produce new online courses. Thrun had already resigned his tenured faculty position earlier that year to run Google X, the company's research center. So when the university said no to credits, he finished out the course, awarded the not-Stanford statements of accomplishment, and walked away.

At this point, everyone in Palo Alto was paying close attention to Sebastian Thrun and CS221. The venture capitalist business model depends on backing a lot of companies with the hope that a few pay off with spectacular returns. VCs look for "20X" investments, i.e., twenty dollars back for every dollar in, which makes up for all the worthless investments in the dead pool. (Describing multiples this way is a common Silicon Valley verbal tic; 20X is pronounced "20-ex," a tenfold increase in customers is "10-ex," etc.) The payoff, moreover, has to come within a defined amount of time, usually no more than ten years after the initial investment. There are normally two ways to get there: a sale to a larger company, or an IPO.

Neither scenario requires profitability per se. What buyers want to see is *momentum*, a steep upward path of exponential growth in users and customers. That's exactly what the graph of new CS221 users looked like. The venture capital firm Charles River Ventures kicked in $15 million for Thrun's new start-up, which he called Udacity. In January 2012 the company announced plans to develop a whole suite of courses, led by Thrun and his colleagues, that would be free and online.

Unsurprisingly, the other venture capitalists chose not to leave Udacity and Charles Rivers alone with the $4.6 trillion education market. Sebastian Thrun was not the only rock star AI guru at Stanford. He was succeeded as director of the university's AI laboratory by a professor named Andrew Ng, who had followed the well-trod path to Palo Alto via computer science degrees from Carnegie Mellon and MIT and a PhD at nearby UC Berkeley. Ng also had a cool side job at Google, directing the so-called Google Brain project, which created a billion-connection artificial neural network spread across hundreds of linked computers. Ng had also taught sections of CS221 and had spent fall 2011 putting his own Stanford class in machine learning online.

A few months after Udacity was loosed upon the world, John Doerr of Kleiner Perkins Caufield & Byers, one of the original investors in Google, announced that he would be joining the board of a new company, backed by KPCB and led by Ng and a colleague from the Stanford computer science department named Daphne Koller. The company was called Coursera. And while Udacity was busy building a bunch of new courses from scratch, Coursera had a different plan. It was going to try and build the digital higher-education platform to rule them all.

LIKE ANY SUBCULTURE, the Silicon Valley start-up world operates within a tightly defined set of aesthetic guidelines. People speak to one another in code—20X!—wear the same clothes, buy the same smartphones and computers, and work in offices that look remarkably alike. So I was a little surprised upon arriving with Michael Staton at Coursera's offices to see that it was not located inside a converted industrial space and did not involve taking a freight elevator to a reception area/fixie bicycle storage space. Coursera is actually in a conventional office building along a commercial strip outside Palo Alto. The company seems a little more serious about its business. This may be the point.

We sat on comfortable couches for a few minutes drinking the free designer sodas before we were ushered into a conference room to meet with

Daphne Koller. She's middle-aged with unstyled graying hair and wore a T-shirt and blue sweatshirt, unzipped, with comfortable sandals. They were the kind of clothes you wear in a subculture that ostentatiously rejects the idea of caring about the kind of clothes you wear.

At this point Coursera had been up and running for a year and had enrolled three million students around the world in more than four hundred courses, a number that it keeps constantly updated on the front of its website like the national debt ticker in Times Square. Coursera didn't build any of those courses itself. Rather, it got some of the world's most famous universities to build them, and throw in their incredibly valuable brand names, for free, in the bargain.

The profusion of news articles about Udacity, Coursera, and other MOOC providers produced a wave of panic among the hybrid university administrative class. As organizations driven by status competition, universities are terrified of being left behind their peers. As soon as "free online course" became associated with "Stanford," everyone who wanted to be like Stanford—which is to say, everyone—rushed to get in the game. The trustees at the University of Virginia went so far as to abruptly fire their recently hired president for insufficient entrepreneurialism after reading an op-ed in the *Wall Street Journal* about MOOCs. Most university leaders weren't quite so stupid, and Virginia eventually hired their president back after being denounced in the press. But the die was cast, and Coursera built a business model out of offering hybrid universities a credible answer to the question "What are you doing about online education?"

From the moment Coursera and Udacity were created, people began asking how they would make money. This was in some respects the wrong question to ask about an Internet start-up, because the idea was that if you create a free service so elegant and spectacular that the whole world flocks to your virtual doorstep—if 20X multiplies on itself over and over again—you will figure out a way to make billions of actual dollars through the sheer force of attraction and scale. That's what Google and Facebook did, and so, an endless parade of would-be Zuckerbergs say, we'll do it, too.

But I asked the question anyway, and Koller was ready for it. She recommended a YouTube video by a Wharton business school professor who explains why Coursera is a "blue ocean" company. Koller believes Coursera is growing into a "huge addressable market" and said something along the lines of: If only 2 percent of all the people in the world are willing and able to pay $74 for a service, that's $10 billion a year, which is a lot of revenue for a company that can fit all of its employees into one part of one floor of a commercial office building in Palo Alto. Her point was that the world is *really big* and there are a lot of people in it who need education, so you don't need to charge them a lot of money to get to some-large-number-ex and everyone gets rich.

I mentioned that, in contrast to Coursera's strategy of growing very quickly by leaving the educational work to brand-name universities—many of whom relied on a standard model of recorded lectures—Carnegie Mellon's OLI system has a very intensive approach to course development that involves a lot of time, money, and diagnosis of learning pathways for the AI. Koller started shaking her head, as if to disagree with the idea that Coursera was offering an inferior service. I asked her why, and she said, on the positive side, OLI is using cognitive science and artificial intelligence to build programs that adapt to individuals' learning styles, and that was way ahead of its time. But she believes the OLI model is too rigid and solitary. To explain what she meant by that, she mentioned that she had a daughter in elementary school who is (surprise) really good at math. Koller's daughter had been enrolled in Stanford's Education Program for Gifted Youth (EPGY). This is the program that Patrick Suppes first began developing back in the 1960s—the basis for his famous article in *Scientific American*. It's still in operation today.

EPGY is sophisticated but inflexible, said Koller, and after a while she and her daughter started watching Khan Academy videos instead. They were more satisfying, because the experience was more "Web 2.0," which is a way of describing online environments in which large numbers of people communicate and collaborate, learning and making together. Suppes's original Teletype math program came before Doug Engelbart and his team showed the world what the future of networked collaboration would look like. People like forming communities with other people.

Koller was right about the virtues of Web 2.0. But this is also what you have to say when you're a platform and don't have the time, money, expertise, or business model to build, as Coursera claims to, "the world's best courses, online, for free." When such courses actually come to exist in the near future, they will combine the best of both worlds: flexibility, sharing, and collaboration married to sophisticated AI built around the latest theories of cognition and learning. One of the stranger aspects of the Stanford-based MOOC phenomenon is that, while it was led by some of the world's great experts in AI and computer science, there is—so far—little if any AI in the MOOCs themselves.

I asked Koller what she thought the next five years would look like at Coursera. She said there would be three main developments ahead. First, Coursera would build 5,000 courses, which she saw as feasible given that the company offered more than 300 after a year. In five years Coursera is planning to have available, in her words, "an education in anything for anyone anywhere." Second, so-called blended learning, in which students on traditional college campuses learn through a combination of in-person and Web-based teaching, will be the norm, she believes. She quoted Edwin Slosson's well-known alleged quip that lecture notes are a way of transmitting information from the lecturer to the student without it passing through the minds of either one of them.

Third, there will be a transformation of the study of human learning, from a series of anecdotes to real-data science. Suppes had written about this, too. "The power of the computer to assemble and provide data as a basis for [educational] decisions," he wrote, "will be perhaps the most powerful impetus to the development of education theory yet to appear."

As we finished the interview, Michael Staton mentioned to Koller that Learn Capital was putting together a new pool of investment money. A few months after we spoke, Coursera announced a new $43 million round of investment from a group of Sand Hill Road funders, the investment arm of the World Bank, and Learn Capital. In March 2014, the company hired Richard C. Levin, who had recently completed a twenty-year stint as the president of Yale, as its chief executive.

We walked back to the lobby and I passed a world map on the wall with strings connecting places all across the globe to the names of colleges and universities that are offering courses through Coursera. It was also, implicitly, a map of Coursera's target market: everyone on earth. I knew that Koller's goal of creating 5,000 courses was not a randomly chosen number. According to the U.S. Department of Education, one-third of all the course credits earned by people with bachelor's degrees in America come in just thirty courses, the workhorse introductory classes like Calculus, Biology, Physics, Marketing, Corporate Finance, Accounting, Statistics, Spanish, English Comp, and Econ 101. Five thousand courses would cover a huge percentage of all credits currently earned.

In other words, while an education in anything to anyone anywhere may sound utopian, an education in most things to most people in most places is a concrete, realistic goal that can be accomplished using existing technology in the near future. The question is not whether it will happen but who will make it happen.

A FEW MONTHS LATER, I returned to Palo Alto and made my way to a large house on the outskirts of the Stanford campus. Sixty-two years before, Patrick Suppes had arrived with his newly minted Columbia PhD and bought the property in a neighborhood that was reserved for faculty and administrators. He still lives there today, at the age of ninety-three, holding the title of professor of philosophy, emeritus.

While we had briefly corresponded by e-mail, I was unsure of what to expect, because ninety-three is by any measure a lot of years. What I found was someone who talked with the energy of a man a half century younger. Suppes is recently remarried to a woman whose son has just started his freshman year at Stanford. He was in the midst of publishing various books, monographs, and articles on subjects related to learning, mathematics, and psychology.

Suppes had been watching the rise of MOOCs with keen interest as Koller, Ng, and Thrun were feted in magazine features and asked to speak at high-profile conferences worldwide. He is very sure of himself and seemed to relish his elder scholar's prerogative to speak freely. Suppes's biggest complaint about the people running the hyped-up MOOC companies is that, unlike him, they don't seem to have done the hard work of studying the theoretical literature of learning science or conducting experiments to contribute anything new to the field.

Daphne Koller, Suppes said, "has not studied education at all. She's completely naïve about the history of what's happened." She is, he allows, "smart about some things in computer science, though not all. But she doesn't know what the hell she's talking about in education and doesn't seem to realize it."

Indeed, in the two years that followed the explosion of interest in Stanford-birthed MOOCs, some people began to back away from their most outsized claims. Thrun in particular struggled with the fact that the large majority of students enrolling in courses offered by his company, Udacity, which he tried to run part-time, failed to finish.

But in a larger sense that didn't matter. Because Sebastian Thrun's great innovation had nothing to do with teaching or learning. It came from punching a gaping hole in the psychic wall that separated elite higher education from online learning. His decisive act was disrupting the *idea* of the eternal, rare, and expensively place-bound hybrid university. Once the notion of "free online Stanford course" became embedded in the public mind, and hundreds of other well-established liberal arts colleges and research universities rushed into the breach for fear of being left behind, there was no going back. Like it or not, they began lending their expertise, money, and credibility to the great project of building the University of Everywhere.

And while Coursera may not be integrating the latest AI into its courses today, it can in the future, and it's not the only would-be education platform king. The knowledge of how to build great online learning environments is out there, and it has existed in various forms for some time. What's different today is that, unlike traditional universities, education start-ups have strong financial incentives to use that knowledge on behalf of as many people as they can.

That's why, despite his feelings about the new generation, Suppes remains firmly convinced that he was right all along. Even back in the 1960s he could see the shape of things to come. "It was trivial that we could do this technologically," he said. "That wasn't the issue." The challenge was unraveling the principles of neuroscience and cognitive psychology and using them to give all students exactly the education they need while overcoming the barriers of inertia and bureaucracy that keep the hybrid university in place.

"It's going to be painful," he said, when that day finally, inevitably, comes. "The consequences of really teaching everything you can do well with computers were terrifying for a lot of us once we thought about it carefully." For college education, he said, "we probably should expect a revolution."

It is certain that the capitalists and visionaries of Silicon Valley will try to finance and instigate that revolt. If the current MOOC companies end up in the dead pool, others will rise in their place. The $4.6 billion yellow circle is simply too big and education is too lucrative and information centered to be ignored.

What's less certain is how the hybrid universities that have dominated global higher education for the past century will respond. Will they withdraw into the high reaches of the ivory tower while the siege engines around them grow stronger? Or will they try to break out and build something new on open ground?

Back on the other side of the country, in the birthplace of American higher learning, plans were under way that would help to answer that question, one way or the other.

8

Imaginary Harvard and Virtual MIT

There are a number of free genetics and biology courses available on the Internet. Coursera offers one taught by a professor from Duke. But I decided to take 7.00x for one reason: It came from MIT, one of the great science and engineering universities. With a 9 percent acceptance rate, it's also one of the most selective; among elite research universities, only Stanford, Princeton, Columbia, Harvard, and Yale let in a smaller percentage of students who apply. In addition to learning more about genetics, I wanted to learn more about myself. Could I hold my own in a course designed for the best and the brightest? And what, exactly, was it about MIT's courses that made the smartest kids in the world clamor to get in the university's doors?

Fortunately, MIT's commitment to rigorously translating *The Secret of Life* experience into an online learning environment made it easy for me to compare my performance to the freshmen in Cambridge. 7.00x featured exactly the same problem sets, midterms, and final exams administered to the MIT undergrads. The six problem sets were collectively worth 20 percent of the course grade, while the two midterms were worth 25 percent each and the final exam 30 percent. The online problem sets gave students a limited number of tries to earn points, after which a detailed explanation of the right answers would become available. The midterms and final, by contrast, gave only one chance at each problem. This was nerve-racking because the questions were scored instantly, so if you were bombing, you knew *right away*. I stumbled a little on the biochemistry in the first midterm but rebounded on genetics and managed to score 90 percent.

At that point, the course dove into the really cool stuff: recombinant DNA and the mechanics of cloning using restriction enzymes to cut out specific sections of DNA, paste them into plasmids, and grow them on petri plates in a kind of biochemical purification. That brought us to DNA sequencing and every episode of every police procedural broadcast on CBS since the late 1990s. I made a stupid mistake about the way DNA sequences are read biochemically and tripped up on the very last question, but pulled through with an 89 percent on Midterm 2.

All of which brought us to the climax of the course: genomics and the Human Genome Project. We learned how, in the years since the project was completed in the 1990s, scientists have been able to map the origin of species by documenting specific genetic sequences common among multiple organisms following a chain of evolution back millions of years. We saw how the process of medical discovery has become increasingly rationalized through large-population genetic analysis, yielding new studies about the nature of things like mental illness, some of which were literally published while the 7.00x class itself was in progress. Medicine was being steadily transformed by new information.

A few days after the last lecture, I sat down in front of the final exam. My course average was sitting right at 89 percent and I really wanted to get it over 90. But it was not to be: I got stuck once again on biochemistry and scored an 85. Combined with the two midterms and the problem sets, that yielded a final score of 87 percent—a solid if unspectacular B.

That meant I could pass an MIT-grade class, albeit only at the freshman level. But I still wondered whether I was missing something, a crucial distinction between the experience of being a Cambridge-based MIT undergraduate and an online student. I got on the phone and spoke with a half dozen MIT students about the class. For the most part, their experience was just like mine. They went about the course the same way: watching the lectures, doing the problem sets, asking questions of fellow students, taking the tests.

Still, the brand names of MIT and its partner institutions in the edX consortium, most prominently Harvard, were crucial to the success and public understanding of the endeavor. What was it about those institutions that mattered so much? After completing the second midterm, I decided to head to Cambridge to see for myself.

WHILE CAMBRIDGE has the standard bars and burger joints of a college town, other parts are unusual. There are an inordinate number of stores selling clothing in the classic New England high collegiate style, with sherbet-colored pants and loud plaid jackets, red bow ties, and a shop full of nothing but hats. The sign on the J. Press store says "Washington, New York, Cambridge, New Haven," i.e., the city where all the power is, the city where all the money is, Harvard, and Yale. A newsstand next to the train station in Harvard Square was selling the latest issue of *U.S. News & World Report*'s guide to America's best graduate schools. Harvard had programs at or near the top of almost every list.

As I walked toward the campus I was struck by how many gates enclose Harvard. The gates were open and anyone could walk through them, but they were barriers nonetheless, architectural messages that were not hard to understand. I stepped over the threshold into Harvard Yard and stopped for a moment to take in the old redbrick buildings, five stories high, with chimneys and white windows overlooking an expanse of lawn dotted with oak trees and a few remaining elms. I was struck by an odd sense of déjà vu, in part because I'd seen pictures and in part because I was looking at the original form that thousands of other colleges and universities had copied over the centuries as they tried to evoke and live up to the original. The "university yard" at George Washington University was trying to be this.

There were, as on any college campus, a lot of students walking back and forth between buildings, most of them staring at their mobile phones. Unlike other campuses, there was also a clot of elderly Japanese being led about by a small woman holding an umbrella over her head. Nearby, a group of thirty children crowded around a bronze statue of a sitting man as a woman gestured and spoke in a language that wasn't English. As I walked toward the university's main library, I passed a large, blondish German couple wearing fanny packs who were clutching a thick book with a lot of photographs on a cover that said, *DK Eyewitness Travel Guide: USA*. They were tourists, I realized—all of them. And then it hit me: *I* was a tourist. I was standing in the middle of a tourist attraction. It may be an American university, but for many people it's a place to visit.

So I did what tourists do: I hired a guide.

Back at Harvard Square, I gave a few dollars to a smiling young woman who handed me a sticker that said, "Trademark Tours presents, Harvard University, est. 1636." A part of me that I was displeased to acknowledge did not want to wear that sticker. Because if you're good enough to get into Harvard, you don't have to take the tour. This kind of status anxiety is an enormous motive force in American higher education. It drives people to act and spend in ways that make no rational sense otherwise.

My guide's name was John. He was a freshman from Iowa City, majoring in history. I asked the two tour promoters, who were standing next to him wearing Harvard shirts in front of a sign on Harvard Square, if they were students there, too, and they both shook their heads. "I'm not that cool," said the woman, who attends Boston College. The young man looked slightly embarrassed and said, "Suffolk County Community College." John said, "I've been at Cambridge since last fall," which is code I recognized after years living and working among Ivy League graduates in Washington, D.C. Saying "Cambridge" instead of "Harvard" is how

Harvard graduates draw attention to their alma mater by pretending to not invoke its name.

I was the only person there for the 12:30 tour, so it was just me and John for the next hour. We walked along the edge of campus and then inside one of the gates. He pointed to Harvard Hall and said it is the third Harvard Hall, built on the ashes of the second, which was built on the rubble of the first. Unlike a certain rival university whose name rhymes with "Fail," he said, the buildings at Harvard look old because they actually *are* old. "I didn't realize how old until I got here," he said, "when they pointed out that we were the *fourth* Class of '16."

We walked to the statue of John Harvard, which was surrounded by more tourists, and famously manages to tell three lies in only four words on the inscription: "John Harvard, Founder, 1638." The university was actually founded in 1636, Harvard donated the land but died at age thirty-one and didn't himself found it, and the statue isn't of him at all. No images of Harvard the man survive, and the statue was cast more than two hundred years after his death.

From there we walked across Harvard Yard, which is encircled by dorms that house freshmen. John pointed toward them while running down the standard list of famous Harvard alumni: Natalie Portman lived in that dorm; that's the one where Tommy Lee Jones and Al Gore were roommates; this is where JFK and Teddy Roosevelt both lived; that's where Bill Gates and Mark Zuckerberg bunked before dropping out. At several points John mentioned the extent to which various dorms have different degrees of luxuriousness and proximity to the main campus, which apparently matters quite a lot at Harvard, mirroring the intense and essentially insane status competition that consumes elite universities.

As we circled around and through various buildings under a brilliant spring sky, John told me a series of tales about Harvard: how the Widener Library was endowed by the mother of an alumnus who drowned aboard the *Titanic*, which is why students had to pass a swimming test for many years before graduating; how Gertrude Stein gave a clever one-sentence answer to a final philosophy exam and got an A plus; how Conan O'Brien managed to set the Harvard and Cambridge police against each other in furtherance of his plot to steal the sacred editor's chair of the *Harvard Crimson*; how the Charles River pedestrian bridge I had walked across earlier that morning was the scene of Quentin Compson III's suicide in *The Sound and the Fury*; how Franklin Roosevelt's biggest regret in life was not getting "punched," or selected, for a Harvard social club; how that was the dorm where the Chinese premier's daughter lived last year, which has its own panic room; and how the Phoenix social club's competitor made its building available for the unflattering portrayal of Phoenix in *The Social Network*.

Later, a Harvard alum told me that many of these stories are apocryphal at best. But that fact missed the point. John had given me what I, a tourist, really wanted: a tour of Imaginary Harvard, the Harvard of the public mind. In the real university, it's cold most of the year. Most of the people live and study outside the wrought-iron gates that surround Harvard Yard. Almost no one who attends is a household name.

But reality doesn't really matter, because Harvard has become one of those places where the imaginary version is much more important than the real version. The Harvard that matters most is the Harvard of the movies: *Good Will Hunting, Legally Blonde, Soul Man, How High.* Imaginary Harvard is the template for all of the other, lesser universities, with their quads and yards, their founders' statues, their circled seals with mottos in Latin and the oldest plausible date of founding in rounded letters along the bottom. Imaginary Harvard has become the reflexive aspiration for striving students worldwide—people who have never been to Cambridge and don't have the foggiest idea of what an education there actually means, but understand that it is, somehow, incredibly important.

Being the nation's first, richest, and best has been to the university's enormous advantage over the years, decades, and centuries, and never more so than today. But when I was there I sensed a kind of nervousness about the whole endeavor. To me there was a vibration of insecurity underneath the eternal ruling-class veneer. Because while being allowed inside the gates may be an accomplishment in itself, it carries great and increasingly unmanageable expectations. When an educational institution becomes grotesquely swollen with money, pawed at by tourists, possessed of an immensely valuable brand name the popular meaning of which it can't control and the benefits of which it cannot bestow on nearly everyone who wants them, the pressures of that threaten to distort and split the place open at the seams. Harvard was never meant to be this wealthy or important. It all happened more inadvertently than anyone imagines, a combination of first-mover advantage, just the right sequence of industrialization and globalization, Cold War government spending, the rise of the information economy, and not getting bombed into rubble during World War II.

But Real Harvard continued getting richer even as Imaginary Harvard grew larger and weirder and more important, because the hybrid university severely restricts your freedom of movement, and really there was nothing else to do. It's hard to argue for dramatic change when the fourth Class of '16 is lining up outside the gates—and there were tens of thousands of young people who hoped they'd be part of that group.

That's the way it was until 2011, when the one university in the best position to challenge Harvard for supremacy decided to take the most important attribute about itself and give it away for free to anyone, anywhere.

THE MASSACHUSETTS Institute of Technology is a straight two-mile drive from Harvard, up Broadway to the banks of the Charles. It is an odd accident of history that two of the world's great universities are both located inside the same seven-square-mile minor municipality across the river from Boston, and that—despite sharing the advantages of vast wealth and the brightest students and scholars—they are about as different as two elite universities can be.

MIT is much the younger of the two, founded during the Civil War. There are no walls around it, and its buildings look neither old nor fake-old. For a long time they didn't look like much of anything. The university is infused with a culture of practicality, reflecting its 1861 charter as "a school of industrial science, and aiding generally, by suitable means, the advancement, development and practical application of science in connection with arts, agriculture, manufactures and commerce." The similarity to the purposes of the Morrill Land-Grant Act, enacted a year later, is not coincidental.

This dedication to practicality positioned MIT to play a leading role in the twentieth century's great scientific and engineering triumphs. Vannevar Bush was one among scores of thinkers in eastern Cambridge who probed the secrets of the universe and built the infrastructure of the Information Age. While the ecosystem of money and high technology was developing in Silicon Valley, a parallel system evolved along Route 128 outside Cambridge. Companies like Digital Equipment Corporation and Wang Laboratories were worth billions in the 1970s and 1980s, employing Harvard and MIT engineers and producing some of the leading computer technologies of the day. Those firms ultimately fell to the forces of disruption, but Cambridge remains one of the biggest centers of start-up tech outside of Palo Alto.

The official MIT tour is short on celebrity references. What the tour guides like to talk about, besides the standard discussions of meal plans, campus safety, and the Olympic-caliber workout facilities that have become commonplace at modern universities, is practical jokery. Or, in the MIT vernacular, "hacks"—a series of inventive, elaborate, and ultimately benign pranks that embody certain elements of the MIT culture.

MIT is proud of its hacks. There's a whole corridor in one of the engineering buildings describing them. Like when one new president arrived for his first day of work and found that the entrance to his office suite had been carefully closed off by a newly installed wall. Or when a bunch of students somehow put a fully assembled campus police car on top of the domed administration building. Or when another group of students dressed up a white van with the logo of a "cannon cleaning company," stole the Caltech cannon, drove it back across the country, and fit it with a giant MIT class ring.

In a sense, the hack stuff is just an evocation of Imaginary MIT, a way to make the university seem interesting and fun to the outside world. Most students don't have the wit or the time to de- and reassemble police cars, because they're too busy slogging through problem sets. But the difference between Imaginary Harvard and Imaginary MIT is instructive. One is built around wealth, status, and celebrity. The other combines the quest to understand deep, profound, and beautiful principles of reality with the engineer's practicality in making things *work,* of staying rooted in objectivity and not the artificial rules and frames of reference that human organizations impose upon us. The most celebrated hacks are elegant. It's no coincidence that "hacker" is high praise in Silicon Valley. It means you're the kind of person who grabs the new tools of information technology and makes the world the way you believe the world should be.

So it was not surprising, in retrospect, that of the two great universities in Cambridge, MIT was the one that decided to hack higher education itself.

THE IMPLOSION OF COLUMBIA's Fathom.com venture in the early 2000s left MIT the de facto leader of Internet education among elite universities. Over the next ten years, millions of people visited the MIT OpenCourse-Ware site and downloaded course materials. But the sudden storm of media attention around the free Stanford courses made it clear that the next stage in online learning had arrived. The cloud, mobile devices, social networking, and the ongoing march of cheaper, better computers had opened up possibilities that hadn't existed ten years before. In December 2011, while Sebastian Thrun was busy administering final exams to tens of thousands of online students in CS221, MIT announced the creation of a new nonprofit organization that would provide free Web-based courses—not "materials"—online. They named it MITx.

The creation of Sebastian Thrun and Peter Norvig's Udacity in January 2012 and Coursera two months later meant that, within five months, three new organizations backed by deep-pocket funders and the brand equity of world-class American research universities had been created to give away college courses to anyone, anywhere, for free. Even from the lofty vantage of Harvard Yard, it was hard not to notice.

Harvard had, to that point, avoided any involvement with free education on the Internet. It offered a few online courses, in exchange for thousands of dollars in tuition, through its Summer School program. "Online course credit can be transferred to many schools," it said, while neglecting to mention that one of the schools that did *not* accept online credits earned at Harvard Summer School was Harvard College itself. While MIT, Yale, and other elite schools were experimenting with sharing their educational resources online, Harvard was conspicuously absent.

But you don't hold the rank of America's best college for almost four centuries without knowing when the time has come to follow the crowd so you can lead them. While it was all well and good to have the most money, the most precious commodity in higher learning is status. All of sudden the institutions Harvard competes with for students, scholars, and that precious sense of default preeminence in the public mind were being praised in the *New York Times* for taking higher education into the digital future.

Which is why, in May 2012, Harvard and MIT held a rare joint press conference to announce the creation of a new venture called edX. Like Stanford, MIT had an artificial intelligence laboratory, and so, following the pattern, its director, Anant Agarwal, had been tapped to run MITx. Now that it had been expanded scant months later to include Harvard and a select group of other world-leading universities, Agarwal was elevated to run the whole enterprise.

He was not shy about his ambitions. "There is a revolution brewing," he said at the press conference, "in Boston and beyond." He believed that this was the "the single biggest change in education since the printing press." From there the conference cut to videos of university higher-ups declaring that "Harvard and MIT recognize the incredible effect that technology is having on education today" while generic Coldplay-style music played in the background and the camera swooped across keyboards and digital screens. Then Agarwal kicked it over to the tense-sounding president of Harvard, Drew Gilpin Faust, an eminent historian of the Civil War and American South who until that day had displayed little interest in anything involving computers or otherwise expanding Harvard's educational offerings beyond its hallowed grounds. She was followed by the smiling president of MIT, Susan Hockfield, and then back to Agarwal, who, in case the audience wasn't quite feeling the sheer scope and importance of it all, proclaimed that edX was going to "educate a billion people around the world."

Agarwal was born in India and went to college at the Madras campus of the Indian Institutes of Technology, which are arguably the most selective colleges in the world. An American teenager stressed out about acing the SATs and getting past Harvard's 8 percent admission rate should feel lucky compared to the half million Indian math and science prodigies who take the IIT's entrance exam every year knowing that only the top 2 percent will make the cut.

In our conversation, Agarwal hit most of the same notes I heard from Daphne Koller. He said edX had "blown through all of their projections" on student enrollment, growing to eighty-five full-time employees working on technology and engineering, education services, learning design, editing, and videography. I asked him how many courses edX was planning to build over the next five years, and he started to talk like a computer scientist who is used to exponential growth. They would double the number of courses every few months, he said, until they hit something around 5,000—the same number Coursera was shooting for, a number representing the vast majority of all the credits earned by American college students today, given away for free, to anyone, anywhere, in half a decade or less.

But there were also real differences between the two organizations. Coursera may be run by Stanford professors in Palo Alto, but the porous border between Stanford and Silicon Valley is still a demarcation of a certain kind between organizations for which money matters most and organizations for which status matters most. Coursera is a for-profit company backed by venture capitalists who would like to get 20X returns on their investment in a short amount of time. So Coursera was trying to be the king of all higher-education platforms while leaving the issue of educational quality up to the colleges themselves.

EdX was also running a higher-education platform, and Agarwal noted with some satisfaction that Stanford itself had recently decided to use the edX learning management systems for its own foray into free online learning. But edX is also a nonprofit organization whose biggest investors are Harvard and MIT themselves. Harvard didn't invest $30 million in edX because it wants to get 20X back in five years. It already has $33 billion and a stable of highly paid full-time investment managers for that kind of work. Harvard spent $30 million because it wants to still be seen as the world's greatest university in five years, and fifty years, and when the fifth class of '16 walks through the Cambridge gates.

Which is why edX, more than anyone else in the business of providing free education to anyone, anywhere, appears to be genuinely focused on the *quality* of the courses it provides. The hybrid university model had traditionally hidden the quality of individual courses behind the university-encompassing light of wealth, fame, admissions selectivity, and the collective scholarly renown of the faculty. Not all of what happened behind closed classroom doors lived up to those lofty reputations, but it was hard to parse the brilliance that students brought into Harvard with the brilliance that they emerged with four years later.

Now those universities would be opening their virtual doors to the entire world. If the classes were substandard, people might start to realize that the universities in their minds were actually . . . imaginary. The whole virtuous cycle of everyone wanting to be in the place everyone wanted to be would be at risk.

That's why Agarwal kept coming back to the word "rigor" as we talked. MIT isn't just a place full of the coolest gadgets and smartest people. It's also a university that, somewhat unusually, takes the idea of undergraduate education seriously.

So when MITx emerged and edX quickly followed, it wasn't that hard to figure out how to make the new free online courses rigorous enough to deserve the MIT name. The university simply took the very good, very difficult courses it was already offering and translated them, as accurately as possible, onto the edX platform.

WALKING INTO the Brain and Cognitive Sciences Complex that night altered my understanding of 7.00x in a few ways and solidified it in many others. It was a little strange to recognize the faces of young men and women I had been watching for months on my computer. Lander himself arrived a few minutes before class was scheduled to begin, and an edX publicist introduced us. He asked me how the class was going and was I sticking with it, and I said yes, I had just turned in the fourth p-set the night before. He grinned, said "All right!" and put up his hand for a high-five. "You're learning molecular biology!"

In debating the educational value of lecture videos, some people argue that there's something about being *in the room* that mere video can't replicate. Based on what followed, I can say this: live and taped lectures really aren't the same. Live lectures are definitely worse.

It's a simple point to make, but there's a lot to be said for the Pause button. A big part of taking notes for 7.00x involved drawing fairly complex diagrams and stopping to write out certain key points and ideas, which is hard to do if you're also trying to keep up with the next point the lecturer is making. Lander packed a lot into an hour, with barely a wasted word. The videos are shot by multiple cameramen with professional equipment in great audio and full HD. The lecture hall only seats one hundred people, yet sitting near the back it was harder to see, harder to hear, and more distracting than watching at home. The kid with pink hair next to me kept fiddling with his iPhone and was clearly bored. I much preferred sitting down to watch lectures at a time and place of my choosing, headphones on, notebook in hand.

At the end of the class, a group of ten or so students gathered around Lander in the well of the lecture hall to chat and ask more questions. Lander is an optimistic, garrulous person, and a number of his students clearly had an intellectual crush. The same was true for the online community. A student in Prague wrote, "I feel almost like prof. Lander is a part of my family because I see him often on my computer." From Baguio City in the Philippines: "I want Prof. LANDER to teach me anything every week for the rest of my life . . ."

I understood the feeling, and part of me was a little jealous that I couldn't join the after-lecture colloquy. But not so much that I would have paid $5,000 in tuition for the privilege. Whatever value relationships with the TAs and professor might have yielded, I was able to get a good grade without them. And even if I had been willing to pay $5,000, MIT can't and won't take my money, partly for reasons of sorting and selectivity and institutional prestige, but also because of pure logistics. There's only one person who led the Human Genome Project, and the number of people who can form a group around him after class can't ever be more than ten.

THE NEXT DAY I came back to MIT, took the campus tour, and then grabbed an above-average sushi lunch at a restaurant in the Frank Gehry–designed student center. (After years of boring buildings, the university has lately taken a hard turn toward the great architectural fantasies of the twenty-first century.) While eating, I glanced over at a young woman about twenty feet away, sitting with her elbows in front of her, talking cheerfully with two other young women on the other side of the restaurant table.

Except, I realized a moment later, the two women were not in the student center at all. They were projected in life size on a curved high-definition video screen on the other side of the table. There was a small transparent umbrella three feet above the young woman who was actually there, acting as a speaker projecting the sound of her lunchtime companions' voices so that she could hear them perfectly and nobody around her could hear them at all. By all appearances the electronic mediation had no effect on their human interaction. The setup, I later learned, is called a "wormhole," and the two women on the screen weren't even elsewhere at MIT: They were 3,000 miles away, at Stanford University.

From there I walked to the chemistry building to meet my cousin—Bernard Carey's nephew—who grew up in small-town Pennsylvania, went to Boston College on a scholarship, then got an administrative job in the MIT chemistry department. While most college classes consist of students sitting in rooms, listening to teachers, some require more hands-on work. I wanted to see what that kind of learning looked like at MIT.

We walked down into the labs, where we put on safety glasses. A woman in a white lab coat was removing solvent from a solution by using a rotary evaporator that put the solution into a vacuum, thus lowering the boiling point so that just a mildly-above-room-temperature level of heat was enough to suck the solvent away and leave a purified compound. She was trying to figure out a way to synthesize the poison that African tree frogs secrete, in a way that doesn't involve killing thousands of African tree frogs. I asked her: With the wonders of modern technology, wasn't there some kind of universal chemical-making machine—the equivalent of a 3-D printer—where you just type in the compound you need, press "Enter," and it appears on a table nearby? She struggled a little to be polite while saying no, there is no such thing. Even the companies that synthesize chemicals in large batches for places like MIT are still pouring buckets of one substance into larger buckets of another substance by hand.

We went to another lab where one woman had her hands stuck inside enormous black rubber gloves that allowed her to manipulate objects inside a box full of nitrogen gas, thus avoiding having the things inside be affected by contact with air. Another machine was separating and chemically analyzing the compounds and depositing them via a robot arm into a waiting array of sterile test tubes. Nearby, there was a simple chalkboard where people had scrawled images of molecules, including the standard carbon hexagon that had become familiar to me through the chemistry part of 7.00x.

A graduate student told me that he was working on surface chemistry, trying to come up with a more universal process of bonding things to surfaces, which, he explained—and he had clearly thought about this a lot—is a lot more difficult than working with liquids, which can be easily manipulated via pouring them into glass beakers and feeding them through tubes into machines. In particular, a single "monolayer" of molecules on a surface is *really small* and has very little mass compared to the object it's attached to. As Nobel Prize–winning physicist Wolfgang Pauli once said, "God created solids, but surfaces are the work of the devil."

The grad student had a slight foreign accent, suggesting that he was among the legions of very smart people drawn to America by our world-beating research institutions. There are many practical applications of surface research—he mentions somebody improving the insides of ketchup bottles so ketchup doesn't stick to them as much—but he is focused on inscribing molecule-size wires onto surfaces, which would increase the number of circuits per unit of surface. In other words, MIT's research is contributing to the ongoing extension of Moore's law, which is the underlying motive force driving the entire Silicon Valley business model and the higher-education technology revolution. Universities like MIT are both building the technology that makes this possible and, with the advent of edX, using it to hack the underlying business model of their own institutions.

Except, probably not *this* institution. Because while many aspects of the hybrid university—like curricula and p-sets and HD video of really good lectures—can be readily translated into digital form, spending hours standing at a bench, feeding liquids into an expensive machine, isn't one of them. I asked Eric Lander whether any of the thousands of professors teaching genetics felt threatened by the possibility that 7.00x would put them out of work. I noted that a group of philosophy professors from San Jose State University (motto: "Powering Silicon Valley") had written an open letter to Harvard philosopher Michael Sandel objecting to the possibility of their university offering Sandel's well-known Justice course on the edX platform. "Professors who care about public education," they wrote, "should not produce products that will replace professors, dismantle departments, and provide a diminished education for students in public universities."

Lander chuckled. "That's the philosopher's guild saying that. I haven't heard anything like that in molecular biology. Most molecular biologists are practicing scientists, so nobody thinks their livelihood is being impaired."

Instead, Lander thinks we should create "a handful of really great biology courses where we get two or three lectures on the human vision system from the guy who's an expert on that, and then two more from the expert on neuroscience," and so forth. Lander's experience with the Human Genome Project was formative: Thousands of scientists from around the world worked with billions of dollars in government funding to collaborate on a project that made a gift of knowledge to humanity. This wasn't in everyone's short-term best interest. When President Clinton announced in 2000 that the human genome couldn't be patented, the market value of for-profit biotech firms trading on the NASDAQ dropped by billions of dollars in a matter of days.

"I would love to take the same approach to teaching biology," Lander told me, "with 'open source' materials to create really great courses." The San Jose State professors had said, "The thought of the exact same social justice course being taught in various philosophy departments across the country is downright scary—something out of a dystopian novel." I asked Lander about this. "Of course there should be more than one biology course," he replied. "Maybe there should be five or six or seven. But there doesn't need to be a thousand or more."

THE HARVARD Department of Molecular and Cellular Biology looks like the building Indiana Jones taught in. Along the top of the redbrick front walls spanning three sides of a courtyard are a set of friezes depicting various animal species. The front doors are flanked by two life-size statues of rhinoceroses. I walked in to meet with the professor who's leading Harvard's involvement with edX. His name is Robert Lue.

Lue is from Jamaica and seemed young for the number of titles and accomplishments he has racked up. He spoke with unusual depth about the science of learning, more so than the entrepreneurs and computer scientists driving much of the education technology revolution. "I've always been very interested in distance education," he said, specifically "science visualization." He gestured toward a picture from *The Inner Life of the Cell*, a short animated video that he helped produce that has been viewed millions of times by students around the world. It is, he declared, the most-viewed science animation in history.

Lue teaches Harvard's introductory biology course and became fascinated with how complicated educational design can be if you really take it seriously. He told me that learning can be enhanced by "reversal of misconception." For example, he asked me, of the following four things, which contributes the most to the mass of a tree: air, water, soil, or sunlight? I said sunlight, because I thought of energy being transformed into mass. That's a common answer, he said, and people also say soil a lot. But they're both wrong. The right answer is air, because that's where the carbon comes from, and trees, like people, are carbon-based life-forms. We're mostly made up of the little carbon hexagons that the people in the MIT chemistry department scribble on their chalkboards.

Because people think air is light and soil is heavy, they think soil is the likely answer. But they're wrong. There is a *lot* of carbon in the air. And when people learn what they thought is true is the opposite of true, they're surprised—and they remember. "Our brains have evolved to respond to change," Lue said. "Change and surprise drive things." In other words, the shock of having our existing, well-worn neural patterns first accessed and then contradicted is a powerful instigator of new learning.

That's why, just a few hours after the fact, I remembered almost nothing of what I had seen in the MIT student center except the girl talking to the two other girls who weren't actually sitting on the other side of the table. Even small details of edge and shade and color were stuck firmly in my mind.

While Harvard employs some of the world's greatest scientists, the university—particularly in its imaginary incarnation—is best known for humanities and liberal arts. It's one thing to visualize the inner life of a cell with a computer, but what about the inner life of a person in all her multitudes? I asked Lue about teaching humanities digitally and he responded by asking professorially, "What are the humanities?" and then answering: The humanities are a series of juxtaposed exposures to very different things—perhaps music, literature, and film—that provoke moments of coalescence and realization. Technology provides many ways to achieve such moments, he said, by contrasting ideas expressed through different media, deepening the context in which students work and consider ideas, and providing opportunities for students to annotate material and share their thoughts and ideas with one another as they occur.

Lue also mentioned one of the basic principles of effective online educational design: constantly assessing the pace and progress of student learning. Carnegie Mellon's OLI courses do this to feed information to their AI-driven cognitive tutors, which personalize the problems students work on and the materials they engage with accordingly. Lue also sees this as a way of engaging students' "metacognition"—that is, their conscious awareness of their own learning. If students become more aware of the pedagogical arc of the course—if they can see the patterns in the big learning picture—they're more likely to learn.

Harvard's edX endeavor, HarvardX, is not without controversy in Cambridge, and Lue is familiar with the arguments. At one faculty meeting, someone stood up and said, "Aren't we building a doomsday machine here?" His response was that edX is the future, it is coming, so we can either be a part of it and lead it or not. "If you're not better than students reading the textbook," he said, "you shouldn't be teaching. If you're not better than the video, you shouldn't be teaching."

Like nearly everyone thinking seriously about the future of higher education from inside a hybrid university, Lue proposes a win-win scenario: Professors take advantage of the new world of free online resources to do a much better job teaching. But there are some with a gloomier view. Clay Christensen, the Harvard business school professor and the high priest of the disruptive innovation theory that is treated like holy scripture in Silicon Valley, had recently characterized so-called blended courses—professors combined with computers—as analogous to steamboats with sails. The first steam-powered boats to cross the oceans were fitted with sails as a precaution while the steam technology became more powerful and reliable, and because it's hard to go from one way of working to another way overnight. But nobody moves freight across the ocean with sails today.

Lue smiled. "I've debated Clay publicly on this," he said. "Clay is an economist and I'm a biologist. So while he thinks higher education is a system, I think higher education is an organism. Our environment is changing, so we need to evolve. We need to *deconstrain,* to redefine how our individual components relate to one another. Organisms go extinct when they *cannot mutate.*" As Lander had taught me, the first cells had parts that we've been working on improving for the past three billion years.

Lue has no doubts about whether information technology will be part of the university's next evolution. "HarvardX *is* Harvard," he said, with conviction. "It is us."

Lue was my last meeting in Cambridge, and I left thinking about the reversal of misconception and what the evolution of the hybrid university might actually mean.

In describing how the brain reacts to surprise, Lue said that "everything is a function of risk and opportunity." To survive and prosper in the world with limited cognitive capacity, humans filter waves of constant sensory information through neural patterns—heuristics and mental shortcuts that our minds use to weigh the odds that what we are sensing is familiar and categorizable based on our past experience. Sebastian Thrun's self-driving car does this with Bayesian statistics built into silicon and code, while the human mind uses electrochemical processes that we still don't fully understand. But the underlying principle is the same: Based on the pattern of lines and shapes and edges, that is *probably* a boulder and I should drive around it. That is *probably* a group of three young women eating lunch at a table near the sushi bar and I should pay them no mind.

Heuristics are also critically important to the market for higher education. That's why brands like Harvard and Stanford matter so much, and people like Ben Nelson can raise $25 million in seed funding based on the promise of a for-profit company with a similarly valuable brand. It's hard to see inside the cathedrals of learning and understand just exactly what the rooms and priests are like and what the experience of living as an acolyte there really entails. The brand is the shortcut: Spending four years in Cambridge is *probably* a good idea.

So when we're genuinely surprised, it sticks, because it implies we don't just need to reconsider the small facts at hand. We may need to reevaluate the broad, powerful heuristics that have been guiding us through life. If we were so surprised about this, we might be wrong about other things, altering the mind's ongoing risk and opportunity calculations in a substantial way. What if there's another alternative outside of Harvard and MIT?

If the teaching part of the hybrid university is allowed to evolve with technology into new and interesting forms, does the institution have enough core functions left to survive? Or will people be so surprised by the newly evolved organism that they change their whole way of thinking about what higher learning should cost and should mean? What part of the organism is most likely to provoke that kind of surprise and change, expanding the public consciousness to embrace the University of Everywhere?

The answer, I realized, was the part that has little to do with teaching and everything to do with how colleges make money: the college credential.

9

Less Like a Yacht

I graduated from college in 1992 with a bachelor's degree in political science. At the commencement ceremony, held in a hockey arena in downtown Binghamton, New York, some university official I had never met handed me a diploma, which I took back among several thousand other young men and women nursing hangovers and wearing cheap polyester robes. I stuck the diploma in an envelope, put the envelope in a box, and carted the box from one home to another for the next twenty-odd years. Since I received it, nobody has ever laid eyes on my diploma but me.

Yet everything important that subsequently happened in my life depended on that piece of paper. Without it, I couldn't have enrolled in graduate school and met my wife. Every job I might ever have wanted required a college degree. I went on to live, work, and socialize almost entirely among other college graduates. I didn't feel any different walking back from the graduation stage than I did walking up. But from the perspective of the rest of the world, I had become a different person altogether. While I couldn't see them all yet, whole new realms of opportunity had opened up to me, just waiting for me to walk up to the entrances with diploma in hand.

This was true despite the fact that almost no relevant information about my college education came with me when I drove away from Binghamton a few days later. All of my tests, notes, and papers were left behind. The university maintained no records of the syllabi that were used in my courses or the standards—if they existed in any recognizable form—that were used to calculate my grades. My transcript, along with my diploma the only official record of my four years in college, is all but indecipherable today. It says things like "PLSCWE 484A." Even I'm not sure what that means.

By contrast, everything important about 7.00x is available for anyone to see. Because the course exists in a digital learning environment, the syllabi, lectures, problem sets, tests, and discussion forums can be saved forever at virtually no expense. Scanning my handwritten notes into a digital file and uploading them onto the Internet took me about five minutes. Anyone can find out exactly what I was taught and, according to the tests, how much I learned.

Yet, as far as the rest of the world is concerned, that twenty-year-old piece of paper remains far more important in establishing my identity—in defining, in the ways that matter most, who I am.

My efforts to understand why this is led me, somewhat improbably, to a yacht.

IT WAS LATE AT NIGHT or possibly early in the morning and I was standing next to Michael Staton on a large and expensive boat. We had arrived many hours and cocktails ago at the Potomac River harbor in Washington's tony Georgetown neighborhood. The yacht was moored near a group of expensive restaurants, and as we climbed up the ship's ladder we were greeted by an attractive young woman wearing a nautical miniskirt outfit who checked our names off a list and then offered us drinks and hors d'oeuvres. She explained that this was the owner's "medium-size" yacht— he has three of them—and it was being kept open all evening in case he decided to return from that night's NHL hockey game with some of the

Washington Capitals and their girlfriends in tow. The ship is a sixty-eight-foot Italian racing number that has been described as the "Lamborghini of the yacht world." The cabins belowdecks are all red walnut, chrome, marble, and white linen. It started to rain after a few hours and we stayed dry under the roof as people outside scurried for cover. The drinks continued to flow and the hostesses remained on alert, but the owner and the hockey players never arrived.

I had ended up on a yacht in the middle of the night because I was trying to understand the future of college degrees. MIT's OpenCourseWare initiative had tapped a huge demand for free online college materials—and had no effect whatsoever on the economics of higher education, because it did not offer credits that could be used to get a college diploma. Courses without credits, Fathom.com had discovered, were worth little in the open marketplace. Without college credits and degrees, or something like them, none of the venture-financed start-ups or nonprofit MOOC providers had much hope of truly disrupting higher education.

That's because people don't borrow tens of thousands of dollars to merely acquire the knowledge and skills taught in college. They pay for the keys to a lifetime of educational opportunity and financial reward. Without a college degree, workers are categorically excluded from the most lucrative parts of the labor market. Such jobs don't just pay more at the outset. They offer many more opportunities to acquire additional knowledge and skill on the job, which leads to more money and more chances to learn. Without a college degree, people can't get another, better college degree, the legacy of Charles Eliot's decision to make bachelor's degrees a requirement for graduate school. Credentials also offer security. College graduates are much less likely than others to lose their jobs during economic downturns; this was especially true during the Great Recession. Graduates who do face unemployment are much more likely to be rehired as the economy recovers.

For more than a century, the hybrid university has had a government-backed, culturally reinforced monopoly on the sale of increasingly valuable credentials. That, more than anything else, is the reason that colleges and universities have been able to continue raising their prices year after year. Average inflation-adjusted tuition and room and board charges at private four-year colleges and universities more than doubled from 1983 to 2013, from $18,143 to $40,917 per year. Public university prices rose at an even faster pace. Anyone can write a textbook or start a tutoring company or charge people for the privilege of listening to a ninety-minute lecture twice a week. Only colleges as we know them today can sell college degrees—and for increasingly large amounts of money.

But a credential is just information. Like modern financial currency, the value of that information is nothing more than what people collectively attribute to it. If everyone agrees that a 2.5-by-6-inch piece of U.S. government-printed paper with George Washington's portrait on the front can buy a dollar's worth of goods and services, then it can. If everyone agrees that an 8.5-by-11-inch piece of paper with the name of a hybrid university on the front is the only thing that will give you access to the jobs worth having, then people will beg, borrow, and steal to get one. There's no law of nature that says this is the only way to communicate educational information to employers. We could collectively agree to something else.

Even as information technology is being used to create new ways of helping people learn, it is also creating new ways of helping people signal the nature of their learning to organizations and other people. Out in Silicon Valley, the same philosophies of openness and collaboration that are being used to build the software that's eating the world are also being applied to college credentials. And back in Washington, D.C., one of the original pioneers in giving away online courses was starting to think about the credential part of the equation.

HIS NAME IS MICHAEL SAYLOR—the man who owned the yacht. Saylor was born in Dayton, Ohio, in 1965 and spent his early years following his Air Force sergeant father around the world from one military base to another. The family settled back near Dayton when Saylor turned eleven, and he was in most respects a typical midwestern boy, with a bicycle, paper route, and a budding enthusiasm for Rush and Pink Floyd. Saylor thrilled to stories of Greek and Roman philosopher kings and loved comic books and science fiction, especially the work of Robert Heinlein, who infused a muscular, patriotic libertarianism into his tales of rocket ships and wars against monsters from space. In one Heinlein book, *Have Space Suit—Will Travel,* a high school senior gets in a spaceship and saves humanity from alien hordes, winning him a scholarship to MIT. That, apparently, was where you went to college if you wanted to fly and build spaceships. So after Saylor graduated as valedictorian of his high school class, he packed his bags and made the trip to Cambridge.

Four years later, after graduating with a degree in aeronautical engineering plus the history of science, technology, and society, Saylor got ready to enlist in the Air Force. But a medical exam revealed an undiagnosed heart murmur. He would have to make his way on earth. Saylor quickly zeroed in on what was becoming the central challenge for businesses in the late 1980s: what to do with the rising tide of digital information.

As computers were becoming cheaper, more powerful, and more connected, businesses converted many of their administrative systems from paper files to electronic databases. In theory, that meant they could know much more, much faster, about their customers. But as Herb Simon and Vannevar Bush and all the other smart people who had thought about information and modernity had realized, simply having access to data was not nearly enough. The hard part was figuring out what do with it, how to filter and process and understand. In 1989, when he was twenty-four years old, Saylor and a friend from MIT founded a company designed to solve that problem. They called it MicroStrategy.

MicroStrategy dug into the databases that companies had been accumulating, often by accident, and gave them useful intelligence about their business. Victoria's Secret, for example, was stocking the same number of the same kind of bra in every store. It turned out that women in different parts of the country have different preferences for bra colors and sizes. MicroStrategy analyzed the inventory data and told Victoria's Secret it could make a lot more money by varying inventory accordingly.

That kind of work was enough to make MicroStrategy a thriving technology company. Saylor played the venture capital game shrewdly, keeping the lion's share of the company's stock for himself. He also had grander visions than mere business intelligence. At MIT he had learned about the structure of scientific revolutions, how inventions like the printing press had profoundly changed not just the act of learning but whole systems of politics and philosophy. The world was on the verge of another such change, Saylor believed, and MicroStrategy software would be the key tool for making sense of the new information—not just for businesses but for every single person on earth.

It was a grandiose, almost messianic message and it rang perfectly for the times. MicroStrategy went public in 1998, with the MSTR symbol listed right next to Microsoft on the soaring NASDAQ index. By the middle of 2000 the company was worth $15 billion and most of it was owned by Michael Saylor. The future seemed limitless, and education was high on his list of human endeavors sure to be transformed by the wave of intelligent software. In March 2000 he announced plans to spend $100 million of his own money to create a free Internet university based on video lectures by the smartest people in the world. "A cabdriver in Bombay," he said, would be able to get "95 percent" of an Ivy League education. The university would educate "everyone, everywhere."

One week later, under a directive from the Securities and Exchange Commission, MicroStrategy announced that it was revising downward statements it had made about how much money it had earned in 1999. The timing was terrible, coming less than two weeks after the NASDAQ had peaked and the dot-com bubble had begun to rapidly deflate. MicroStrategy's share price collapsed, and Saylor's theoretical net worth declined by $6 billion in a single day, by some measures the largest such loss in history, a fact that would eventually be immortalized as a question in *Trivial Pursuit*. While admitting no wrongdoing, Saylor settled SEC charges of reporting inaccurate financial results by paying a multimillion-dollar fine. Most of his fortune was gone, and the $100 million for the free university along with it. The cabdrivers of Bombay would have to wait.

But unlike many of the dot-com–era ventures that evaporated in the post-bubble reckoning, MicroStrategy always had a viable business that involved actual customers paying real money for services. Saylor steadily rebuilt the diminished firm, and while he didn't have $6 billion anymore, there was still plenty left for yachts. MicroStrategy moved into an office tower in the Tysons Corner business district in suburban Washington, D.C.

When I came to visit, one of Saylor's assistants arrived in the lobby to bring me up to the top floor. As we entered the elevator, she pulled out an iPhone and touched an icon on the screen. This, she explained, was an application developed by MicroStrategy that allows smartphones to store and authenticate information about personal identity. She tapped another button, which told the elevator who she was and thus gave us permission to go to the top floor. We exited and turned left toward a set of tall, windowless doors covered in fabric. She fiddled with the iPhone for another few seconds, a small light on the wall turned green, and the doors opened to the executive suite.

After a few minutes I was led into Saylor's office. I asked him if anything had happened in the last thirteen years to change his mind about the wisdom or feasibility of creating a free online university.

"No, my thinking has not changed," he said. Saylor is somewhere on the very far reaches of the statistical distribution of human certainty. He is tall and handsome, which—along with the hundreds of millions of dollars—tends to mask a generous level of engineering-student social awkwardness. He's a classic MIT rationalist, someone who sees the world for what it is, and what it should be, and struggles most with managing the emotional residue of constant frustration that the two can't be made the same, sooner. Owning and running your own company is a nice way to get yachts and mansions and pretty girls, which Saylor has enjoyed in abundance. But I sensed that the biggest advantage for Saylor is having enough control over the environment he lives and works in to keep the irrationality of the world at a manageable level.

"When I went to MIT in 1983," he said, "it was the most expensive college in the world. My grandma had enough money in the bank to pay for the first four weeks of classes and then it would have bankrupted my family. So I had to indenture myself to the United States government. I joined the Air Force ROTC, because I really didn't have any other choice."

Like all MIT freshmen, Saylor was required to take introductory physics as part of the General Institute Requirements. The course was taught by a Dutch physicist named Walter Lewin, who demonstrated the principles of classical mechanics with a series of props and exercises that he had refined through the years. In one, a grapefruit-size steel ball hung from a wire hurtled across the lecture hall, only to stop, bound by the laws of physics, inches from Lewin's face. In another, Lewin himself was suspended from the wire. The lectures became famous. He was the Abelard of Newtonian motion.

Newton's laws don't change much from year to year. At the level of freshman mechanics, they haven't really changed since the *Principia* was published in 1687. So MIT did the logical thing by recording Lewin's lectures and broadcasting them twenty-four hours a day using the best available technology, which in 1983 was a cable television system local to MIT.

This made an impression on Saylor. "Many people's perception of higher education is you have this personal tutor who's helping you through all this," he told me, "but my experience was not that at all. If there are four hundred people watching one guy lecture, then how interactive could that be?"

In 1999, MIT recorded a fresh version of Lewin's lectures, which Saylor couldn't help but notice were exactly the same as those he had indentured himself to watch back in 1983. "Why not just upload that stuff to the Internet and make it freely available?" he thought. "Instead of it costing students $50,000 a year, why not $50 a year?" In fact, Lewin's lectures on mechanics, electricity, magnetism, and vibrations would become some of the most popular features of MIT OpenCourseWare and are now the foundation of a series of courses offered by edX.

As MicroStrategy recovered from the crash and Saylor's fortunes rose along with it, he decided to make good on his original promise. With the cost of everything technological falling, he didn't need to spend $100 million anymore. Today, Saylor University at Saylor.org offers nearly three hundred courses on the Internet, all of them free, for anyone, anywhere.

Saylor finally had done what had seemed obvious and rational to him thirteen years before, which was to replicate his undergraduate experience of reading books, watching lectures, studying course notes, and taking tests. He considers this to be a solved problem and as such not interesting to talk about. Instead, he wanted to discuss things that are more complicated and important, like college credentials and the way people and machines process information.

The human mind is good at many things, like finding patterns in a complex array of stimuli and applying them to other patterns that have been stored in the brain. Sebastian Thrun became famous for teaching a computer to do something that anyone with a driver's license can already do: drive a car without running into objects, falling off cliffs, or crashing into other cars.

There are other jobs, however, that people do very poorly. One of them is to understand differences in size. We cannot escape our own lived experience, the centrality of ourselves in interacting with the world around us. This makes it hard for us to really comprehend things that are much smaller or larger than we are. The average person is between 1.5 and 2.0 meters tall. We understand how big four meters is, and eight meters, and a half meter, and a tenth of a meter. But once you get out to 100,000 meters or 1,000,000 or 1,000,000,000, it all just merges, cognitively, into "very far away." The difference in size between a quark and an atom is about the same as the difference in size between a golf ball and the moon, but for most people "atom" and "quark" both register as, indistinguishably, "very small."

This is particularly problematic when the scale of very large things is changing rapidly—like, for example, the number of circuits that can fit onto a silicon wafer. The average person's understanding of such trends often lags behind the reality of what the world has become. People are even worse at making rational predictions about scale-driven changes. We assume, wrongly, that our future lives will be like those we live today.

One of the characteristics that distinguishes Saylor and the other rationalists who gravitate to Cambridge and Silicon Valley is that they're good at keeping scale properly in mind. To illustrate this point and how it relates to the thorny problem of personal identity and college credentials, Saylor said, "You've crossed the Golden Gate Bridge, right? You know the story of that bridge and how much it cost to build. That was done one hundred years ago. How many people in the world do you think were qualified for the job of architecting that bridge when they started looking for the person to design it? Like, five or something? How many could there have been?"

To be able to build the Golden Gate Bridge in 1920, Saylor said, a person would need to come from a rich family, have an expensive university education, and be lucky enough to have certain innate intellectual talents. Then they would have needed to build a first bridge and then a second bridge. "How many guys would have built five bridges, or even one bridge, like that in their life?" he asked. "That's the credential you would need before you could be considered for the Golden Gate Bridge. There might have been five guys to choose from on earth.

"What if there were fifty? What if there were five hundred, or five thousand? The future is all about putting the program to build that bridge on a tablet computer that costs $200. Then give that program to a billion people. Now let's see if there isn't an eight-year-old girl in western China who's the world's best bridge builder."

Which is all well and good, but who, I asked, is going to hire an eight-year-old girl in western China to build a suspension bridge? Colleges don't just teach people how to do things. They give out trusted credentials that prove people's bridge designing and other skills. The college diploma is an integral part of the labor market. Doesn't that matter?

Michael Saylor had an answer for the credential problem, too. Unsurprisingly, it was built around software—the same software, in fact, that brought me up the elevator to his office.

AMERICAN COLLEGES AND UNIVERSITIES grant over four million degrees a year. In round numbers, they break down to one million associate's degrees, two million bachelor's degrees, one million master's degrees, and two hundred thousand doctorates (which include a lot of doctors and lawyers). The bachelor's, master's, and doctoral titles are centuries old, dating back to the guilds of masters and scholars in Paris and Bologna.

Before colleges all became the same, they tried different approaches to credentialing. When Thomas Jefferson's University of Virginia opened in the 1820s, it offered no university-wide degrees at all. Instead, each of eight autonomous schools—anatomy, ancient languages, law, mathematics, medicine, modern languages, natural history, and natural philosophy— gave independent credentials signifying that students had mastered defined bodies of work. Students weren't labeled according to how much time they had been studying, i.e., freshman, sophomore, etc. Their academic identities were a function of how much and what they had learned.

But when colleges and universities settled into their current form in the late nineteenth century, the structure of American college degrees settled with them. Professional administrators dedicated to the glory and well-being of their institutions took control, and they established rules and regulations accordingly. The foundation of credentials became time: three hours a week spent in class over a standard fifteen-week semester yielded three credit *hours*; 120 credit hours earned a four-year degree.

Time-based degrees reinforced the power of scarce, expensive institutions. The degrees said very little about what you had learned. There were grades, of course. But the hybrid university was built around giving professors academic freedom in teaching along with research, which meant that all those As, Bs, and Cs were the product of, to the outside observer, unknowable standards, methods, and professorial idiosyncrasies. Grade inflation steadily erased whatever small meaning grades might have had. The median grade earned by Harvard undergraduates today is an A minus, and the most frequently awarded grade is a straight A. There's a reason that most of the fancy script on a diploma is dedicated to *where* you learned, and for how long.

Once again the hybrid universities benefited enormously from timing. As the hybrid model took over, the world was becoming bigger, richer, more populous, more specialized, and more complicated. The administrators were gaining power in many other walks of life besides higher education. They needed a way to define and protect their status, and college degrees fit the bill. As the great German sociologist Max Weber wrote in 1922, "The elaboration of diplomas from universities, business and engineering colleges, and the universal clamor for the creation of further educational certificates in all fields serve the formation of a privileged stratum in bureaus and in offices." Such certificates, he wrote, "support their holders' claims . . . to the monopolization of socially and economically advantageous positions."

Colleges did their part by making certain kinds of degrees a prerequisite for valuable professional education. You couldn't go to law school or medical school or business school or get a doctorate without first getting a bachelor's degree. The professions and universities came together, hand in glove.

Officially, a diploma signifies that the bearer has completed a defined course of study. But if that's all it meant, it wouldn't matter very much. In reality, diplomas mean many different things, depending largely on where they come from. Some signal a certain level of underlying cognitive ability. Elite colleges select for smartness by running annual high-stakes admissions tournaments that rely in significant part on student performance on standardized tests like the SAT, with the rest coming from academic performance in a relatively small number of elite public and private high schools. The single most important message that a Harvard diploma imparts is not that the person got *out* of Harvard. It's that he or she got *in*. That's why "Harvard dropout" and "Harvard graduate" are almost identical in what they say about a person.

Diplomas also suggest that people have undergone a kind of acculturation, that they have proceeded through a rite of passage for entrance to the upper middle class. In addition, college degrees signal that people have successfully navigated a defined and lengthy organizational process by signing up for the right courses, attending (presumably) many of the classes, figuring out what it takes to pass the classes' final exams, and showing up for the finals—"faithfulness, docility, and memory," in Hutchins's phrase.

The value of this information in the labor market has increased markedly. The difference between the average wage for people with a bachelor's degree and people with only a high school diploma doubled between 1977 and 2005, even as the supply of diploma bearers increased substantially. This occurred in part because of skill-biased technology change and the decline in real wages for low-skill workers. College credentials have also been locked in place as a required part of many large professions. Teachers, for example: There are 3.7 million elementary, middle, and high school teachers in America. Almost every one of them has a bachelor's degree, and nearly half have a master's degree. This did not happen because tens of thousands of school principals individually decided that it was impossible for someone to succeed in the classroom without first spending four years in a hybrid university. It happened because state laws mandate that you can't teach in a public school without a bachelor's degree, and union contracts say you can't make the maximum possible salary without a master's degree.

Employers were also faced with another version of a familiar problem: how to sort through a lot of information with limited resources and limited time. Brassiere inventory management is a snap compared to figuring out human beings. As information technology destroyed jobs that involved simple and repetitive tasks, like painting car parts or shelving paper files, and globalization moved other low-skill jobs overseas, the American jobs that remained fell into several large categories. Some required creativity, judgment, and pattern recognition. Others involved interacting with other people by providing services of different kinds.

It's hard to tell if someone you don't know personally will be good at either of those kinds of jobs. Living anonymously in large communities is a peculiar modern condition. As transportation and communications became cheaper and people increasingly moved from one urban and suburban area to the next, companies hiring employees were faced with the difficult task of selecting from among large numbers of complete strangers.

Companies did what everyone does in that kind of situation: They looked for certain key signals and markers that limited the amount of information they had to process so they could make a good enough decision in a reasonable amount of time. They "satisficed." College degrees served this need reasonably well. Large modern organizations are built around rules and structures and procedures. To succeed in them, people need to be able to fit into an organizational culture. They need to show up on time in the morning and stick around until the end of the day. People with college degrees are, by definition, pretty good at this. Plus they've been acculturated. People like to hire people who are, in their experiences and ways of thinking, much like themselves.

To be sure, some college programs, like nursing and accounting, are closely tied to professions and signal verifiable skills. Forty-four percent of associate's degrees are awarded in programs that teach specific work-related knowledge. And certain kinds of scholarly majors are designed to prepare people to be professional scholars. People get bachelor's degrees in medieval history so they can get doctorates in medieval history. In this sense, a medieval history degree is just as "vocational" as a certificate in welding.

But for a large number of people, the college degree is overwhelmingly a signal of general cognitive ability, acculturation, aptitude for becoming part of a large organization—and nothing else. The diploma itself has about as much information as captured prisoners of war are required to disclose under the Geneva Conventions: name, rank, and serial number (or academic major). The accompanying college transcript, and the one from high school that preceded it, is similarly grudging, composed of little more than departmental abbreviations, numbers suggesting placement in a broad hierarchy of upper- and lower-division courses, and grades of entirely indeterminable origins.

Once the hybrid university organized itself around the elective system, it lost the ability to make any plausible claims that its graduates had common, identifiable academic traits. The few exceptions, like Columbia and the University of Chicago, just served to emphasize the overwhelming larger abdication of responsibility for defining what a liberal education actually means.

The credentialism that Max Weber warned about was magnified by the decline of the blue-collar labor market and the rise of the white-collar middle class. All manner of programs and courses of study were shoehorned into the time-based, college-located educational mold. Objectively speaking, it is unlikely that the programs of study necessary to prepare people for careers in agriculture, architecture, biology, business, communication, computer science, education, engineering, English, fitness studies, French, history, homeland security, library science, linguistics, mathematics, philosophy, public administration, theology, and the visual and performing arts all require exactly four years—not three or one or five and a quarter—to complete.

Stephen Joel Trachtenberg likes to make the instructive if possibly apocryphal point that when Henry Dunster left Cambridge, England, in 1640 to become the first president of Harvard, Cambridge had four-year bachelor's degrees. So Harvard adopted the same standard. A few years later Cambridge switched to three-year degrees, which it still uses today. Dunster's predecessor, Nathaniel Eaton held the title of headmaster. He had been ousted after allegations of beating students and having his wife put goat dung in their hasty pudding. If Mrs. Eaton had kept the pudding dung-free for a few more years back in the colonial 1630s, Harvard would have copied Cambridge's three-year bachelor's degree and American students today would be saving hundreds of millions of dollars in tuition and time every year.

The college degree missed a great deal of important information about people, particularly what they actually learned in college. But it offered some useful signals, it was universally understood, and companies didn't have to pay anything out of pocket to maintain the degree-granting apparatus. Most important, there was no alternative that offered the same combination of ease and limited expense. Some companies found it worthwhile to invest in additional formal testing of job candidates. But this usually came after an initial screen for degrees, because formal testing is expensive. While companies knew there were probably some people out there who never graduated from college and might be great employees, it wasn't worth the money to find them.

This hurt a very large number of people. Only a third of Americans over the age of twenty-five have a bachelor's degree, and America has a higher percentage of bachelor's degree holders than almost any other country in the world. Those whose highest credential is a two-year associate's degree make up another 10 percent, although most of those are "academic" degrees, which aren't good for much other than transferring to a four-year college and getting a bachelor's degree—which, by definition, those people haven't done.

People among the degree-lacking majority of Americans know a great deal. They have acquired knowledge and skills through reading books and learning on the job and doing the things people do throughout their lives to learn. But because the systems we have created to grant or deny access to opportunities for rewarding work and further education have been built around the hybrid university degree, those people are systemically short-changed. They are paid less than degree holders with identical skills and are denied chances to become worth more. Education is one of the great virtuous cycles: The more you learn, the more you are able to learn. The best part about getting a job that requires a bachelor's degree isn't the extra money you get paid in the first year. It's the opportunity to start a career, join a class of people, find a mate similar to you in outlook and earning potential, and acquire valuable knowledge and skills in subsequent jobs throughout your working life.

The current system of getting into college and then the good parts of the labor market is a lot like being invited onto a yacht. You have to know the right people. It helps if you have some money. There's a lot of free booze, and the accommodations are unnecessarily expensive. When the economy turns bad, you're sheltered from the storm—at least for a while. You get to sip cocktails served by attractive young women while everyone outside runs for cover.

What most people need is a system that's more like getting up the elevator and onto the top floor of Michael Saylor's office building. That requires a MicroStrategy software program called Usher. It allows organizations to issue secure digital credentials that can be stored on a mobile phone. The credential might allow you access to physical places, like specific floors of a building or certain parts of a networked computer system. It lets you authenticate documents with a digital signature and send them to other people. The credentials can be permanent or temporary, expiring after a certain amount of time.

Saylor calls this "deep identity." Services like Facebook have allowed people to create shallow social identities: where you live and work, what you look like, who your friends are. It's not very secure but it doesn't have to be, because the stakes are low.

Other kinds of identity are more important. The government controls your political identity. It decides what borders you can cross, what services you can access, and whether and where you can vote. It determines whether you must enter a prison and whether you can leave. Your political identity determines whether the government can kill you without a trial. It can be literally a matter of life and death.

Huge corporations control your financial identity. The amount of money you have is just digital information in a computer somewhere. Your access to credit is controlled by three private credit bureaus, Equifax, Experian, and TransUnion. There are lots of problems with credit reports and botched credit scores, but because money matters, at least there's a semblance of a system. Your financial identity is somewhat deep.

Once your citizenship and financial worth are established, what's the most important information about you? Your educational identity: what you know and what you can do. As the global economy continues to integrate and more businesses operate in cyberspace, your educational identity will become ever more important. Educational identities will be especially important for people who live far from the cathedrals of learning.

Who controls your educational identity? No, it isn't you. It's the college you attended—if you attended college. The diploma and transcript from your alma mater are meager and forgeable, leached of useful information and locked away by university registrars. But at least they're something. They make a difference—sometimes, all the difference.

And if you didn't attend college, who controls your educational identity? Nobody, because it doesn't exist. Of all the things you've learned in your life by reading, talking, thinking, and working—all of the hard-won patterns in your mind—most of it doesn't matter when the time comes to build a relationship or get a job or gain access to more education. Just as people won't take your word for it when you try to cross a border or take out a loan, they need proof when it comes to high-stakes decisions about jobs. Because our system of educational credentialing has been constructed around the selfish interests of archaic institutions, whole realms of individual human knowledge are being excluded from the workings of our economy, undiscoverable and obscure.

Overcoming the college diploma's tick-like embeddedness in the labor market will require the creation of credentials that have huge advantages over the traditional diploma. In part, getting there will be helped along by the manifest flaws of existing college credentials. The rest will be driven by the new possibilities of information technology.

Because what people like Michael Saylor have realized is that giving businesses the ability to mine their inventory databases is a trivial achievement compared to giving people the ability to communicate the breadth of their knowledge, skills, and ability to organizations and other people. Once that happens, and employers start to recognize the value of that information, the cornerstone of the hybrid university economy will begin to crumble, and the University of Everywhere will take its place.

10

Open Badges

A month after returning from Cambridge, I found a message from edX in my e-mail account. It included a link to an electronic file containing an image that looked at lot like my college diploma. It was rectangular, with a colored border. The name of the issuer, MITx, was on top. The document said that **Kevin Carey** had successfully completed **7.00x: Introduction to Biology—The Secret of Life**, a course of study offered by **MITx**, an online learning initiative of **The Massachusetts Institute of Technology** through **edX**. The document was dated on the top and on the bottom it had the signature of Eric Lander, Professor of Biology at the Massachusetts Institute of Technology and Professor of Systems Biology at Harvard Medical School. There was even a note that said "Authenticity of this certificate can be verified at https://verify.edX.org/cert/ffda1bd75cd947ccae0c205b50724270," which, if you click on it, takes you to an official edX website declaring: **This is a valid edX certificate number for KEVIN CAREY.**

I had what hundreds of thousands of people around the world wanted but until now couldn't get without winning a high-stakes admissions tournament, paying a large sum of money, and moving to Cambridge,

Massachusetts: an official certificate of learning from one of the world's greatest universities.

I was not alone. By 2014, tens of thousands of students had completed MOOCs offered from Coursera, Udacity, and the growing edX consortium, which had expanded to include, among others, UC Berkeley, Rice, Georgetown, the University of Texas, Wellesley, Dartmouth, Cornell, Caltech, the University of Washington, and a host of world-class international universities, including Australian National University, Kyoto University, IIT Bombay, McGill, Seoul University, and the University of Hong Kong.

And beyond the MOOCs, something even more radical and decentralized was emerging: a brand-new credentialing system growing out of the same dynamic Silicon Valley culture that had spawned all of the other technological tools that were revolutionizing higher education.

NETSCAPE'S $3 BILLION IPO in August 1995 remains one of the most significant business events of the last half century, launching a wave of venture-funded Internet start-up firms that continue to reshape the economy and everyday life. But as a Web browser company, Netscape was swiftly crushed by Microsoft. Less than ten years after its launch, Netscape was a forgotten subsidiary of AOL, with only 2 percent of people on the Web applying its software.

Many of the people who worked for Netscape were scarred by the experience. Hacker culture places extraordinary value on "open" philosophies of information. Knowledge is power, and one of the ways that authoritarian regimes and large organizations maintain their wealth and privilege is by controlling access to information. Wresting power from such people was how you made the world the way you thought the world should be. The Web browser was the greatest portal to knowledge in human history. Having it owned and controlled by a giant corporation rankled.

So as Netscape shrank into oblivion, some of its employees created a nonprofit foundation called Mozilla, with the logo of a giant red thunder lizard. The Mozilla Foundation birthed a new Web browser called Firefox. It was "open-source" software, which means that the underlying code was available for anyone to download, copy, and improve.

The open-source ethos is both moral and practical. In a world that is increasingly run by highly sophisticated computer programs, no single person working alone can build sufficiently great software from scratch. Computer programmers work in virtual communities where chunks of code are shared, modified, and re-shared for anyone to use. That's why Marc Andreessen's venture capital firm has invested $100 million in a company called GitHub, whose website allows computer programmers to store, share, and collaborate on open-source code. Programmers can see what other people are working on, create new and improved versions, and share their work with the larger community. By 2014, GitHub had four million registered users worldwide collaborating on ten million repositories of code. That's more than double the total number of college professors in the United States.

Openness also allows different kinds of software to interact. The creation of ARPANET back in the 1960s was only nominally about the physical hardware that allowed electronic signals to move among Palo Alto, Santa Barbara, Los Angeles, and Salt Lake City. The goal was creating common software protocols so when the information was broken up into pieces in one place, it could be perfectly reassembled, microseconds later, in another. That's what the *tp* stands for in the "http://" that sits in front of website addresses: "transfer protocol." Openness isn't some hippie sharing ideal. It is, practically speaking, vital to making the modern world function.

The first, freely available version of Firefox was released in 2004. It was downloaded by 100 million people within a year. That was the year that Internet Explorer's market share began to decline. Google released its own free browser, Chrome, at the end of the decade. At the same time, people began using smartphones and tablets to access the Internet instead of desktop computers preloaded with Explorer. Today, the majority of people accessing the Internet use software that is free and open-source.

But the people at the Mozilla Foundation understood that giving people access to all of humanity's information was not enough to make the world the way the world should be. People also needed to be able to access and control information about *themselves*. Human interaction was increasingly taking place in cyberspace. Social networks allowed people to control their online identities for family and friends. In certain kinds of virtual environments, often involving video games, people could create whole new online personas. You could become an Elven mage in World of Warcraft and carefully display all of your earned skills, experience, and accomplishments for anyone to see.

But for the things that mattered most in real life—the skills, experiences, and accomplishments that got you a raise or allowed you to start a career—the world was still stuck in the late nineteenth century. All you had was a couple of 8.5-by-11-inch sheets of paper—actual, physical paper—written in an obscure code by an organization that wouldn't even give it to you unless you asked for permission, wrote a check, and paid any outstanding parking fines: your diploma and college transcript.

This method of transmitting information was so archaic and obscure that colleges themselves didn't trust what college diplomas and transcripts had to say. The law, business, medical, and graduate schools run by the hybrid universities all required people with bachelor's degrees to take standardized multiple-choice tests as part of their application. A bunch of As on the transcript wasn't enough to grant you acceptance. Who really knew what they meant? Colleges also adopted a guilty-until-proven-innocent approach to credits earned from other colleges. The majority of all people with bachelor's degrees have taken courses and earned credits from more than one college. Yet the experience of transferring from one college to another usually involves your new institution refusing to accept many of the credits earned at the old.

So with the for-profit Web browser vanquished, the Mozilla Foundation turned to its next project: using the principles of openness to replace the college diploma.

MOZILLA'S PROJECT, called Open Badges, is designed to create an alternative system of credentials that is controlled by no central authority. Firefox took access to the world's digital information away from powerful incumbent organizations and gave it to the people. Open badges are designed to do the same thing for information about people themselves.

Open badges can be created by anyone. Mozilla itself doesn't offer them. Instead, the foundation developed a set of common protocols that allow other organizations to create them, so people can collect and display badges earned in different ways and times in a single place. A transfer protocol, in other words, for personal information. The badges themselves are round and consist mostly of stylized images that represent the skills and knowledge badge holders have earned.

But the real power of badges lies beneath the images. Mozilla designed the digital badges to be portals to a trove of additional information. This is called "metadata," which is another way of saying "information about information." When you take a picture with a smartphone, all you see on the screen is an image. But the digital file containing that image includes lots of additional information. If your phone has a GPS chip, the file has the exact geographic coordinates of where the photo was taken. It also stores the date and time you took the picture, the size of the file, and various color and focus settings associated with the image.

Digital badges work the same way. Click on a badge and you'll see what organization issued it and when. There might be an expiration date associated with the badge and a link to a website that explains exactly what the person with the badge had to do to earn it, including a portfolio of class work and scores on a variety of tests and assessments. Traditional college credentials have no such readily available information and assurances, which is why there is a robust industry in fake degrees. Say you're an employer looking at résumés from Columbia College of Missouri; Columbia State University; the University of Missouri in Columbia; Columbia University; and Columbia State Community College. It's not obvious that one of them (Columbia State University) is a diploma mill founded by a nightclub hypnotist named "Doctor Dante" who once hired a hit man to assassinate a rival hypnotist and was also, briefly, Lana Turner's seventh husband.

Once the basic protocols were established, Mozilla helped sponsor a contest to see who could create the most interesting badges. Some of the participants were traditional colleges. Purdue University created badges in subjects like "Fundamentals of Atomic Force Microscopy" to accompany a series of short online courses it offered to anyone, for free, online. That particular badge contains a picture of a blue-and-white circle, roughly one inch in diameter, embossed with the stylized image of an atomic force microscope bouncing a laser beam off a cantilever into a photodiode, which is how scientists take photographs and measure the size of very small (nanoscale) things. UC Davis offers a series of badges through its sustainable agriculture program, recognizing skills, competencies, and experience in areas like "community nutrition education" and "agricultural pests of California."

But most of the contest participants weren't colleges at all. Disney-Pixar, Intel, and the Smithsonian signed up. So did NASA, the National Oceanic and Atmospheric Administration, and the Corporation for Public Broadcasting. The Girl Scouts created a digital sash for mobile phones, which some teenage girls are known to use. A veterans group created a badge system for returning servicemen and women to visually represent the training they received while serving in the armed forces. The National Manufacturing Institute collaborated with a youth development organization to create an "M-Badge" system to "recognize the critical skills that are learned in settings other than educational institutions but are highly sought by manufacturers." Many organizations, large and small, help people learn. Only some of them are colleges and universities.

Open badges sit at the intersection of evidence, learning, human-computer interaction, and information technology. Unsurprisingly, Carnegie Mellon developed some of the most sophisticated new credentials. The university had already created a program that helped many people not enrolled at CMU—including high school students, hobbyists, schoolteachers, and people at other colleges—learn computer science. It also had learning scientists on the faculty who were interested in studying how credentials help, or hinder, student motivation.

The CMU designers apportioned all of the computer science expertise they were teaching among a series of digital badges. Traditional college credentials come in two arbitrary sizes: the course, typically in units of three credit hours, and the degree. Neither of these has anything to do with learning per se. Course credit hours are based on the amount of time that passes during semesters defined by agricultural seasons. The degree is based on the number of years young European men spent maturing into bachelors four hundred years ago.

The CMU computer science badges, by contrast, are based on the acquisition of actual knowledge and skills related to computer science. Many of them are smaller than the equivalent of a course or even a single credit hour. The smallest are represented by little slices of a circular badge. A student might earn several slices in a single learning session. Teachers can see real-time statistics showing exactly how far each student has come.

The small badges are based on another potent source of evidence about human behavior: video games. One of the ways World of Warcraft motivates people to work incredibly hard at battling wizards, orcs, and dragons is by creating opportunities to "level up" and gain new opportunities to earn better skills and battle more magical foes. The game shows people exactly what they must accomplish to reach the next level and displays their progress on the screen. Players show off their levels to their peers as ways of asserting status in online communities. At its peak in 2010, twelve million people were playing World of Warcraft worldwide.

The Carnegie Mellon researchers were interested in whether students learning computer science could be motivated in the same way. They modified one of the university's AI-driven cognitive tutoring programs so it awarded digital badges both for learning specific skills and for sticking with the program for a certain amount of time. The tutor helped students use mathematical principles to program a virtual robot located on a distant asteroid. The researchers found that badges did increase motivation, albeit in some interesting and complicated ways.

Motivation and learning are highly connected but also distinct. The kind of practice necessary to achieve real expertise, to build and strengthen neural patterns to a high level of depth and sophistication, requires a great deal of hard work. People are not driven to work in the same way that they like to eat and play and chat. Work requires motivation, and there is a whole field of psychology and human behavior devoted to understanding why some people have the grit and self-regulation necessary to stay on task and finish the difficult work that makes all the difference in learning.

Researchers have identified different kinds of motivation. In part, people are motivated to learn because they want to be smarter and more able. But people are also motivated to *perform,* to be seen as having certain levels of knowledge and skill, particularly in relation to their peers. This "performance motivation" can be positive or negative. People want to be seen as having done well, but they also want to avoid being seen as having done poorly. The grading systems that nearly all colleges use in the United States—A, B, C, D, F—are implicitly designed to stimulate performance motivation. Most of what a 4.0 grade point average says about a person is that she did better in class than most of her peers.

The Carnegie Mellon researchers found that different badges stimulated different kinds of motivation, depending on how much knowledge and skill students brought to the exercises. Students who were relatively low performing before starting the exercises were motivated to avoid the perception of being a poor performer. They perceived, correctly, that they had not reached the same academic level as their peers. The badges motivated them to keep working so they could achieve tangible evidence of performance that other people could see. The high-performing students, by contrast, were primarily motivated to acquire new skills. They cared little for the badges that were awarded for persistence; what they wanted was evidence that they had learned something new.

The CMU badges team mapped out their badge sequence in a way that was designed to educate students about the nature of their education. This is what Harvard's Robert Lue was talking about when he described the need to engage with students' metacognition—their awareness of their own learning. Just as metadata is information about information, metacognition is thinking about thinking. If badges help people see how each new concept builds on those that came before, like a scaffold ascending a wall, they are more likely to reach greater heights of understanding.

The CMU badges were also designed to be "machine discoverable." This reflects another profound technological change in the nature of human interaction. Until all of the computers and mobile devices were connected to one another, people had a certain kind of control over information about themselves and went about finding information about other people in a certain way. The only way to see someone's college transcript was to ask them for it. The same was true for most other important information about people. It was yours, and people had to ask you for permission to see it.

From a privacy standpoint, this makes a great deal of sense. One of the great anxieties of the Information Age is the way our identities seem to have left our control, adrift on an ocean of accessible digital information.

But there are certain kinds of information that a person might want to be as un-private as possible. Like, for example, "I am very good at programming robots." In this situation, the old system is terribly inadequate. It's all well and good that people can ask you for evidence of your robot-programming skills. What if they don't know they should ask? At any moment in time there might be tens of thousands of robot-programmer jobs available around the world. What if you don't know who to send your information to?

The solution to this problem is "search"—that empty white box on your laptop or mobile phone that allows you to type in a word or phrase and scour the entire Internet in a fraction of a second, for free. We all take "search" for granted now, and it comes in a variety of forms beyond Google and Bing. There are sophisticated automated programs—essentially, robot searchers—designed to sift through oceans of online data on quests for very specific kinds of information, like "people who are very good at programming robots." So the CMU badges won't just be designed for *people* to look at, although they will be very good at that. They will also be designed for *machines* to discover in their constant search for information.

The idea of machine discoverability applies to more than one aspect of the traditional college degree. For elite colleges like Harvard, Stanford, and MIT, an important part—arguably, the *most* important part—of the credential is the admissions process. Nobody really knows what goes on behind the ivy-covered walls, and some of it is unsavory. But the corruption of admissions preferences for legacies and wealthy donors notwithstanding, an elite degree suggests that the bearer entered a high-stakes cognitive-ability-plus-motivation-plus-social-capital tournament—and won. That is real information. If it weren't, an Ivy League diploma wouldn't be so valuable.

But this process, too, could work a whole lot better than it does. College admission relies on an outmoded process of exchanging information. Elite colleges have a strong desire to admit high-quality students, and they compete intensely with one another to snag the best of the best. But while engaging in that competition, they are limited to the applicant pool, the people who decide to send them information. As much as the news media likes to hype the increased number of people vying for slots in selective schools, it is still a very small number in the grand scheme of things.

Harvard received 35,000 applications in 2013, a record amount; 3.4 million students graduated from American high schools in the same year, and that doesn't include the tens of millions more who graduated in other years, or not at all, but might be great candidates for Harvard. It may be hard for Ivy-obsessed parents and students to believe, but there are actually a large number of very bright students in America and around the world who don't realize they might successfully apply to an elite college or university.

The traditional college admissions process involves people sitting at desks, reading through large stacks of paper, or images of pieces of paper, that include a lot of information that is hard to understand. The admissions officer's challenge mirrors that of employers: What to do with all of this information? High school transcripts are just as opaque and irregular as college transcripts. SAT and ACT scores provide a narrow window on the reality of the student mind. People are complicated and it's hard to understand them.

Thus, college admissions officers are overwhelmed by both the quantity and imperfections of the information they have about the students who apply, even as that pool represents only a small fraction of students who *could* apply. The confusion and subjectivity of the process create the kind of ambiguity in which the corruptions of hereditary admissions privilege can thrive. It also allows families with a lot of money and social capital to game the system in less obviously immoral ways. Certain expensive high schools, public and private, are known to be feeders into elite colleges. Admissions consultants, test prep tutors, and essay writers can be hired for thousands of dollars in fees.

It is an information problem, and like many others the possibilities of solving it have been altered by information technology.

In Palo Alto, I visited the headquarters of a company called Brilliant, which is run by a couple of University of Chicago dropouts. The company's goal is to identify people age eleven to eighteen who are smart but frustrated when it comes to science and math. Brilliant offers free math games and problem sets for people to work through, letting them accumulate a score, compare themselves to others, win prizes, and virtually connect with fellow math enthusiasts around the world. By the time we met, Brilliant had signed up more than 65,000 students from 135 countries. Only 10 percent were from the United States and Canada.

The initial audience for MOOCs reflected a similar hunger for intellectual challenge. When I asked Eric Lander what surprised him the most about teaching 7.00x, he said, "I was struck by how many really good thirteen-year-olds there are out there." There are a lot of people in the world and enormous differences among them in what they want to learn. When Anant Agarwal rolled out the very first edX course, in circuits and electronics, he made the final exam highly difficult—"MIT hard," in his words. Only a few hundred people out of tens of thousands got a perfect score. He and the edX designers were eager to learn who they were.

It turned out that the budding circuits and electronics genius was not an eight-year-old girl in western China. It was a fifteen-year-old boy in Mongolia named Battushig Myanganbayar. It is an understatement to say that Ulan Bator is located very far from the American cathedrals of learning. But Battushig was lucky. As he was growing into adolescence, the Mongolian government was building a new information network. With a third of the populace living nomadically and the lowest average population density in the world, a wire-based network didn't make much sense. So the government invested in wireless technology good enough to handle edX courses. Battushig also had the good fortune of attending a high school run by an MIT graduate, the first from Mongolia, who decided to challenge his brightest students with the circuits and electronics course. Not long after posting his perfect score, Battushig was accepted as a sixteen-year-old freshman to MIT.

Another top-scoring circuits and electronics student was a sixte-year-old self-described "computer geek" from Jabalpur, India, named Amol

Bhave. Impatient to keep learning and eager to connect with other people like him, Bhave decided to use open source videos and online resources to create his own MOOC in signals and systems. He was also accepted into MIT's next freshman class.

Elite colleges enjoy the money and status that bribe- and legacy-based admissions bring. But they also like to assemble classes full of interesting and unusual people. They admit students whose parents paid for the right admissions consultant, not because they really want to, but because Battushigs have historically been hard to come by. Now they are about to become much easier to find. Partly through the MOOCs elite colleges themselves are offering. Partly through companies like Brilliant that are designed to attract the best and brightest. And partly because information about prospective high school students will become increasingly machine discoverable. Instead of waiting for applications to arrive, colleges will be able to conduct extensive searches of data that students and parents choose to make available. Instead of leaving the process entirely in the hands of admissions officers armed with nothing more than a desk, a cup of coffee, and a stack of paper to evaluate "holistically," colleges will be able to analyze that data and make informed judgments about who is most likely to come to campus and thrive, both during their college career and afterward.

If this only changed the makeup of the freshman class at MIT, it wouldn't change much. As long as elite institutions are bound to physical places, they will only ever touch a tiny sliver of humanity. But since the "won the admissions tournament" part of a college degree is independent of the actual experience of going to college, it can exist entirely on its own. The more people can engage with openly available, rigorously designed coursework, the more people will be able to credibly say, "I'm good enough to get into Harvard." The whole theory of the Minerva Project is that a new organization can pair a highly selective, uncorrupted admissions process with an educational experience that is similarly world-class.

———

THE FINAL ELEMENT of the Carnegie Mellon badge system focuses on the workplace. All of the little badges that are automatically doled out for motivational purposes in the CMU computer science course eventually roll up into larger badges that describe a collection of skills like "advanced programming." Ultimately, those pieces fit together into a badge that also serves as a certification. The small badges help people learn by improving their motivation. The certification helps people demonstrate what they've learned to other people—specifically, people who want to hire, say, robot programmers. CMU designed its robot-programming certification badge to match the requirements for the National Instruments "Certified Lab-VIEW Associate Developer" title. National Instruments was founded by a group of University of Texas at Austin graduates in the 1970s and sells hundreds of millions of dollars' worth of highly technical computer hardware and software every year. The certification is an industry-standard entry-level credential in a visual programming language that's used to control things like self-driving cars.

Traditional time-based college degrees and transcripts are very bad at signaling this kind of specific, relevant information. Employers use degrees in their hiring processes because of habit, or government regulation, or because it's a cheap way to screen candidates for broad qualities like faithfulness, docility, and memory. But that still leaves them with enormous information deficits, which means that the labor market doesn't work as well as it could. Employers can't find the best people, and people can't find the best jobs.

One of the people who described this problem to me was a young Silicon Valley entrepreneur named Danny King. King is originally from the United Kingdom and runs a start-up called Accredible along with his college classmate. Accredible is a tool for displaying information about yourself. It allows you to create "certs" into which you can upload evidence of what you've learned—a kind of self-created digital badge. Accredible lets you link to your various online identities (Twitter, Facebook, LinkedIn, Google, etc.) in order to strengthen the evidence that you are who you say you are. For the same reason, you can show Accredible your driver's license or government ID—your political identity as a tool for strengthening your educational identity.

People can also upload videos of themselves taking exams to confirm that they took them. Fraud is definitely a challenge for online education. It's also a challenge for conventional education. It's hard to know if traditional college students actually wrote the papers they submit, which is why there's a multimillion-dollar term-paper-writing industry that long precedes the Internet. A student taking an exam remotely while being simultaneously monitored by a video camera and having her keystrokes recorded, as some online students are, is being subjected to much more scrutiny than a terrestrial student who simply shows up at a large lecture hall.

Accredible certs can also include testimony from peers. Sometimes the most powerful evidence you can communicate about yourself is the endorsement of other people. Anyone who's watched *Downton Abbey* on PBS will recall various moments of high drama related to whether a servant will leave the household with a personal letter of recommendation from the head butler or lady of the house. That's largely how formal credentials worked before mass higher education. They were personal recommendations from people whose positions or social class gave them authority. The rise of the hybrid university and the general bureaucratization of things transferred much of that authority to large organizations and the people who ran them. This allowed administrators to monopolize all of the socially and economically advantageous positions.

The way the Internet allows people to connect with one another and share information creates new sources of authority that can be used to validate credentials. As is often the case, the computer programmers are leading the way. While GitHub allows programmers to share code, the website Stack Overflow allows them to share advice. The site's two million registered users award fellow members "reputation" points and a variety of badges based on answers to questions posed by fellow computer programmers. The more insightful and helpful your questions and answers, according to the collective wisdom of Stack Overflow, the more points you receive. Tomasz Nurkiewicz, an Oslo software engineer and one of fewer than two hundred people who have earned a "Legendary" Stack Overflow badge, told me, "I received numerous job offers from people who either saw my profile with reputation and all the badges, or were particularly impressed by one of my answers." Like Mozilla badges, Stack Overflow badges have metadata. You can click on them and see exactly what kind of answers garnered so much respect from peers. Rather than guessing what a vague credential like "bachelor's of computer science from Big State University at Anytown" means, employers can use digital badge metadata to find exactly the person they need.

AFTER TALKING TO DANNY, I logged onto the Accredible website and started uploading information about my work in 7.00x. I included the certificate with MIT's name on the front, Eric Lander's signature, and the link to the MIT website that proves the certificate is real. I uploaded all of my course notes: sixty-three pages of diagrams and quotations from all of Lander's lectures. I included a picture of my score on each of the homework assignments, midterms, and finals. I put up the syllabus and the course schedule so people could see which topics were covered and how the course was designed. And I uploaded each of the nine problem sets so people could see exactly what kind of work I had to do in order to build all those new patterns and networks of understanding in my mind.

It was the most credible, discoverable evidence of learning I had ever produced—other than, perhaps, this book.

The newly emerging credentialing systems will be a crucial part of the University of Everywhere. They will match freely available educational resources in their technical specifications and larger ethos of openness. They will allow people to control and display information about themselves in new and powerful ways, by assembling credible evidence of knowledge and skills gained in a variety of contexts—in college, in the workforce, in life. Some of that evidence will come in the form of peer assessment, some through formal tests and examinations, some through broader experiences and proof of work well done. The digital learning environments themselves will be built to make evidence of learning sophisticated and abundant instead of obscure. Educational identities will become deep, discoverable, mobile, and secure.

All of this will happen largely outside the control of traditional colleges. Or, in cases like edX, the new credentials will be granted by institutions with so much money and prestige and social capital that they are likely immune from the forces of disruption.

What happens then?

11

The Weight of Large Numbers

When Eric Lander and his colleagues set about mapping the human genome in the 1990s, they didn't know exactly *how* the information would ultimately benefit mankind. They were just sure it would—and they were right.

An enormous number of medical ailments have genetic origins. Until the secrets of DNA were unlocked, understanding such diseases and problems was mostly a matter of guesswork. Patterns could be observed in families where certain kinds of inheritable diseases, like cystic fibrosis, were prevalent, or in broad similarities between syndromes. But much of it was just speculation, and often yielded little insight that could help patients heal.

The genetics revolution is changing all of that before our eyes. In the middle of my 7.00x course, the prestigious medical journal *Lancet* published a groundbreaking genetic study of tens of thousands of people. It found that a range of distinct psychiatric illnesses, including schizophrenia, attention-deficit disorder, depression, autism, bipolar disorder, and hyperactivity, have common biological origins—not from a single gene, but from the complex interactions among many different genes. To make this discovery, researchers had to sequence and compare the DNA of tens of thousands of people. In 2001, it cost $100 million to sequence a single human genome. In 2011 it cost about $10,000, and the price tag is falling. Scientists achieved a 10,000-fold reduction in the cost of gene sequencing in just ten years, utterly changing the economic possibilities of genetic diagnosis, analysis, and learning.

This means that in the future doctors will be far better equipped to treat the *causes* of mental illness rather than the symptoms. Eric Lander calls this "rational medicine." Something similar will happen with technology and learning. When large numbers of people begin working in digital learning environments, they will create the information necessary for "rational education." Computers will be able to sequence the unique learning patterns of millions of people. They will find that, while each person's neural patterns are different, they aren't wholly distinct from one another. Common elements will emerge. Educational designers will be equipped to act from the causes of human learning, or lack thereof, rather than the symptoms.

Rational education is emerging from profound changes of *scale*: The number of people engaged with digital learning environments and the amount of data they generate will increase by orders of magnitude in a short amount of time. It is the collective weight of those large numbers, rather than the actions of any single person or organization, that will ultimately build the University of Everywhere.

Some of those numbers are embedded in the trajectory and force of technological progress. Moore's law and its storage equivalents haven't been repealed yet. Smart people standing in front of laboratory benches will continue to grapple with devil surfaces and find ways to make computers faster and more powerful. We will be able to move, process, and store more information for less money.

Other large numbers are educational. Existing colleges and universities offer a staggering number of courses. There is almost no subject so esoteric or obscure that you can't find it offered for three credits somewhere. This hides an important fact: Most students don't fill their course schedules with the esoteric or obscure. They take a relatively small number of similar courses in pursuit of a relatively small number of similar degrees.

On any given day, hundreds of thousands of American college students are enrolled in different versions of the same courses. Some, like introductory mathematics, science, economics, psychology, and language, are taken by millions of students as part of their general education requirements at colleges of varying quality. Others are taken by the legions occupying popular majors such as political science, accounting, and psychology. Many are taught with the same textbooks.

EdX, Coursera, Udacity, and Saylor.org aren't the only organizations working to build high-quality versions of the first 5,000 courses and give them away for free. There is an entire open educational resources (OER) movement dedicated to achieving this goal. Proceeding from the logic and ethos of open-source coding, websites like Oercommons.org have gathered and indexed tens of thousands of courses, lectures, and "learning objects"—chunks of content, problems and assessments that focus on a defined learning objective and that can be incorporated into different kinds of learning environments. The volume and quality of OER will surely continue to improve.

Another large number is the size of the global student population: It's big and getting bigger. The American market for higher education is tiny compared to the rest of the world and will continue to shrink as a percentage of the whole population.

The last half century has seen dramatic growth in the world economy. In 1981, World Bank statistics found that over half of all the people on earth—52 percent—lived below the global poverty line of $1.25 per day. By 1990 that proportion had dropped to 43 percent. By 2010 it was down to 21 percent. Even as the total world population grew by 3.5 billion people, the absolute number of people in poverty dropped by 700 million over thirty years.

Emerging from poverty means a life where the absolute necessities of food and shelter are not constantly at risk. Once people achieve that level of security, their aspirations expand. They want comforts and culture. Most of all, they want a better life for their children, one without the specter of poverty. The members of this emerging global middle class understand that this requires education.

How will this change the demand for higher learning? According to one set of estimates from the Organisation of Economic Co-operation and Development, there were about 1.8 billion people in the global middle class in 2009. These are households that spend well above the global poverty line, between $10 and $100 per person per day.

According to those estimates, the global middle class will grow to 3.3 billion people by 2020. By 2030 it will be 4.8 billion strong. That's an increase of three billion people in a single generation. Even after adjusting for the risks of global calamity, inadequate primary and secondary education, and other factors, the number of *additional* people who will want a college education over the next twenty years could exceed the number of people who have ever been to college in all of human history.

They're not going to learn at anything resembling a hybrid university. In recent decades, countries like Saudi Arabia and South Korea have invested heavily in building their own versions of the American research university. They see them as engines of economic development and markers of national pride. China alone has built hundreds of universities that enroll millions of students.

But "millions" is still a small number compared to "billions." The hybrid model is unavoidably expensive. It requires large buildings and classrooms and administrators and faculty armed with PhDs. The parts of the world where the middle class is growing most quickly don't have anything like the kind of money necessary to build out an American-style higher-education infrastructure. *America* is struggling to afford an American-style higher-education infrastructure, and America is the richest country in the world. Most American students enroll in community colleges and public universities that can barely maintain their facilities and keep financially afloat. The hybrid university ideal that is so deeply embedded in the public consciousness has only ever served a small number of students, and only ever will.

What many of those billions of middle-class people do have, or will have, is access to telecommunications. So will millions more in poverty. Computers will continue to become less expensive and more powerful, and communications networks will grow. The eye-popping enrollment numbers in MOOCs have been mostly driven by global demand. One million students signed up for Coursera classes in the company's first four months of operation. Nearly two-thirds were from 195 countries other than the United States. The student roster for MIT 7.00x was a cross section of humanity exceeding a diversity-focused admissions officer's wildest dreams: the South American med students, the Indian homemaker, the Sri Lankan college dropout, the Ukrainian software engineer, the nurse in the Philippines, the eighth-grade girl.

BILLIONS OF PEOPLE being educated this way will create large amounts of electronic data. This will allow unprecedented analyses of human learning. Colleges and universities are in the business of knowledge creation. Yet nearly all of the information they generate about learning itself is lost. Every year, millions of students enroll in courses and, in doing so, make things. They write papers, take tests, submit homework assignments, ask their teachers for help, and talk to one another. Nearly all of that information is subsequently dispersed or destroyed. There are few if any repositories of student work for researchers to examine, or records of classroom discussions to explore.

The hybrid university is congenitally uninterested in applying its formidable analytic powers to its own educational mission. In part, that's because it would rather not produce definitive evidence of the educational failures that inevitably occur in organizations that sublimated their teaching obligations to research back in the nineteenth century. But it's also because high-quality analysis requires certain conditions, including large numbers and experimental design.

There are several ways to find meaning in a complex system. One way involves conducting an experiment. You take a collection of students and randomly assign them to two different groups. Each undergoes an educational experience that is identical, with one exception. Perhaps a different textbook is used, or a class schedule, or a system of problem sets. Then you measure how much the students in each group learned. If Group A learned a lot more than Group B, you can say with confidence that the one factor you changed made the difference.

This kind of research is complicated. If the experiment isn't designed correctly, the conclusions will be faulty. The design requires some control over what courses students take and how professors teach. But under the elective system, students take whichever courses they like. More important, the culture of academic freedom, extended to teaching, prevents the university from controlling the educational environment in different classes. Individual professors and academic departments create curricula, administer exams, grade papers, and assign textbooks as they like.

The number of students studied also has to be sufficiently large. While there are big lectures and small seminars in American higher education, many classes are essentially medium-size, between thirty and one hundred people. That's large enough that the experience of being taught isn't much different than being in a thousand-person lecture. The ability to be Aristotle to someone's Alexander declines rapidly as the number of Alexanders grows larger than one. At the same time, the typical college class is small enough that it becomes more difficult, statistically speaking, to extract meaningful conclusions from even a well-designed experiment.

Research also requires some way to systematically gather, organize, and analyze information. This is difficult and expensive when the information is recorded on paper idiosyncratically. Or, in the case of student interaction with teachers and other students, not recorded at all. Part of the learning process happens outside of the classroom and campus, in dorm rooms and coffee shops.

The new digital learning environments will radically alter these limitations. Much more information can be gathered: every log-in, keystroke, discussion question, test, essay, and problem set. Computers can track not just what students do but what order they do it in. When you have 50,000 students instead of 50, your ability to draw statistically meaningful conclusions from experimentation increases exponentially.

Hybrid universities are not, in any honest sense of the term, teaching organizations. When the college experience isn't dominated by the semi-random choices of autonomous scholars who haven't been trained as teachers, it's a lot easier to make experimental changes in the learning environment. Education research today is a single-celled organism compared to what it will evolve to be.

The ability to gather large amounts of data creates other ways to improve education. Experiments are powerful, but they require researchers to make choices about what factors to vary and observe. What if they don't know what to look for? What if the things that matter most in learning aren't what we think they are?

Peter Norvig, who co-taught the famous Stanford CS221 class that launched MOOC mania, has a solution to this problem. He and two coauthors recently name-checked a well-known article called "The Unreasonable Effectiveness of Mathematics in the Natural Sciences," which "examines why so much of physics can be neatly explained with simple mathematical formulas such as $F = ma$ or $E = mc^2$. Meanwhile, sciences that involve human beings rather than elementary particles have proven more resistant to elegant mathematics." "Perhaps when it comes to natural language processing and related fields," they wrote, "we're doomed to complex theories that will never have the elegance of physics equations. But if that's so, we should stop acting as if our goal is to author extremely elegant theories, and instead embrace complexity and make use of the best ally we have: the unreasonable effectiveness of data."

Learning and human cognition are definitely among the "related fields." Theorists like Vygotsky, Piaget, and their intellectual descendants have improved our understanding of learning in many important ways. But even the most advanced theories of cognitive psychology pale in comparison to the complexity of billions of unique people working to learn in fields that vary across the whole expanse of human action and knowledge.

Norvig's point is that, rather than search for one educational theory to rule them all, it may be far more profitable to look for specific, unpredictable insights in the troves of electronic information now piling up around us, and in data that can and will exist in the near future, as more people learn in digital environments. With this kind of "machine learning," computers search for probabilities and patterns within large data sets and, once they find them, automatically refine future analyses.

Analyzing that data will require money and very smart people. That's why Google, which makes billions of dollars analyzing data from its search engine, hired Norvig as its research director. Indeed, money is another area where large numbers point toward profound change in the nature of higher learning.

In talking to people about information technology and higher education, I was struck by how badly those who work in colleges and universities tend to botch the question of financial scale. They do it for the same reason people always get scale wrong: They are bound to a faulty point of reference.

A typical college class doesn't cost very much to offer. There are different ways to come up with estimates, like the cost of hiring an adjunct professor in the open labor market, or one-fourth of a professor's semester salary plus standard overhead rates. Regardless, the numbers range in the thousands or low tens of thousands of dollars and no more.

Developing a course using the labor-intensive Carnegie Mellon OLI process can cost several hundred thousand dollars. Higher-end MOOC providers like edX cite similar amounts. Inevitably, these numbers are discussed as if they are large, and thus a barrier to widespread adoption and development of high-quality online courses, as if there are just not enough money in the world to create really good digital learning environments that can help more than a fraction of all students.

Which doesn't make any sense at all. The right point of comparison isn't what it costs to teach one introductory biology class for one semester in one college. It's what it costs to teach *all of them,* to millions of students in tens of thousands of sections in thousands of colleges over a number of years. That number runs into many millions of dollars.

Or we could compare course development costs to what universities spend on things they actually care about, like grand academic buildings, recruitment-friendly recreational facilities, and money-losing quasi-professional sports teams. Such things cost an order of magnitude more than teaching a course—millions, not thousands, of dollars. And that's for a single college or university.

These expenditures are by no means limited to elite institutions. Take Northern Arizona University, a classic example of how isomorphism made hundreds of American colleges and universities all act and look the same. Founded in 1899 as a "normal school" that trained women to become schoolteachers, the Flagstaff campus underwent the standard transformation from teachers college to college to university over the course of the twentieth century. In the 1990s the university hired a veteran computer scientist who had served long stints in academia and industry to chair the electrical engineering and computer science department: my father, Bernard Carey.

Flagstaff sits at nearly 7,000 feet of elevation in a huge pine forest at the foot of the San Francisco Peaks. Bernard loved the rugged countryside and enjoyed mentoring bright young engineers, much as he had been taught at the Mellon Institute many years before. But he was frustrated at his faculty's disinterest in any kind of serious examination of education. When he proposed some basic experimentation in teaching an introductory course that routinely flunked large numbers of students, his faculty explained that this violated their academic freedom and reported him to the dean.

Bernard also couldn't help noticing that NAU was spending millions of dollars on new facilities even as the state was slashing operational support to the university and raising student tuition by more than 50 percent. In 2011 the university announced that "Northern Arizona University's new Health and Learning Center just might take your breath away," followed by a description of how "on the second floor, an indoor jogging track circles above the gym and indoor climbing wall and dashes by the high-tech cardio theater, mirrored weight room and expanse of exercise equipment. . . . After class or a bit of exercise, guests can catch their breath at the third floor café, which serves sandwiches and drinks along with a panoramic view of the San Francisco Peaks through floor-to-ceiling glass walls and the outdoor terrace." The total cost of the 272,000-square-foot building: over $100 million, paid primarily through extra student fees.

This is in no way unusual. Northern Arizona ranks in the middle of the second tier in the annual *U.S. News & World Report* college rankings, which means *hundreds* of colleges and universities are richer, more selective, and more famous. Spending $100 million on a fancy gym is completely unremarkable in contemporary American higher education. Yet $10 million for a really good online biology course that could serve millions of students is seen as an outlandish, unaffordable expense. If an anonymous benefactor handed a typical university that amount for that purpose, most college presidents wouldn't even know how to spend it.

Compare this with the millions of dollars and large numbers of people companies routinely devote to creating other kinds of software. In 2013, Rockstar Games released Grand Theft Auto V, reportedly the most expensive video game ever made. A team of 250 people worked for five years developing an elaborate virtual city of missions, levels, bank heists, and carjackings. The total cost was $115 million, enough money to garner headlines in mainstream business publications— or build a snazzy workout facility at a second-tier public university in northern Arizona. While students and faculty in Flagstaff were enjoying panoramic views, Grand Theft Auto V had more than $1 billion in sales in its first three days on the market. Meanwhile, annual venture capital investment in education technology is rising even as state and federal governments continue, despite recent cutbacks, to spend hundreds of billions of dollars subsidizing higher education every year. That's just in the United States. Hundreds of billions more are spent abroad.

What all of these large numbers add up to is this: billions of dollars available to create digital learning environments and matching credentials designed to teach a relatively small number of courses and subjects to billions of people, resulting in trillions of data points available to be analyzed using techniques that will become increasingly sophisticated over time. The weight of these large numbers will eventually grow so heavy that it will overwhelm even the formidable barriers of regulatory protection, public subsidy, and cultural habit that protect the cathedrals of learning.

This turning point might result from some kind of rapid change in the collective consciousness, a kind of mass experience of the contradiction and surprise that Robert Lue identified as a key element of learning. This happens sometimes. The newspaper industry went from its most profitable year ever to widespread financial Armageddon in less time than it takes an undergraduate to earn a bachelor's degree.

Or it might happen through a slower, grinding attrition that lasts a decade or more. But in either case, this is neither an avoidable nor a distant scenario. The University of Everywhere is on the horizon. It's going to emerge while the current generation of young people mature into adulthood—not the generation after that.

Organizations such as edX, Coursera, Udacity, Saylor.org, OLI, and a range of others like the United Kingdom's long-established Open University will continue to create and refine an ever larger catalogue of college courses that anyone in the world with an Internet connection can take, for free. Over time those courses will be organized into sequences that approximate the scope of learning we associate with college majors. MIT is already moving in this direction, starting with a seven-course sequence in computer programming that begins with introductions to coding, computational thinking, and data science and then moves to software construction, digital circuits, programmable architectures, and computer systems organization. The length of the course sequences will vary depending on the field, profession, or kind of work. Some will involve a few courses; others will be dozens long. Neither the courses nor the sequences will be constrained by the artificial limitations of semester hours or years spent attending school. They will be as long or short as they need to be.

The actual experience of taking these courses will be familiar in some ways. Education in the future will still involve reading books, writing papers, solving problems, talking to other people, and getting out into the world. Nobody is going to have information uploaded into their brain via coaxial cable, *Matrix*-style. We will still watch the Abelards of our time lecture, weaving characters, ideas, and emotion into narratives of enlightenment. We will still exchange ideas with other people about what we're learning. Some of them will be fellow students, people who share our passions and struggles. Some will be masters and experts, people who can diagnose and inform, provoke and inspire.

In other ways the courses will be quite different, built around immersive digital learning environments. These environments will not be designed by lone individuals. Instead, the best will be created by teams of people specializing in different aspects of the learning experience. They will be shaped, tweaked, and assembled using open-source components shared by millions of educators collaborating in the educational equivalent of GitHub—coders working in the operating system of human cognition. They will benefit from network effects: The better they are, the more people will use them, generating more data and more money that can be used to make them better still.

Organizations competing for students—some existing colleges, many others businesses and nonprofits yet to be created—will incorporate increasingly sophisticated artificial intelligence into their educational designs. The AI will diagnose the strengths and weaknesses of each individual learner and customize his or her education accordingly, constantly challenging and motivating people to work harder and better without breaching the threshold of frustration and failure. The machine-learning techniques developed by people like Peter Norvig will analyze the oceans of information being generated by millions of students and continually optimize and improve what students experience and how much they learn.

Meanwhile, a thriving ecosystem of nonprofit and for-profit organizations will develop around the core education providers, offering students a range of services to support, facilitate, and improve their educational experience—counseling, tutoring, advising, study groups, course notes, learning aids, supplementary texts and videos, and much more—each offered by technology-driven organizations that specialize in a specific aspect of higher education.

There will be fits and starts, successes and failures. But the long-term trend is obvious and unavoidable: A larger and larger percentage of the education that has been historically confined to scarce, expensive colleges and universities will be liberated and made available to anyone, anywhere. That means that students in the future will have peers from every corner of the earth, of many different ages, backgrounds, and creeds.

At the same time, new systems like open badges will emerge to gather evidence of what people have learned, replacing traditional letter grades and diplomas. Much of that information will be extracted from regular academic work. Because so much of the learning process will be digitally recorded, and because the new learning environments will incorporate badges and credentials to improve student motivation and metacognition, courses will rely less on high-stakes standardized tests to assess what people know. There will be some costs associated with ensuring the integrity of the testing process—for example, hiring people to read students' poems and essays and evaluate portfolios of student work. So while future courses will be free, there may be some charges for assessment. But those costs will be more than manageable. (MIT charges $425, *total*, to assess students and issue certificates in its seven-course computer science sequence on edX.)

This kind of rational pricing—free courses, inexpensive assessments— will be part of a long-term process in which the price of higher education falls to the marginal cost of providing different pieces of the unbundled university. Services that computers can provide for essentially no cost to the next student, such as my 7.00x course, will cost, like that course, nothing. Services that require human labor, such as career counseling, will cost something. But here, too, people will be aided by powerful, productivity-enhancing technology. The total cost of college for many students in the University of Everywhere will be a small fraction of the current market price of higher education.

Evidence of what students have learned in the new digital learning environments will be organized in an entirely new system of credentials—a secure personal educational identity that is controlled by learners, not institutions. Instead of being bound to a college and fixed in a moment of youthful time, these credentials will continually change as people themselves change, reflecting their growing experience, knowledge, and skill sets. Employers competing for the best and brightest will adapt their hiring practices to take advantage of the enormous amount of information available in rich, machine-discoverable credentials. Because the credentialing systems will be open, millions of Americans and many more elsewhere will compete on a level field in the labor market for the very first time, rather than being systematically shut out for lack of an obsolete and elitist degree.

The way that people learn in the University of Everywhere will vary tremendously, because people will not be forced to conform to the outdated traditions and habits of the hybrid university. Some people will learn mostly by themselves, on computers. This isn't the ideal learning environment for many, and it's simply untenable for some. But we live in a big world with a lot of people. Some of them have jobs and families that consume most of their daily time. Some are isolated by geography or medical circumstances. Some live in societies that deny or discourage educational opportunities to members of certain genders, religions, ethnicities, and castes. Some don't have enough money for anything else. Less than ideal will still be far better than nothing at all. If time, money, family, and circumstances didn't matter, I would rather have learned about the secret of life in person in Cambridge, Massachusetts. But all of those things *do* matter, a lot, and I was still able to get an 87 percent.

Moreover, no one is alone on the Internet if they don't want to be. In addition to faster connections and cheaper, more powerful computers, the last decade has seen the rise of the social Web. People form deep and lasting connections with others in virtual environments. They become part of authentic communities. And as technology improves, the nature of those interactions will more closely approximate actual face-to-face meetings. The person sitting at a chair, staring at a monitor, is a cramped and increasingly archaic vision of human-computer interaction. Right now, talking to a life-size virtual image of a real person is the kind of experience you see only in the cafeteria at MIT. In the future, as telecommunications and video technology improve, it will be commonplace, maybe even dull. The conversation might come through an image projected onto a pair of glasses or through ultra-high-definition screens that are large, flexible, and cheap. Whatever way it happens, the experiences of seeing and hearing people who are nearby and at a far distance will increasingly converge. Information will keep moving faster, and experiences once reserved for the elite will become commonplace for the many.

The international learning communities that develop in the virtual education world will have enormous advantages of scale. They will be inexpensive and at certain levels of access, entirely free. Millions of people simultaneously enrolled in a course of study will create data that is analyzable with great sophistication. In addition to customizing the environment for each learner in a way that reacts to what they bring to the environment and how they proceed to learn, educational designers will also be able to shape the way students interact with one another, much as Minerva plans to do with its all-seminar education. In other words, the learning experience will be different but not *solitary*. The future of higher education is not one in which everyone sits by herself in her pajamas, pallid and goggle-eyed, being taught by a machine.

Indeed, many people—particularly those who we now think of as "college age"—will live and learn together under the auspices of organizations specifically and solely dedicated to their education. The coming abundance of inexpensive, highly effective, continually improving digital learning environments will radically change the economic logic of creating new higher-education institutions. Colleges and other learning organizations serving college students won't need to hire hundreds of professors and build scores of pricey buildings to house their offices, libraries, and lecture halls. Just as information technology has made it much cheaper to create a start-up technology company in Silicon Valley, it will make it much cheaper to create a start-up college almost anywhere.

Which means that, in addition to a profusion of digital learning environments online, the University of Everywhere will include tens of thousands of new higher-education organizations—they won't be colleges in the traditional definition of the term—that are physically located in places but have few attributes in common with the traditional hybrid university.

Everyone lives somewhere, and most people live near many other people. Certain kinds of master/student and peer relationships form most naturally and strongly in physical proximity. Most parents will still want to kick their children out of the house when they're grown, and most children will gladly go. So there will always be organizations dedicated to higher learning where people live and learn together. But those organizations will not look much like colleges and universities as we know them today.

The rise of new digital learning environments will supercharge the logic of creating new Minerva Projects. When all the books in the world and a wide array of digital learning environments can be accessed at very low cost from anywhere, people will be free to organize higher-education institutions in ways that make much more sense in terms of cost, size, and the focus of human activity. Great colleges won't have to be scarce and expensive anymore. They will be everywhere.

Imagine a small group of buildings or spaces run by people with a particular educational philosophy and open to anyone who's interested in learning. The educators there focus on mentoring students and helping them form relationships with one another. There are places for people to work person-to-person, or to engage electronically with peers in other cities, states, and countries. Some of the students live nearby and spend hours there every day, learning full-time. Others come in from their families and homes.

It sounds kind of like a liberal arts or community college, except these buildings don't have traditional classrooms, lecture halls, libraries, or academic departments. The educators work within and alongside digital learning environments, but they do not design them alone. Words like "semester" and "credit hour" have no meaning. The organization doesn't control the evidence of what students learn. It isn't in the business of granting degrees with the institution's name in bold type. Having a PhD or an MA or even a BA isn't a job requirement.

Instead, a typical student might be taking one course along with a half million other people around the world and another with three peers and a mentor in the local community. Because it doesn't cost very much money to start such a place, there are dozens of similar organizations nearby. Some may specialize in a particular subject area, offering a few extended educational programs. Others may be organized around different ideas, faiths, occupations, and philosophies of learning.

The future of higher education is one in which educational organizations shrink back to a human scale. They will be big enough to form authentic communities and not so big that interpersonal connections are overwhelmed. Think of the number of churches in a given municipality, some large and wealthy and part of international denominations, others small and local, as little as a single room where friends and faithful meet. That's how many new "colleges" there can be.

Private businesses might create these new learning organizations, or governments, or philanthropists. Andrew Carnegie had the right idea a century ago when he built thousands of local libraries around the world. The Carnegie libraries made sense given the state of the art in educational information technology then: the printed book. Local communities were obligated to invest in the buildings in the form of land and ongoing operating support from public sources. They were also required to make them free for anyone to use.

The world needs the twenty-first-century equivalent of Carnegie libraries—beautiful, peaceful places where knowledge lives and grows and spreads. Places supported and beloved by local communities, open to everyone, that offer people all of the educational opportunities technology will make possible.

A great learning experience at such a scale might seem impossible in view of the colleges we've all experienced in our culture and lives. But gigantic universities are a relatively new, mid-twentieth-century phenomenon. A lot of people learned a great deal in the entire sweep of human history that preceded them. The logic of the hybrid university is comprehensive and self-contained, everything and everyone you need inside the campus walls. The higher-learning places of the future will be portals as much as meeting places, connected to the global University of Everywhere beyond.

12

Your Children and the University of Everywhere

Nearly 150 years ago, Charles Eliot became the most influential college president in American history by asking a question that still weighs on the minds of parents today: "What can I do with my boy?"

For a long time, the answer has been obvious: Make sure he graduates from high school, gets accepted into a good college, and can pay the tuition bills. That was true for my generation, and my father's, and his parents' before. The path to higher education has long been one of the great comforts of the middle class. It left little confusion about what it meant to succeed as a parent. As the economy changed and many blue-collar jobs disappeared, the prevalence of that thinking expanded. As late as 1982, only 57 percent of parents thought their children would go to college. By 2010 it was 92 percent.

This is why the rising cost of higher education has struck such a deep chord of anxiety. People have been told that their children's futures and their success as parents are absolutely dependent on higher education. Yet the price of fulfilling that obligation has grown further and further out of reach.

In one way, the disruptive effects of information technology offer possible salvation. As digital learning environments become more sophisticated and open credentialing systems replace the traditional college degree, the upward trajectory of college tuition over time will flatten and start to descend. "Enough to put my kids through college" will cease to be cultural shorthand for "a mind-bogglingly large amount of money." People will start to think of higher education as a particularly sophisticated kind of information service instead of membership dues in a country club. What they're willing to pay will change accordingly.

But the savings in money will have a price in complication. The established college system outsources a great deal of hard work and responsibility to traditional educational organizations, regulatory systems, and broad cultural habits. Especially for middle- and upper-income families, there is zero ambiguity about what college is, which colleges are best, when students should go, and how to get there. The messages that popular culture sends about college and the financial subsidies provided by the government all point toward ivy-covered walls. If that maddeningly expensive yet highly understandable system fractures, where should students turn? Who should parents trust? What should everyone do?

While the answer depends a lot on individual circumstances, here are the four most important decisions to keep in mind when you think about the University of Everywhere.

CHOOSING A COLLEGE

The hybrid university will not disappear tomorrow. The process of disruption will take years, and the aftermath will include institutions descended from existing colleges *and* a constellation of new higher learning organizations, some physical and some purely virtual. Which means that young people fast approaching the end of high school are still going to have to decide whether to attend a traditional college or venture into new arenas. Here's what everyone involved should keep in mind:

Hybrid universities have been ripping off parents and students for decades by shortchanging undergraduate learning. Students are being left to the whims of professors who haven't been trained to teach and aren't accountable for helping students learn. Colleges are not challenging students to work hard and think critically and creatively. All available evidence suggests undergraduates simply aren't learning very much, even as they are being charged ever larger amounts of money and becoming increasingly burdened with debt.

Don't let this happen to you. Some institutions still have authentic educational programs like the MIT General Institute Requirements. The University of Chicago is still colored by Robert Maynard Hutchins's thwarted dreams, requiring undergraduates to study the humanities and liberal arts. It's a lot of work, and the university lacks a social scene centered on booze and big-time sports (Hutchins eliminated the football team in 1939), leading students to wear T-shirts calling the U of C "Where Fun Comes to Die." This is a good sign. Colleges give nineteen-year-olds too many reasons to have fun and not enough to study consistently and thoughtfully.

Of course, most students aren't going to MIT or Chicago. But there are hundreds of programs and departments at all manner of colleges and universities, large and small, public and private, elite and less selective, that have made deliberate choices about what students should learn. This clarity of purpose is the single most important quality a program can have. Choose a college with a coherent sense of what it's trying to accomplish on behalf of students. This quality is rarer than you may imagine.

Historically, the main justification for maintaining thousands of course options and giving undergraduates nearly unlimited choice in selecting their courses was to give young people opportunities to explore various intellectual territories during their formative years. This was always self-serving: It justified the employment of large numbers of autonomous scholars focused on research instead of teaching. With the advent of the University of Everywhere and tens of thousands of rich, well-designed college courses available to anyone, anywhere, for almost nothing, the laissez-faire elective system makes no sense at all. Students and parents should be paying tuition at colleges that are willing to work for it by making undergraduate learning their number one priority and acting accordingly. Don't pay huge amounts of money for services that the Internet will give you for free.

For an example of the kind of college you should be choosing, look to the land of 10,000 lakes. In 2006 the state of Minnesota decided to create a new public university in Rochester, home of the world-renowned Mayo Clinic. Instead of spending billions of dollars to build another hybrid university, the University of Minnesota Rochester rented cheap space in an abandoned food court in a mall located two blocks from the Mayo Clinic and renovated it into offices and classrooms. It leased a few floors in nearby apartment buildings for students to live in, and memberships at the YMCA for exercise and recreation. It re-created the room in the traditional campus library where students like to sit in comfortable chairs and connect to the Internet with their tablets and laptop computers, and left out the other 95 percent of the building, including the books.

Instead of hundreds of degrees programs, the university offered exactly two: a bachelor of science in health sciences and a bachelor of science in health professions. Instead of choosing from among a phone book full of electives, students take a defined curriculum for the first two years. The professors charged with teaching chemistry, biology, statistics, philosophy, and creative writing coordinate their courses on a week-by-week basis so the various concepts interlock and reinforce one another. There are no lecture halls: When I visited, the classrooms I saw held thirty people at most. Yet the whole enterprise is amazingly inexpensive. UMR is able to provide a first-class education at the standard Minnesota public university tuition of $13,000 plus a fraction of what the state spends subsidizing traditional institutions.

I asked many of the UMR students, nearly all of whom came from Minnesota, if they had regrets about attending a college without fraternity houses or football games or rows of taverns offering drink specials on

Wednesday nights. Traditional universities complain that they need expensive amenities to compete for today's entitled, hedonistic students. But the UMR students seemed perfectly happy. They have parties and extracurricular activities, including something called "boot hockey," which involves boots instead of skates and brooms instead of sticks. But mostly they're busy working. When I asked them how much time they spent working on academics outside of class, the typical answer was thirty to thirty-five hours per week. According to the nonprofit National Survey of Student Engagement, only 6 percent of freshmen at the biggest, most prestigious research universities work that hard. Eighteen-year-olds are highly sensitive to expectations and organizational culture. If you give them a lot of work and commensurate support, they'll do it. If you give them little work, a lot of free time, and an elaborate social infrastructure centered on alcohol consumption, they'll react accordingly.

The UMR educational design is commonsensical and entirely impossible in a hybrid university structured around departmental autonomy and academic freedom. It was built a lot like the Minerva Project, because both organizations are what you get if you start a college in the twenty-first century and make logical choices about what structures and practices will help students learn at a reasonable cost. People don't build new American hybrid universities anymore because they're too expensive. They also don't make any sense.

Be wary of traditional colleges and universities that aren't moving quickly and creatively to use technology as an integral part of undergraduate teaching. The standard administrative response to IT has been to let individual professors decide how, or if, to use powerful new teaching tools. Given how long academic careers can be, that means that some classes might be several generations away from reaching the high-tech world we know today. That's not nearly fast enough. This doesn't mean you'll be limited to colleges and universities with a technical orientation. For example, Davidson College, a small liberal arts institution in North

Carolina, has a long tradition of high academic standards, has a strong commitment to the humanities, *and* was one of the first liberal arts colleges to join edX.

For hundreds of years, students have expected the college degrees they've earned—and paid large amounts of money for—to still mean something decades after they graduate. That's less likely if the college goes out of business because it didn't adapt to the changing economics of higher education. Colleges that act as if the Internet is just another fad that can be waited out or absorbed into an essentially unchanged organizational model are going to disappear in the long run. No student or parent should let their money and hard work disappear with them.

GOING TO COLLEGE

Four years can seem like a long time if you're young, but it is actually a brief interval when it comes to learning what you need to become an enlightened person and productive citizen. Once a student enrolls in a college, be it a small liberal arts college or a large state university, the most important decision she can make is how to spend that precious time. Some people know who they want to be at an early age, and for them the path toward medical school or the scholarship of medieval history is well defined. But for most students, college is a time to come to understand how to learn and develop, in Newman's phrase, "a union and concert of the intellectual powers."

The best way to do this is to stick to the classics: arts and sciences. While Arum and Roksa's *Academically Adrift* made headlines for finding low average levels of learning among college students, the study also found important distinctions between academic majors. The data they collected indicated a strong correlation between how hard students were asked to work and how much they learned, which is consistent with everything we know about neuroscience and cognitive psychology. The most challenging and rewarding programs were in the traditional liberal arts, such as philosophy, history, and literature, along with science, math, and engineering. The least work and least learning happened in programs like business and education, which are two of the most popular majors among American college students today.

The reliable, mechanistic old college system has allowed a large number of people born into middle- and upper-middle-class circumstances to comfortably ride along established pathways to prosperity without having to work especially hard. As the higher-education system opens up to many more people, this will change. Elite college admissions will become increasingly less game-able. The number of students who can live on the MIT campus is limited. For every additional Mongolian genius who gets admitted, that's one fewer spot for the smart-but-not-brilliant young man whose parents spent a lot of money getting him into the right private high school. Instead of waiting for 35,000 students to apply and picking among them by reading stacks of paper, elite schools like MIT, Princeton, and Stanford will electronically search among tens of millions of potential students worldwide. A critical mass of high schools will allow students to make evidence of their learning machine-discoverable, and more people will build up portfolios of digital badges and other credentials online to attract the attention of universities around the world.

The millions of students who faithfully make their way through less selective colleges earning generic degrees in business, education, political science, psychology, and so on will also be at risk. Those degrees have granted permanent and exclusive access to graduate-level education and desirable professions, not because the credentials themselves are particularly meaningful, but because they are more meaningful than anything else that is universally accepted and, in a narrow way, understood. When the value of the generic bachelor's degree fades, students' lack of learning will be exposed. Most of them will be left with little but debt and lost time.

The message for all students should be: Put down the bong and get to work, because the number of curious, eager-to-learn peers around the world with the means and ambition to get a great college education is about to increase a thousandfold.

PAYING FOR COLLEGE

Most of the future is hard to time. No one can predict at this point exactly when the weight of large numbers will knock the hybrid university off its foundations. The political and regulatory protections surrounding the hybrid university are functions of politics, which always oscillate on the edges of luck, personality, the business cycle, and majority coalition building. Potentially world-changing education technology companies can rise or fall based on a few semirandom changes in the venture capital environment, the labor market, or the ins and outs of acquisition and IPO.

All of which means that now is not the time to cash in your 529 college savings plan and buy a sports car. Even in the new landscape of higher education, students will still have to pay rent somewhere. More important, higher learning in the future will take place over a much longer time period than we 'commonly think of today. As the world's labor market becomes more demanding and traditional college degrees are replaced by open credentials, people won't be able to complete their formal education in their early or midtwenties. They'll need to keep experiencing—and in some circumstances paying for—education.

A good rule of thumb is this: Spend your hard-earned money to pay for your or your child's education, not someone else's ambitions. There are a small number of colleges and universities—probably fewer than fifty in the United States, total—that are of such exalted reputation and proximity to power that their name alone on a degree is worth the price of tuition. Don't finance some other college's dreams of joining that club. Focus your limited resources on high-quality educational programs that enlighten your children and prepare them for careers, not a comfortably undemanding extended adolescence.

Remember, too, that colleges have absolutely no conscience when they are encouraging students and parents to borrow large sums of money for tuition. Living at a public university and learning in the University of Everywhere are cost-effective ways of finding yourself when you're twenty. Borrow money only for an education that will yield enough of a return in the job market to allow you to pay your loans back.

PREPARING FOR COLLEGE

For parents with younger children or no children yet, the University of Everywhere will be more fully realized and thus less familiar. These parents should start rearranging their thinking about college right away. It will be very important for their children to be able to thrive in the new digital learning environments. Given how much time young people already like to spend staring at glowing rectangular screens, this can seem like a terrifying prospect for parents who've grown up in and succeeded at traditional colleges and universities. While these changes may be daunting, remember that (a) much of the time that kids currently spend in front of screens can be repurposed for more productive use (see, for example, *Grand Theft Auto V*), and (b) digital learning environments don't require students to spend all of their time staring at computers. The better technology gets, the more true this will be.

Parents of young children should keep in mind that their pride and joy will be competing and collaborating with other students around the world, the generation born out of the great rise of the global middle class. Most of the new entrants will be more likely than American students to adapt to the new digital learning environments, because they won't have access to the rich schools and colleges that Americans enjoy. The

University of Everywhere will be their best and probably their only option. These will offer life-changing opportunities for students to engage with people from other cultures and simultaneously grow into the global learning communities that will increasingly define large parts of higher education and the world of work beyond.

It will also be crucial for students to accumulate discoverable evidence of learning. Whether it's Mozilla Open Badges or Accredible certs or something else that hasn't been invented yet, the future will require people to gather, organize, and control information about what they learn, in order to build their educational identities. Trusting economically obsolete organizations with your educational credentials is a risk nobody should take—today or tomorrow.

More broadly, the future of education involves substantially more academic work. This reality is easy to miss in the hazy utopian thinking that ofter surrounds promises of technological progress. Technology will make education better, but not *easier*. Students working in personalized learning environments will experience less of the frustration that comes from incompetent, homogenous educational design. But they also will have fewer opportunities to float along a river of mediocrity and low expectations. They will be less able to rely on the inherited privilege of being born into the right family and social class to move ahead. Rational education will be unforgiving in many ways. The academic standards that emerge from global learning communities will rise to the achievement of the most capable and dedicated students in the world. There won't be any room to hide or slack off.

There is not now and there never will be a substitute for the deliberate practice necessary to gain real expertise. The higher-learning organizations of the future will give students the right kinds of hard work to do, and they will recognize that work by awarding credible evidence of accomplishment. But they won't do students' work for them. What parents can do is to help their children build the intellectual and emotional tools they will need for these demanding and rewarding tasks.

AND WHAT ABOUT EXISTING COLLEGES, with all their glories and flaws? In the long run they will rise or fall based on their ability to decide what they're good at and create an economic model that supports the cost of doing exactly that, and nothing else.

The hybrid university was specifically designed and exquisitely refined as a mechanism for avoiding such difficult choices. The whole point of it was to lash together three very different purposes in a way that concealed the contradictions and subsidies between them. As the historian Laurence Veysey said, the university throve on ignorance, shielded by a hypnotic mode of ritual idealism, with each group refraining from too rude or brutal an unmasking of the rest. We are headed for a time of brutal unmasking.

Institutions that are primarily built to perpetuate the ruling class will persist (assuming there are no larger revolutions). The human instinct to divide into social classes organized around power, money, and exclusivity will not be disrupted by information technology. It will help to have enormous amounts of financial and social capital. Harvard is building a doomsday machine for *somebody*—just not itself.

Research will continue to be research, and the logic of scholarly academic freedom holds. Whether those scholars need to live and work in the same physical place—and whether they'll be able to afford to have careers as scholars—will depend a lot on the disciplines. If chemists still need to stand in front of benches and manipulate expensive machines, then they will congregate in something like a "research institution." Since learning to be a chemist involves lab time, chemistry education, particularly at the graduate level, will happen there, too. The same is true for the fine and performing arts and other hands-on fields.

It's less clear why poets and historians need to be organized in departments on campuses, particularly when the disciplines have become ever more divided and specialized. Walk down the hall of a humanities department on a college campus today and what you'll find is a lot of offices that are closed or empty because the people who technically occupy them are working alone or with their laptops somewhere else, on topics so specialized that they have little or nothing to do with the interests of their fellow professors and students. Information technology has already changed scholarship, strengthening connections within the Invisible College of academics who are ultimately loyal and accountable to their peers, not their institutions.

Nor do research institutions necessarily need undergraduates. Universities like to make a show of undergraduate involvement with basic research while alleging that it's vital for professors to be on the cutting edge of their fields in order to effectively teach lower-division courses. This is 95 percent bunk, another myth furiously told and retold in order to paper over the structural illogic of the hybrid university. As William James said of the PhD holder: "His moral, social and personal characteristics may utterly disqualify him for success in the class-room; and of these characteristics his doctor's examination is unable to take any account whatever."

There will be exceptions, as there should be. It's a good idea for MIT to have both undergraduates and world-class research facilities in the same place, because of the culture and mission of the institution. But if that's the standard, many existing research universities won't meet it.

What's likely is that many scholars will continue to work in organizations that are located in the kinds of places where scholars like to live. New York City, with a population of more than eight million, contains only two first-tier research universities, Columbia and NYU. That's the same number as the state of Iowa, population three million. Given that New York City is a global capital of finance and culture with an enviably low crime rate, it could easily house ten times the numbers of organizations that support high-level scholarship.

The city is also a huge potential market for new educational organizations built from the ground up to serve undergraduates. Universities like NYU and George Washington shoved their way into the top tier of contemporary prestige by selling, first and foremost, their locations. As Plato said: "The city educates the man." Indeed, in late 2013, Carnegie Mellon provost Mark Kamlet stood with New York City mayor Michael Bloomberg to announce that a new CMU technology program focused on media and design would be opening in 16,000 square feet of renovated space in the Brooklyn Navy Yard. Brooklyn is a thriving hub of intellect, culture, and entrepreneurialism with a population of 2.5 million within the largest city in America. If Brooklyn can have an NBA basketball team, why can't it have new start-up universities, research institutions, and higher-learning organizations? The answer is that it can, and it will.

Who will work at these new and distinct research and educational organizations? The federal government is still working from Vannevar Bush's blueprint for investing in university-based science research. Researchers with external sources of funding will continue to do their work as they always have.

But many scholars receive no such funding. This is particularly true in the humanities, which have shrunk relative to the rest of higher education as the structural economic forces favoring job training and research have altered the proportions of the hybrid university over time. There's no National Institute of Philosophy in Washington, D.C., doling out millions of dollars per year to support the study of Kantian deontology. The tens of thousands of scholars working in fields without external funding are being supported by student tuition, government subsidies, and, in a relatively small number of institutions, endowment earnings. When the hybrid model breaks apart, that money will disappear. Where these scholars will go and how they will support themselves are questions that today have no easy answers.

There is no escaping the fact that the inefficient hybrid university model has served as a shelter and benefactor for important scholarship with no immediate value in the free market or obvious source of external patronage. Ideas that challenge and provoke conventional thinking are, by definition, less likely to garner enthusiastic support in the here and now. As a society, we have chosen colleges and universities as our principal mechanism for protecting and transmitting our inheritance of civilization to future generations. That the financial cost of this was obscured by hidden subsidies within university budgets was a feature, not a bug; it protected scholarship from vulgar politics and the unforgiving demands of the market. While colleges as we know them today can be passing strange, they also nurture the kinds of odd passions and inspired eccentricities that can be washed over by a tide of lower-cost service. People entering academic fields have long taken the economics of higher education for granted, never asking where, exactly, the money comes from to support the sabbaticals and teaching loads that allow half their time to be spent on research.

That kind of ignorance will be dangerous in the future. The scholarly hierarchy that separates top institutions and departments from others is likely to widen even as the number of tenure-track jobs declines. According to the U.S. Department of Education, the total number of tenured professors in the United States increased modestly over the last two decades, from 234,000 in 1993 to 262,000 in 2011. But those numbers represent a significant decline in tenured professors as a percentage of all professors. As more people graduated from high school, more high school graduates went to college, and a wave of baby boomers' children reached college age, colleges responded largely by hiring more adjunct faculty, part-time workers who don't necessarily have PhDs and earn as little as $3,000 per course.

The promise of high-quality digital learning environments is that they will increase the productivity of academic labor. Using technology to help people do more of what they do better is the basic formula for growing human prosperity and reducing economic deprivation. It also causes millions of people to lose their jobs through no fault of their own. By hiring adjuncts, universities kept the ratio of college teachers to students relatively constant while reducing how much college-level teachers were paid. Future learning organizations are going to use fewer people to teach more students. To the extent the tenure tournament continues to exist, it will become even more treacherous and cruel.

Meanwhile, the large majority of students attend colleges whose main job is teaching, not research, including community colleges, liberal arts colleges, and public universities that train few people to become PhDs. These institutions have benefited from the social prestige and financial support afforded to the hybrid university. They have ridden the long wave of increased prices for college and university degrees. But they have also suffered from the fact that the hybrid university on which they were modeled was not designed to succeed at their teaching mission. They were forced by regulation and convention to hire people whose doctor's examinations took no account of their skill in the classroom.

In one sense, that makes them most vulnerable to competition from new organizations built around high-quality digital learning environments. They don't have some other purpose or revenue source to fall back on. Colleges that continue trying to compete with elite institutions by charging the same tuition and building the same luxury facilities are in for a hard fall. A growing number of schools have already reached this point, struggling to stay solvent from year to year as they raise tuition and curtail financial aid. If they don't evolve, new technology-driven competition will push them over the brink of dissolution.

But in another sense, teaching colleges have a built-in advantage: They're in the growth market of human learning. The people who work there teach because they want to, not because they're forced to as a condition of conducting the research they actually care about. Liberal arts colleges in particular have stayed small and focused on education. Some of them are really good at it. There are also tens of thousands of great instructors in the nation's community colleges who know far more about teaching than the typical tenured scholar at a large research university, and they are eager to adapt whatever technological tools that can help their students learn.

For these institutions and educators, the key to survival will be putting the weight of large numbers in their favor.

Some of those numbers are the same that fuel the dreams of venture capitalists and entrepreneurs. Many of the billions of people about to join the global middle class assume that America has the best colleges and universities in the world. Rather than run out the string on a broken business model for another five or ten years, U.S. colleges should start thinking in terms of smaller amounts of money multiplied by much larger amounts of people. Institutions worried about diluting the exclusivity of their "brand" should ask themselves whether they are truly among the small group of colleges in the business of serving the ruling class—and whether they truly want to be.

But the most important large number working in favor of both existing colleges and all of the new higher-education organizations to come is *time*, specifically *lifetimes*, during which people always need to learn.

Of all the reasons that liberal education got the short end of the stick during the great late-nineteenth-century shakeout and continued to be subordinated to job training and research throughout the twentieth century, the most important may be a simple lack of time. You can train someone to start a career as a Web developer in nine weeks. You can prepare someone for a legal career in a couple of years. Getting a legitimate PhD in a tough research field can take nearly a decade. But liberal education? If you take its meaning at all seriously, liberal education is the work of a lifetime.

The people who best understand this work in the oldest continuously operating learning institutions in the world, those that far predate even the most ancient European universities: organized religions. To contend against those giants, the passion and pride of man, you don't teach people some things and then set them loose at age twenty-one, confident that your work is done. You bring them back *every week*, in a community of learners, for the rest of their lives. To apprehend the great outlines of knowledge, the principles on which it rests, the scale of its parts, its lights and shades, its great points and its little—that's not a goal to accomplish. It's a state of being toward which to always strive.

The current higher-education business model consists of charging students and their parents a great deal of money for a short amount of time and then maintaining an ongoing relationship based on youthful nostalgia, tribal loyalty, professional sports entertainment, and occasional begging for donations. The more complicated the world becomes, the more that intelligent machines usurp traditional human roles, the more people need to learn throughout their lives. The more people escape the isolation of poverty, the more they *want* to learn throughout their lives.

To prosper, colleges need to become more like cathedrals. They need to build beautiful places, real and virtual, that learners return to throughout their lives. They need to create authentic human communities and form relationships with people based on the never-ending project of learning. They need to do it in ways that are affordable and meaningful for large numbers of people. The idea of "applying to" and "graduating from" colleges won't make as much sense in the future. People will *join* colleges and other learning organizations for as long or as little time as they need.

Large numbers of learners make this possible. When you talk to professors teaching MOOCs, none of them say they're doing it to make a lot of money or advance their careers. Instead, they're thrilled by the prospect of reaching tens of thousands of people all over the world who want to learn, of seeing how their ideas resonate in different cultural contexts, of experimenting in ways that were never possible before the advent of technology. Colleges that look beyond the crumbling, ivy-choked confines of the hybrid university will find a world of possibility for anyone who is genuinely committed to helping people learn.

For nearly all of recorded history, the great gift of higher education has been locked away from the vast majority of people. It still is today. That happened in part because knowledge is power and societies that control people through enforced ignorance have no place for open institutions of learning. But it mostly happened because the structures of higher education were limited by available technology. Writing gave people a way to leave their intricate neural patterns for others to absorb. The printing press allowed those patterns to be replicated and distributed at manageable expense. Each advancement reinforced the logic of the university as a rare place: masters and students and books, surrounded by walls that protected the knowledge within.

Now we are grappling with new technologies that break that logic apart. The costs of this transition will be more than made up for by the sheer number of people who will, for the first time, be able to realize the gifts of personhood that are their human right. Many of those who have lived and learned in colleges as we know them cherish their memories and institutions. But the way we know them is not the only way they can be. Our lifetimes will see the birth of a better, higher learning.

ACKNOWLEDGMENTS

Many of the ideas in this book first germinated in the pages of *Washington Monthly,* a magazine of modest circulation and outsized influence on American journalism and civic life. The *Monthly*'s editor in chief, Paul Glastris, gave me my first magazine assignment and has been a friend and mentor ever since. He allowed me to write, and I am grateful.

My literary agent, Gail Ross, did me the favor of rejecting various book proposals until I found the one I was meant to write all along. Her belief in this project and skill in communicating its ideas helped it exceed all of my expectations.

My editor, Jake Morrissey, helped turn a long manuscript into a book that people not pre-obsessed with the American university's many peculiarities might want to read. David Chesanow's patience and attention made it better still. Their colleagues at Riverhead Books have managed a first-time author's many questions with warmth and professionalism.

Linda Perlstein and Charlie Homans read every word of the first draft and helped me excise many writerly tics, strange digressions, and half-formed notions. I count both as friends and model practitioners of what great nonfiction writing can be. Michael Staton was incredibly generous with his time and hospitality, ferrying me around the environs of Silicon Valley and helping me understand the fascinating things to be found there.

Many other people helped with research and writing. Chad Aldeman, Marvin Ammori, Steve Coll, John Gravois, Mary Alice McCarthy, Ben Miller, Bror Saxberg, Mitchell Stevens, Elena Silva, Steve Teles, Tom Toch, and others provided insights that helped improve the book tremendously.

My colleagues at the New America Foundation are a daily source of insightful thinking and dedication to the cause of improving education for all people. Liz McMillen and Dianne Donovan at the *Chronicle of Higher Education* have given me a monthly forum to speak to their matchless audience of educators and scholars.

Most important my wife, Maureen, has inspired and supported me at every turn. Her passion, intellect, integrity, and sense of humor are examples that I aspire to reach. We met on a college campus twenty years ago, and I have never been so fortunate since.

NOTES

1: THE SECRET OF LIFE

1 *a mandatory course for all MIT freshmen:* MIT's General Institute Requirements are described at http://web.mit.edu/catalog/overv.chap3-gir.html.

2 *When the* Boston Globe *listed the 150 most important things ever done at MIT:* Sam Allis, Hiawatha Bray, Scott Helman, and Carolyn Johnson, "The MIT150," *Boston Globe*, May 15, 2011.

7 *inflation-adjusted tuition at public universities has more than tripled:* College Board, *Trends in College Pricing*, 2013.

7 *By 2004, Americans owed nearly $250 billion in student loans:* Donghoon Lee, *Household Debt and Credit: Student Debt*, Federal Reserve Bank of New York, February 28, 2013.

8 *By 2012, 71 percent of students graduated with an average debt of nearly $30,000:* Matthew Reed and Debbie Cochrane, *Student Debt and the Class of 2012*, Institute for College Access and Success, December 2013.

8 *Only a third of working-age American adults have a bachelor's degree:* United States Census Bureau, "Educational Attainment in the United States: 2013 (CPS 2013)," Detailed Tables, https://www.census.gov/hhes/socdemo/education/.

8 *a percentage that grew slowly:* U.S. Department of Education, National Center for Education Statistics, *The Condition of Education, 2013*, http://nces.ed.gov/pubsearch/pubsinfo.asp?pubid=2013037.

8 *Less than 40 percent of students enrolling:* U.S. Department of Education, Institute of Education Sciences, National Center for Education Statistics, *Digest of Education Statistics, 2012*, Table 376.

8 *hundreds of colleges and universities fail to graduate:* U.S. Department of Education, National Center for Education Statistics, Integrated Postsecondary Data System (IPEDS) Graduation Rate Survey.

8 *Only 34 percent graduate or transfer:* Lutz Berkner, Susan Choy, and Tracy Hunt-White, *Descriptive Summary of 2003–04 Beginning Postsecondary Students: Three Years Later,* U.S. Department of Education, National Center for Education Statistics, 2008.

9 *only 11.6 percent earn one within six years:* Alexandria Walton Radford, Lutz Berkner, Sara Wheeless, and Bryan Shepherd, *Persistence and Attainment of 2003–04 Beginning Postsecondary Students: After Six Years,* U.S. Department of Education, National Center for Education Statistics, 2010.

9 *In 2005 a U.S. Department of Education study of adult literacy:* Justin D. Baer, Andrea L. Cook, and Stéphane Baldi, *The Literacy of America's College Students,* American Institutes for Research, 2006.

9 *The study was written up in the* New York Times*:* Sam Dillon, "Literacy Falls for Graduates from College, Testing Finds," *New York Times,* December 16, 2005.

9 *The results were shocking:* Richard Arum and Josipa Roksa, *Academically Adrift: Limited Learning on College Campuses,* Chicago: University of Chicago Press, 2010.

9 *the nonprofit Organisation for Economic Co-operation and Development published a groundbreaking study:* OECD Skills Outlook 2013: First Results from the Survey of Adult Skills, 2013.

10 *A study published by the National Bureau of Economic Research:* Philip S. Babcock and Mindy Marks, *The Falling Time Cost of College: Evidence from Half a Century of Time Use Data,* National Bureau of Economic Research working paper, April 2010.

10 *The numbers were mind-boggling:* Author's calculation based on the College Board, *Trends in College Pricing 2013,* percent increase in inflation-adjusted tuition, fees, and room and board from 1998–99 to 2013–14 applied to 2013–14 to project costs in 2028–29.

2: A SHAM, A BAUBLE, A DODGE

17 *After visiting Bologna, Charles Dickens remarked:* Charles Dickens, *Pictures from Italy* London: Bradbury & Evans, 1846.

18 *Standards for teaching were established in code and contract:* Descriptions of early university life in Bologna and Paris presented in this book, as well as the broader state of medieval higher education in Europe, rely substantially on Charles Homer Haskins, *The Rise of Universities,* Ithaca, NY: Cornell University Press, 1957. The book is based on a series of lectures originally delivered in 1923.

19 *In 1167, England's Henry II forbade English students from studying at the University of Paris:* "Brief History of the University," University of Oxford, http://www.ox.ac.uk/about/organisation/history.

21 *professors at the University of Paris outlawed silent reading:* George P. Landow, "Newman and the Idea of an Electronic University," in John Henry Newman, *The Idea of a University,* Frank M. Turner, ed., New Haven, CT: Yale University Press, 1996.

22 *They sent a letter back to England:* As quoted in Andrew DelBanco, *College: What It Was, Is, and Should Be,* Princeton, NJ: Princeton University Press, 2012.

23 *English authorities kept tight control over the founding of colleges:* John Thelin, *A History of American Higher Education*, Baltimore: Johns Hopkins University Press, 2004, p. 44.

24 *Harvard graduated a class of seventy-seven students:* Helen Hannon, "As the Civil War Finally Ends, a Relieved, Sad, Graduation Day," *Harvard Gazette*, June 4, 2009, http://news.harvard.edu/gazette/story/2009/06/as-the-civil-war-finally-ends-a-relieved-sad-graduation-day/.

24 *As late as 1880, only twenty-six colleges enrolled more than two hundred people:* Thelin, p. 90.

24 *The 1852 catalogue for the University of Pennsylvania lists the name:* University of Pennsylvania, *Catalogue of the Trustees, Officers and Students of the University of Pennsylvania: Session 1851–52.*

25 *three ideas battled for supremacy in defining what exactly college should be:* The framework of understanding the nineteenth-century development of American higher education in terms of competing liberal arts, research, and practical education ideas was developed by the historian Laurence Veysey in *The Emergence of the American University*, Chicago: University of Chicago Press, 1965. Veysey's book is a monument of careful scholarship and remains vital to understanding higher learning in America. Like all subsequent writers on the subject, the author is in his debt.

26 *"for a holiness class which is rendered unclean by material concerns":* Veysey, p. 61.

27 *"The Johns Hopkins University provides advanced instruction,* not professional*":* Veysey, p. 149.

28 *a debate at the heart of the liberal arts idea:* See, for example, Bruce Kimball, *Orators and Philosophers*, College Board, 1995.

29 *In 1869 he wrote an article for the* Atlantic: Charles W. Eliot, "The New Education," *Atlantic Monthly,* February 27, 1869.

30 *"Do you want to be cogs on a wheel":* Veysey, p. 93.

35 *In 2012, American colleges and universities granted nearly 140,000 bachelor's degrees:* U.S. Department of Education, National Center for Education Statistics, Integrated Postsecondary Data System (IPEDS), "Bachelor's Degrees Awarded by Six-Digit CIP Code Among All Title IV–Eligible Institutions," accessed on September 9, 2013.

3: THE ABSOLUT ROLEX PLAN

38 *As the journal* Nature *reported:* Firas Khatib et al., "Crystal Structure of a Monomeric Retroviral Protease Solved by Protein Folding Game Players," *Nature Structural & Molecular Biology,* September 18, 2011.

38 *The federal government spent $2.7 billion:* National Institutes of Health, National Human Genome Research Institute, "The Human Genome Project Completion: Frequently Asked Questions," http://www.genome.gov/11006943.

43 *He began work in a doll factory, sweeping floors:* Stephen Joel Trachtenberg, *Big Man on Campus: A University President Speaks Out on Higher Education,* New York:

Touchstone, 2008. Details of Stephen Joel Trachtenberg's life are from this book and personal interviews with the author.

45 *one popular world university ranking puts Humboldt at 126th worldwide:* QS World University Rankings, 2013.

46 *students and professors from the university participated in a mass book burning:* Humboldt-Universität zu Berlin, "Short History," http://www.hu-berlin.de/ueber-blick-en/history/huben_html/huben_html#nobel.

47 *"The most striking thing about the higher learning in America":* Robert Maynard Hutchins, *The Higher Learning in America,* New Haven, CT: Yale University Press, 1936.

50 *"My mistake was that I thought I was a successful evangelist":* As quoted by Harry S. Ashmore, introduction to Robert Maynard Hutchins, *The Higher Learning in America,* Piscataway, NJ: Transaction, 1995.

50 *One explanation was offered by a pair of Yale sociologists:* Paul J. DiMaggio and Walter W. Powell, "The Iron Cage Revisited: Institutional Isomorphism and Collective Rationality in Organizational Fields," *American Sociological Review* 48:2 (1983), pp. 147–60.

50 *at least eight professors:* Ewald B. Nyquist, *Life Begins at Forty: A Brief History of the Commission,* Middle States Association of Colleges and Schools, 1961, http://www.msche.org/documents/History-Revisited.pdf.

51 *with more than two million veterans enrolling:* Thelin, p. 263.

56 The *New York Times ran a front-page story about the book:* Gene I. Maeroff, "Value of College Degree Held Declining," *New York Times,* August 14, 1975.

57 *The number of young adults with a bachelor's degree:* Sandy Baum, Jennifer Ma, and Kathleen Payea, *Education Pays 2013: The Benefits of Education for Individuals and Society,* College Board, 2013, p. 41, http://trends.collegeboard.org/sites/default/files/education-pays-2013-full-report.pdf.

58 *By 2005, the college advantage had doubled to 80 percent:* Jonathan James, "The College Wage Premium," Federal Reserve Bank of Cleveland, August 8, 2012.

58 *an average of almost one new community college per week:* Arthur M. Cohen and Florence B. Brawer, *The American Community College,* San Francisco: Jossey-Bass, 2003, p. 15.

60 *public research universities spend 79 percent more per student on education:* Sandy Baum and Charles Kurose, "Community Colleges in Context: Exploring Financing of Two- and Four-Year Institutions," in the Century Foundation Task Force on Preventing Community Colleges from Becoming Separate and Unequal, *Bridging the Higher Education Divide: Strengthening Community Colleges and Restoring the American Dream,* New York and Washington, D.C.: Century Foundation Task Force, 2013.

61 *only 10 percent of all students who enroll in community college:* Alexandria Walton Radford, Lutz Berkner, Sara Wheeless, and Bryan Shepherd, *Persistence and Attainment of 2003–04 Beginning Postsecondary Students: After Six Years,* U.S. Department of Education, National Center for Education Statistics, 2010, http://nces.ed.gov/pubs2011/2011151.pdf.

63 *"it's a sort of token of who they think they are":* Daniel Luzer, "The Prestige Racket," *Washington Monthly,* August 22, 2010.

63 *the most expensive university in America:* Tom Van Riper, "Most Expensive Colleges in America," *Forbes,* January 19, 2007.

64 *the average debt for GW graduates flew above the national average:* Institute for College Access and Success, Project on Student Debt, "State by State Data," 2014.

64 *they gathered in nearby nightclubs:* Annie Gowen, "George Washington University Fights Its Rich-Kid Reputation," *Washington Post Magazine,* April 11, 2013.

4: CATHEDRALS

77 *On the day my father hit the road for California:* Baum et al., 2013.

79 *"Over the Christmas holiday, Al Newell and I invented a thinking machine":* Byron Spice, "Over the Holidays 50 Years Ago, Two Scientists Hatched Artificial Intelligence," *Pittsburgh Post-Gazette,* January 2, 2006.

82 *In 1973, Herbert Simon and a Carnegie Mellon psychologist named William Chase:* William G. Chase and Herbert A. Simon, "Perception in Chess," *Cognitive Psychology* 4 (1973), pp. 55–81.

83 *In 1982, Simon's coauthor, William Chase, published a study:* William G. Chase and K. Anders Ericsson, "Skill and Working Memory," in Gordon Bower, ed., *The Psychology of Learning and Motivation,* vol. 16, New York: Academic Press, 1982, pp. 1–58.

5: LEARNING LIKE ALEXANDER

89 *young Patrick found himself taking the side of empiricism:* Patrick Suppes, *Intellectual Autobiography,* Dordrecht, Netherlands: D. Reidel, 1979.

90 *In 1930 a group of progressive education reformers came together:* Wilford M. Aiken, *Adventures in American Schooling, Volume I: The Story of the Eight-Year Study,* New York: Harper, 1942.

91 *"even a subject as relatively simple as elementary-school mathematics":* Suppes.

95 *Massachusetts officials named Richard Fairbanks's tavern in Boston:* United States Postal Service, "The History of the United States Postal Service: Colonial Times," http://about.usps.com/publications/pub100/pub100_002.htm.

95 *By 1728, readers of the* Boston Gazette *were told:* Borje Holmberg, *Growth and Structure of Distance Education,* London: Croom Helm, 1986, p. 6.

95 *Yet, as the radio historian Douglas B. Craig later wrote:* Matt Novak, "Predictions for Educational TV in the 1930s," *Smithsonian.com,* May 29, 2012, http://www.smithsonianmag.com/history/predictions-for-educational-tv-in-the-1930s-107574983/?no-ist.

96 *"I believe that the motion picture is destined to revolutionize our educational system":* Hugh Weir, "The Story of the Motion Picture," *McClure's,* November 1922, pp. 81–85.

96 *In 1938, several hundred students put on suit jackets and ties:* Matt Novak, "Before On-line Education, These 15 TVs Were the Classroom of Tomorrow," *Paleofuture*, July 10, 2013, http://paleofuture.gizmodo.com/before-online-education-these-15-tvs-were-the-classroo-733486470.

98 *In 1947 the U.S. Army conducted an education technology experiment:* Ruth Colvin Clark and Richard E. Meyer, *e-Learning and the Science of Instruction*, San Francisco: Pfeiffer, 2008, p. 12.

99 *The U.S. Department of Education has examined scores of online learning studies:* Barbara Means, Yukie Toyama, Robert Murphy, Marianne Bakia, Karla Jones, and the Center for Technology in Learning, *Evaluation of Evidence-Based Practices in Online Learning: A Meta-Analysis and Review of Online Learning Studies*, U.S. Department of Education, Office of Planning, Evaluation, and Policy Development, Policy and Program Studies Service, revised 2010, http://www2.ed.gov/rschstat/eval/tech/evidence-based-practices/finalreport.pdf.

100 *Suppes showed up on the first day of class:* Michael Allen, "Addressing Diversity in (e-) Learning," in *Michael Allen's e-Learning Annual, 2008,* San Francisco: Pfeiffer, 2008.

101 *At the original Dartmouth conference on artificial intelligence:* J. McCarthy, M. L. Minsky, N. Rochester, and C. E. Shannon, "A Proposal for the Dartmouth Summer Research Project on Artificial Intelligence," August 31, 1955.

102 *The use of ACT-R theory in clinical research:* John Anderson and Christian D. Schunn, "Implications of the ACT-R Learning Theory: No Magic Bullets," in R. Glaser, ed., *Advances in Instructional Psychology, Volume 5*, Mahwah, NJ: Lawrence Erlbaum Associates, 2000, pp. 1–34.

102 *There are competing theories of artificial intelligence:* Others identify themselves as part of a "connectionist" approach that emphasizes the role of neural networks in human thinking. Whether this distinction even makes sense is up for debate, and all of the theories are constantly being updated as the discoveries of neuroscience unfold.

107 *In 1997 the well-known management guru Peter Drucker predicted:* Robert Lenzner and Stephen S. Johnson, "Seeing Things as They Really Are," *Forbes*, March 10, 1997.

107 *"the next big killer application for the Internet is going to be education":* Thomas Friedman, "Foreign Affairs; Next, It's E-ducation," *New York Times*, November 17, 1999.

107 *Launched in 2000, Fathom.com was an attempt to gain first-mover advantage:* The history of Fathom.com presented in this book relies substantially on Taylor Walsh (for Ithaka S+R), *Unlocking the Gates: How and Why Leading Universities Are Opening Up Access to Their Courses,* Princeton, NJ: Princeton University Press, 2011.

110 *Sieg pored through the volumes of data:* Author's interview with Wilfried Sieg, March 29, 2013.

112 *a study comparing the learning outcomes of two randomly assigned groups of students:* William G. Bowen, Matthew M. Chingos, Kelly A. Lack, and Thomas I. Nygren, "Interactive Learning Online at Public Universities: Evidence from Randomized Trials," Ithaka S+R, May 22, 2012, http://www.sr.ithaka.org/research-publications/interactive-learning-online-public-universities-evidence-randomized-trials.

113 *more than 125 million people from around the world have logged on:* MIT, "About MIT Open Courseware," http://ocw.mit.edu/about/.

114 *as a series of congressional investigations revealed in 2011 and 2012:* U.S. Senate Committee on Health, Education, Labor, and Pensions, *For Profit Higher Education: The Failure to Safeguard the Federal Investment and Ensure Student Success,* July 30, 2012, http://www.help.senate.gov/imo/media/for_profit_report/PartI-PartIII-Selected Appendixes.pdf.

115 *the average cost of attending a public four-year university increased by roughly 80 percent:* College Board, *Trends in College Pricing 2013.*

6: THUNDER LIZARDS

123 *he came across an article:* John Markoff, "Computer Visionary Who Invented the Mouse," *New York Times,* July 3, 2013.

123 *he finished a PhD in electrical engineering:* Doug Engelbart Institute, "Dr. Douglas C. Engelbart Curriculum Vitae," http://dougengelbart.org/about/cv.html.

124 *In handwritten notes summarizing his speech:* Doug Engelbart, "Augmented Man, and a Search for Perspective," Stanford Research Institute, December 16, 1960.

125 *The team used the tools they developed as they built them:* Douglas Engelbart and William English, "A Research Center for Augmenting Human Intellect," *AFIPS Conference Proceedings of the 1968 Fall Joint Computer Conference* 33, San Francisco, December 9, 1968, pp. 395–410.

131 *Venture capital investment in education technology companies increased:* "Global Ed Tech Financing Hits Record in Q1 2014," *CB Insights,* April 5, 2014, http://www.cbinsights.com/blog/ed-tech-venture-capital-record.

138 *Seventy students were accepted from nearly 2,500 applications, a 2.8 percent acceptance rate:* E-mail from Ben Nelson, May 12, 2014.

140 *"a no-strings-attached grant of $100,000 to skip college":* Thiel Fellowship, "About the Fellowship," http://www.thielfellowship.org/become-a-fellow/about-the-program/.

7: ANYTHING FOR ANYONE, ANYWHERE

149 *As journalist Steven Leckart would later report:* Steve Leckart, "The Stanford Education Experiment Could Change Higher Learning Forever," *Wired,* March 20, 2013.

157 *one-third of all the course credits earned by people with bachelor's degrees:* Clifford Adelman, *The Empirical Curriculum: Changes in Postsecondary Course-Taking, 1972–2000,* U.S. Department of Education, Institute of Education Sciences, 2004, http://www2.ed.gov/rschstat/research/pubs/empircurr/empircurric.pdf.

158 *Thrun in particular struggled with the fact:* Max Chafkin, "Udacity's Sebastian Thrun, Godfather of Free Online Education, Changes Course," *Fast Company,* December 2013.

8: IMAGINARY HARVARD AND VIRTUAL MIT

161 *only Stanford, Princeton, Columbia, Harvard, and Yale:* U.S. News & World Report, "Top 100 Lowest Acceptance Rates," http://colleges.usnews.rankingsandreviews.com/best-colleges/rankings/lowest-acceptance-rate?src=stats.

162 *some of which were literally published while the 7.00x class itself was in progress:* Gina Kolata, "5 Disorders Share Genetic Risk Factors, Study Finds," *New York Times*, February 28, 2013.

170 *"Online course credit can be transferred to many schools":* http://www.summer.harvard.edu/courses/distance-education, accessed on May 8, 2014. Helpfully, Harvard also advises that "your transcript will not indicate if a course was completed online or on campus." Harvard itself is not so easily fooled, clarifying elsewhere that "you may not count courses taken online toward your Harvard College degree."

177 *"an open letter to Harvard philosopher Michael Sandel":* "An Open Letter to Professor Michael Sandel From the Philosophy Department at San Jose State U.," *Chronicle of Higher Education*, May 2, 2013.

177 *dropped by billions of dollars in a matter of days:* Tom Reynolds, "Genome Data Announcement Fuels Stock Plunge, Misunderstanding," *Journal of the National Cancer Institute* 92:8 (April 19, 2000), pp. 594–7.

9: LESS LIKE A YACHT

185 *"Lamborghini of the yacht world":* Amy Argetsinger and Roxanne Roberts, "Saylor Toy: A $3 Million Yacht," *Washington Post*, April 12, 2007.

185 *College graduates are much less likely than others to lose their jobs:* Jaison R. Abel, Richard Deitz, and Yaqin Su, "Are Recent College Graduates Finding Good Jobs?" *Current Issues in Economics and Finance* 20:1 (2014), published by the Federal Reserve Bank of New York.

186 *Public university prices rose at an even faster pace:* College Board, *Trends in College Pricing, 2013*.

187 *where you went to college if you wanted to fly and build spaceships:* Harry Jaffe, "The Seven Billion Dollar Man," *Washingtonian*, March 1, 2000.

188 *"A cabdriver in Bombay," he said:* David Plotz, "Michael Saylor: MicroStrategy's Cult Leader," *Slate*, March 23, 2000.

188 *The university would educate "everyone, everywhere":* Larissa MacFarquhar, "Caesar.com: A Beltway Billionaire and His Big Ideas," *New Yorker*, April 3, 2000.

193 *one million associate's degrees, two million bachelor's degrees:* Digest of Education Statistics, 2012, "Degrees Conferred by Degree-Granting Institutions, by Level of Degree and Sex of Student: Selected Years, 1869–70 Through 2021–22."

193 *When Thomas Jefferson's University of Virginia opened in the 1820s:* Frederick Rudolph, *The American College and University: A History*, Athens, GA: University of Georgia Press, 1990, pp. 125–26.

194 *The median grade earned by Harvard undergraduates today is an A minus:* Matthew Clarida and Nicholas Fandos, "Substantiating Fears of Grade Inflation, Dean Says Median Grade at Harvard College Is A–, Most Common Grade Is A," *Harvard Crimson*, December 4, 2013.

194 *As the great German sociologist Max Weber wrote in 1922:* Max Weber, *Economy and Society,* Guenther Roth and Claus Wittich, eds., Oakland: University of California Press, 1978, p. 1000.

195 *The difference between the average wage for people with a bachelor's degree:* James, 2012.

195 *There are 3.7 million. . . . Almost every one of them has a bachelor's degree:* U.S. Department of Education, Institute of Education Sciences, National Center for Education Statistics, *Digest of Education Statistics, 2012*, Tables 76 and 79.

196 *Forty-four percent of associate's degrees:* United States Census Bureau, "Educational Attainment in the United States: 2012—Detailed Tables," http://www.census.gov/hhes/socdemo/education/data/cps/2012/tables.html.

10. OPEN BADGES

205 *That's more than double the total number of college professors:* Thomas D. Snyder and Sally A. Dillow, *Digest of Education Statistics, 2012*, U.S. Department of Education, National Center for Education Statistics, December 2013, Table 284, p. 411, http://nces.ed.gov/pubs2014/2014015.pdf.

205 *It was downloaded by 100 million people within a year:* "Firefox Surpasses 100 Million Downloads!" Mozilla.org, October 19, 2005, http://www-archive.mozilla.org/press/mozilla-2005-10-19.html.

208 *a diploma mill founded by a nightclub hypnotist named "Doctor Dante":* Thomas Bartlett, "The Hypnotist Who Married Lana Turner," *Chronicle of Higher Education*, June 25, 2004.

210 *twelve million people were playing* World of Warcraft *worldwide:* Adam Holisky, "World of Warcraft Reaches 12 Million Players," *WOW Insider*, October 7, 2010.

210 *The Carnegie Mellon researchers were interested in whether students learning computer science:* Samuel Abramovich, Christian Schunn, and Ross Mitsuo Higashi, "Are Badges Useful in Education? It Depends upon the Type of Badge and Expertise of Learner," *Educational Technology Research and Development* 61:2 (April 2013), pp. 217–32.

214 *the Mongolian government was building a new information network:* Laura Pappano, "The Boy Genius of Ulan Bator," *New York Times*, September 13, 2013.

11: THE WEIGHT OF LARGE NUMBERS

221 *the prestigious medical journal* Lancet*:* Kolata, 2013.

222 *In 2011 it cost about $10,000, and the price tag is falling:* National Human Genome Research Institute, National Institutes of Health, "Cost per Genome 2001–2014," http://www.genome.gov/images/content/cost_per_genome.jpg.

223 *over half of all the people on earth—52 percent—lived below the global poverty line:* World Bank, "Poverty Overview," http://www.worldbank.org/en/topic/poverty/overview.

224 *there were about 1.8 billion people in the global middle class in 2009:* Homi Kharas, *The Emerging Middle Class in Developing Countries*, OECD Development Centre, Working Paper No. 285, January 2010.

225 *One million students signed up for Coursera classes:* "Coursera Hits 1 Million Students Across 196 Countries," *Coursera Blog*, August 9, 2012, http://blog.coursera.org/post/29062736760/coursera-hits-1-million-students-across-196-countries.

227 *"The Unreasonable Effectiveness of Mathematics in the Natural Sciences":* Alon Halevy, Peter Norvig, and Fernando Pereira, "The Unreasonable Effectiveness of Data," *Intelligent Systems*, IEEE Computer Society 24:2 (March–April 2009), pp. 8–12.

230 *"Northern Arizona University's new Health and Learning Center just might take your breath away":* "NAU Unveils Breathtaking New Health and Learning Center," *Inside NAU*, August 25, 2011.

230 *over $100 million:* TaiAnna Yee, "NAU's HAL, An Unnecessary and Costly Improvement," *Where Is Our Money Going? Investigating the NAU Budget Crisis*, April 21, 2010, http://naubudgetcrisis.wordpress.com/stories/naus-hal-an-unnecessary-and-costly-improvement/.

230 *The total cost was $115 million:* Joshua Brustein, "Grand Theft Auto V Is the Most Expensive Game Ever—and It's Almost Obsolete," *Bloomberg Businessweek*, September 18, 2013.

230 *Grand Theft Auto V had more than $1 billion in sales:* Ben Fox Rubin, "'Grand Theft Auto V' Hits $1 Billion in Sales in Three Days," *Wall Street Journal*, September 20, 2013.

12: YOUR CHILDREN AND THE UNIVERSITY OF EVERYWHERE

239 *As late as 1982, only 57 percent of parents thought their children would go to college:* Jamaal Abdul-Alim, "Poll: Expectations of Sending Children to College Growing Among U.S. Parents," *Diverse*, August 26, 2010.

244 *the study also found important distinctions between academic majors:* Arum and Roksa, Table 4.4, p. 105.

252 *the total number of tenured professors in the United States increased modestly:* Author's calculation from IPEDS data.

INDEX